STUDIES IN HISTORY, ECONOMICS AND PUBLIC LAW

Edited by the
FACULTY OF POLITICAL SCIENCE
OF COLUMBIA UNIVERSITY

NUMBER 438

REVELLIERE-LEPEAUX
CITIZEN DIRECTOR
1753-1824

BY

GEORGIA ROBISON

Frontispiece

Bronze bust of Revelliere-lépeaux now standing before the town hall of Montaigu, department of the Vendée, where it was unveiled on June 14, 1886. The photograph, by Douillard Frères, Montaigu-Vendée, is reproduced here with the permission of Mademoiselle Douillard of Montaigu.

L. M. Revellière-Lepeaux

REVELLIERE-LEPEAUX
CITIZEN DIRECTOR
1753-1824

BY

GEORGIA ROBISON

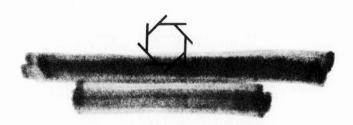

OCTAGON BOOKS

A DIVISION OF FARRAR, STRAUS AND GIROUX

New York   1972

Copyright 1938 by Columbia University Press

Reprinted 1972
by special arrangement with Columbia University Press

OCTAGON BOOKS

A DIVISION OF FARRAR, STRAUS & GIROUX, INC.
19 Union Square West
New York, N.Y. 10003

Library of Congress Cataloging in Publication Data

Robison, Georgia, 1905-
    Révellière-Lépeaux, citizen director, 1753-1824.
    Original ed. issued as no. 438 of the Studies in history, economics, and public law.
    Originally presented as the author's thesis, Columbia.
    Bibliography: p.
    1. La Révellière de Lépeaux, Louise Marie de, 1753-1894.
    2. France—History—Revolution, 1795-1799.
    I. Title.   II. Series: Columbia studies in the social sciences, no. 438.
DC146. L27R6   1972   944.04'092'40 [B]   72-8923
ISBN 0-374-96893-4

Printed in U.S.A. by
NOBLE OFFSET PRINTERS, INC.
New York, N.Y. 10003

To

DORA SLEDD ROBISON

AND

HENRY BARTON ROBISON

ACKNOWLEDGMENTS

THIS study was begun at the University of Chicago at the suggestion of Professor Louis Gottschalk and continued in Paris with the encouragement of Professors Albert Meynier, Bernard Faÿ, and Philippe Sagnac and the late Albert Mathiez and Raymond Guyot; it was concluded at Columbia University under the supervision of Professors Charles Downer Hazen and Carlton J. H. Hayes. Grants of the University Fellowship in History at Columbia University for the academic year 1929-1930 and of the European Fellowship of the American Association of University Women for the academic year 1930-1931 made possible the first stages of necessary research. A very great number of persons in public and private archives and libraries have rendered invaluable assistance in gathering and interpreting materials. It seems appropriate to mention four of these persons who have particularly facilitated the author's work in the west of France where Revelliere-lépeaux was born and reared: M. Marc Saché, former Director of the Bibliothèque de la Ville d'Angers and of the Archives Départementales de Maine-et-Loire at Angers; M. Jacques Levron, present Director of the Archives Départementales de Maine-et-Loire; M. l'Abbé Emile Pasquier, Professor at the Externat Saint-Maurille at Angers; and M. Gustave Pilastre of Mareuil-sur-Lay, Vendée. The author is deeply grateful for this generous personal guidance and for the timely financial grants. Thanks are due, finally, to Dr. Katharine Elizabeth Crane, assistant editor of the *Dictionary of American Biography*, for reading the manuscript at various stages of its preparation for publication.

G. R.

Villa Eze-les-Roses
Eze-sur-Mer, France
September 24, 1936

CONTENTS

ILLUSTRATIONS

TABLE AND MAPS

ABBREVIATIONS

AN   Archives Nationales
ALI   Archives Départementales de la Loire-Inférieure
AML   Archives Départementales de Maine-et-Loire
AV   Archives Départementales de la Vendée
AAE   Archives du Ministère des Affaires Etrangères
AHG   Archives Historiques du Ministère de la Guerre
AL   Archives du Musée du Louvre
BN   Bibliothèque Nationale
BA   Bibliothèque Municipale de la Ville d'Angers
BMN   Bibliothèque Municipale de la Ville de Nantes
BMHN   Bibliothèque du Muséum d'Histoire Naturelle
PR   Parish Register
MLL   *Mémoires de Larevellière-Lépeaux*

13

CHAPTER I

SON OF THE MAYOR

Digne fils d'un excellent père;
Comme lui vertueux époux,
Aux fruits de l'hymen le plus doux
Il a transmis son caractère.

PIERRE-PAUL CLEMENCEAU

IN the days of Louis XIV, toward the end of the seventeenth century, in that part of western France where the old provinces of Anjou and Poitou adjoined, there lived a doctor, a lawyer, a merchant, and a country gentleman. From these four men was descended a great-grandson who studied law, preferred teaching botany, and then became one of the five chief executives of the first constitutional republic of France. The merchant was Jean Reveliere, a seller of cloth, unmarked subject of the king and member of the Catholic Church; the great-grandson, inheriting his name, was Revelliere-lépeaux,[1] a regicide who turned against the Catholic Church and interested himself in the teachings of the deistic cult of Theophilanthropy.

Various branches of the Reveliere family were scattered through the southwestern corner of Anjou in and near Cholet, an important center for the cloth-making industry. Jean Reveliere, the merchant, lived for many years at Le May-sur-Evre, nine kilometers north of Cholet, but eventually he retired with his wife and children to Cholet, where at the age of sixty-four he died and was buried, on May 29, 1699, under the porch of Notre-Dame of Cholet.[2] The only son and name-

---

[1] The orthography of the name is discussed in Appendix A, "Revelliere-lépeaux's Name," *infra*, pp. 273-274.

[2] AML, PR, Notre-Dame de Cholet, 1699, fol. 5 r. His wife, Renée Besnard, and four of their children, Jean, Renée, Agathe, and Marie, were present at the interment. A daughter Louise, aged twenty-three, died two months later (*ibid.*, 1699, fol. 7 r.), and Agathe, aged thirty, died the following year (*ibid.*, 1700, fol. 1 v.).

15

sake of Jean Reveliere, the merchant, was born at Cholet in
1672 [1] and trained for the church, but after having earned the
degree of Bachelor of Theology the younger Jean Reveliere
decided against taking orders. He chose rather to buy and
exercise an office of royal notary at Le May-sur-Evre. In
1707 [2] he was married to Charlotte Gourdon at Montigné-sur-
Moine, a village twenty kilometers west of Le May-sur-Evre,
but for at least five years thereafter he continued as notary at
Le May. By 1714 [3] he had left Le May to establish himself
as notary and counselor [4] at Montfaucon-sur-Moine and to
live in the hamlet of Pont-du-Moine on the outskirts of his
wife's parish of Montigné, just across the river Moine from
Montfaucon. Only by courtesy has the title of doctor been
bestowed upon Jean Gourdon, of Montigné-sur-Moine, whose
daughter Charlotte was married to Jean Reveliere the notary
in 1707. Parish registers describe him as apothecary and sur-
geon, but in a small rural community he may well have played
the rôle of a doctor at times, if he did not entirely replace
such a practitioner.

Jean Reveliere the merchant had slept in his grave under the
porch of Notre-Dame of Cholet for seventeen years before
his grandson and namesake was born at Montigné-sur-Moine
on January 28, 1716, and baptized as Jean-Baptiste-Joseph
Reveliere the same day; [5] but Jean Gourdon, the baby's maternal grandfather, lived on in the same village and, perhaps, in
the same house until within a few days of the boy's fourth
birthday.[6] Although his father, the notary, died before the

---

[1] AML, PR, Le May-sur-Evre, 1686, fol. 14 r.

[2] AML, PR, Montigné-sur-Moine, 1707, fol. 3 v.

[3] AML, PR, Le May-sur-Evre, 1712, fol. 21 r.; Montigné-sur-Moine, 1714, fol. 5 r.

[4] *Notaire, avocat, procureur,* in AML, PR, Montigné-sur-Moine, 1714, fol. 5 r.; MLL, vol. i, pp. 1-2.

[5] AML, PR, Montigné-sur-Moine, 1716-1717, fol. 2 r.

[6] AML, PR, Montigné-sur-Moine, 1720, fol. 1 v.

boy was fifteen years old,[1] Jean-Baptiste-Joseph received a good professional education. Perhaps it was Charlotte Gourdon's ambition for her son; it may have been his own desire to receive a more thorough legal training than his father, whose formal studies had followed theology rather than law; or it is possible that Pierre de Launay, the boy's godfather, himself *licencié ès lois*,[2] influenced Jean-Baptiste-Joseph and saw that he was carefully prepared. Whatever reason or combination of reasons defined his ambition and sent him through law school, the grandson and namesake of the merchant of Le May-sur-Evre was granted the degree of *licence ès lois* by the University of Angers in 1740.[3] He chose, then, to live in Angers. There he came to be known as M. de la Revelliere, the first of his family to spell the name consistently with two *l's* and the first to add the prefix *de la*.[4] This modification of name was in conformity with the fashion of the times. By the middle of the eighteenth century the nobility could no longer assume an exclusive right to the particle, because families of the middle class had found it pleasant to write their names with a prefix and had done so. Revelliere's acceptance of the mode does suggest, however, that he enjoyed sufficient prestige to prevent the *de la* from appearing ridiculous.

In January, 1749, at the age of thirty-two, Jean-Baptiste-Joseph de la Revelliere, bourgeois of the city of Angers, was

[1] Jean Reveliere the notary died later than 1724 (AML, PR, Montigné-sur-Moine, 1724, fol. 2 r.) but before March, 1731 (*ibid.*, 1731, fol. 2 r.).

[2] *Ibid.*, 1716-1717, fol. 2 r.

[3] AML: E 3773; PR, Faveraye, 1781, fol. 2 v.; AV, PR, Saint-Jean-Baptiste de Montaigu: 1749, fols. 2 r., 6 r.; 1753, fol. 3 v.; 1756, fol. 9 v.; 1778, fol. 2 r.; Mairie de Montaigu, PR, Saint-Jean-Baptiste: 1749, fols. 2 r., 4 v.; 1753, fol. 3 v.; 1756, fol. 9 r.; 1778, fol. 2 r.

[4] The record of his marriage (AV, PR, Saint-Jean-Baptiste de Montaigu, 1749, fol. 2 r.) uses the particle, as do other subsequent records. The earliest instance of his own incorporation of the particle in his signature occurs in 1756 (*ibid.*, 1756, fol. 9 v.). The earliest records of the Reveliere family furnish rare instances of the use of the double *l* (AML, PR, Le May-sur-Evre, 1679, fol. 2 r., v.).

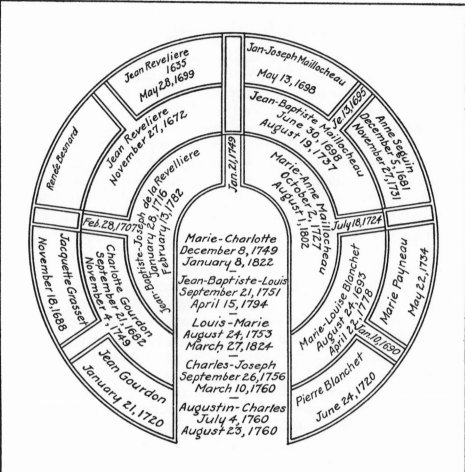

Each circle in this genealogical table represents one generation. The maternal genealogy occupies the right side of the diagram and the paternal genealogy the left side. The subject of this biography, Louis-Marie, is named, together with his sister and brothers, in the central open space. Dates of birth and death under each name, and dates of marriages in the connecting divisions, have been taken from contemporary parish registers.

married to twenty-one-year-old Marie-Anne Maillocheau in the church of Saint John the Baptist in Montaigu, diocese of Luçon, then in the province of Poitou, now in the department of the Vendée.[1] Charlotte Gourdon went to Montaigu to be present at her son's wedding. She may well have been pleased with his choice, for the Maillocheau family, although without pretension to noble blood or immense fortune, was one of the oldest and most respected of lower Poitou. The bride's father, Jean Maillocheau, Sieur de la Daunière,[2] had died twelve years earlier, but he had left three sons so that the line of landed proprietors of La Daunière, which had continued without a break for generation after generation, was not threatened with extinction. Since she was one of six children, the bride could not hope for a large inheritance, but she brought to her husband the offices of *conseiller du roi* and *juge des traites*[3] which had come down from her maternal grandfather. Pierre Blanchet, Sieur de la Bissetière, *licencié ès lois*.[4]

Jean-Baptiste-Joseph de la Revellière used to good advantage the professional opportunity that his marriage afforded. He removed to Montaigu and within ten years had been chosen mayor of the town, an office he filled until his death in 1782. As time passed, he added the duties of *salorge de Bazoge* to his occupations and became influential in the temporal manage-

---

[1] AV, PR, Saint-Jean-Baptiste de Montaigu, 1749, fol. 2 r., v. Information as to his street address in Angers before his marriage is lacking, but this record indicates that he lived in the parish of Saint-Pierre.

[2] La Daunière is the name of a property situated on the Petite-Maine river, in the present-day commune of Saint-Georges, canton of Montaigu, department of the Vendée.

[3] The *juge des traites* settled disputes arising over the payment of internal duties on goods passing from province to province; cf. Marcel Marion, *Dictionnaire des institutions de la France aux XVIIe et XVIIIe siècles* (Paris, 1923), pp. 538-540. *Conseiller du roi* was probably an honorary title; cf. ibid., pp. 138-139.

[4] Mairie de Montaigu, PR, Saint-Jean-Baptiste de Montaigu, 1690, 1720. AML, E 3773.

ment of the church of Saint John the Baptist.[1] Official
records of the administration of Montaigu before the decade
of 1790 have been destroyed. A short paragraph in the memoirs of his second son, Louis-Marie, seems to be the only
surviving account of Jean de la Revelliere, Mayor of Montaigu:

My father was generally recognized to be a man of merit; he
was strictly honest, faithful to his word, and endowed with a keen
sense of delicacy. Although he had made a good academic record,
he did not possess a wide general knowledge; he was, none the less,
by the sole force of his personality, decidedly above the level of
his time and of his fellow citizens. His disposition was affectionate,
his character forceful; he was a person of contrasts, deeply melancholy, or unreservedly gay. He was very polite and at the same
time very stubborn. As mayor of Montaigu for twenty-five or
thirty years, he administered the town firmly and justly.[2]

Marie-Anne Maillocheau, as her son remembered her,

had a great deal of native intelligence; she was infinitely kind and
helpful. Unfortunately, she had, up to a certain point, the faults
of women who have received a limited education and who have
spent their life in the idleness of small towns; she was talkative
and liked to gossip. In spite of these shortcomings, she was an
agreeable companion; her Poitevin frankness and her generous
nature made everyone fond of her, and her perfect conduct might
well serve as a model to all women. Respectful daughter, faithful
wife, she was also the most tender of mothers; like my father,
she was concerned only with the well-being of her children. Like

---

[1] The *salorge* was collector of the salt tax. The word *Bazoge* probably
refers to the district of jurisdiction, perhaps to be identified as the present-
day Bazoges-en-Paillers, commune and village in the canton of Saint-Fulgent,
on the southeastern border of the canton of Montaigu. *Marguiller en exercice*
and *fabriqueur en charge de cette paroisse* are the terms used to describe his
offices in connection with the church; *cf.* AV, PR, Saint-Jean-Baptiste de
Montaigu, 10 février, 1777, and 14 février, 1778.

[2] MLL, vol. i, p. 3; BN, MSS fr., Nouvelles Acquisitions, 21562, pp. 13-14.
This translation and similar ones are the author's.

Madame Primose, of the charming story of the Vicar of Wake-field, she prided herself on making excellent cordials and delicious preserves; my mother, with her currant and cherry wines and her vanity in seeing her children well dressed, had many traits in common with Madame Primrose.[1]

Five children were born to Jean-Baptiste-Joseph de la Revelliere and Marie-Anne Maillocheau, the eldest a daughter and then four sons. The two youngest sons died in 1760, leaving only three children, Marie-Charlotte, Jean-Baptiste-Louis, and Louis-Marie.[2] In the meantime, the unmarried sister of the mayor had left Montigné-sur-Moine after their mother's death and come to Montaigu, where she lived with her brother's family and helped care for Marie-Charlotte who was her niece, godchild, and namesake.[3]

From this aunt the children learned to read and write, but as soon as the two boys were old enough they went every day to study Latin with Father Payraudeau, curé of the parish Saint Nicholas of Montaigu.[4] The lessons with Father Payraudeau proved a grave mistake. The boys were not always models of perfection, the curé was sometimes ill-tempered, and difficulties were settled by the rod. In the end, Louis-Marie suffered more deeply than his elder brother; he had been frail since infancy; more than once there had been a question whether or not he would survive early childhood, but when

[1] MLL, vol. i, pp. 3-4. BN, MSS fr., Nouvelles Acquisitions, 21562, p. 14.

[2] Mairie de Montaigu, PR, Saint-Jean-Baptiste de Montaigu, 1749-1760.

[3] Charlotte Gourdon, widow of Jean Reveliere the notary, died on November 4, 1749, at Montigné-sur-Moine and was buried the following day in the cemetery of Notre-Dame de Montfaucon-sur-Moine (AML, PR, Notre-Dame de Montfaucon, 1749, fol. 5 v.). Marie-Charlotte Revelliere was present at the baptism of her niece and godchild at Montaigu on December 10, 1749 (AV, PR, Saint-Jean-Baptiste de Montaigu, 1749, fol. 6 r., v.). She died at Montaigu in her brother's home on November 11, 1774, and was buried the next day (ibid., 1774, fol. 9 r.; MLL, vol. i, pp. 2, 9).

[4] G. Mignen, Paroisses, églises et cures, Montaigu "Bas-Poitou" (La Roche-sur-Yon, 1900), p. 183. Pierre-Alexis Payraudeau was in charge of the parish of Saint Nicholas from 1746 to 1779.

year after year passed without catastrophe his father and mother took courage. The mayor, fearing that the unusual amount of attention and pampering which Louis-Marie received as an ailing and youngest child would make him a moral weakling, subjected him to severe physical discipline. He was slowly "hardened" to exposure in all kinds of weather and to a great deal of exercise in the open air. Whether Mayor de la Revelliere welcomed Father Payraudeau's methods as an aid to the development of strong character for his sons or was a little careless in supervising what actually went on during their days of study away from home, Louis-Marie was ten years old and Jean-Baptiste twelve before their father realized that both his sons were being miserably intimidated and that Louis-Marie was developing a curvature of the spine, which made him a hunchback.

Once convinced that his choice of tutor was unfortunate, the mayor acted with energy and promptness. The elder son was immediately sent away to a preparatory school for boys at Beaupréau in Anjou, a town of about eighteen hundred inhabitants,[1] northeast from Montaigu. Louis-Marie was removed from the charge of Father Payraudeau to the more kindly supervision and instruction of Father Séguillon. For three years longer he remained at home. He grew more robust, but it became apparent that his back would not recover from

[1] Célestin Port, *Dictionnaire historique, géographique et biographique de Maine-et-Loire* (Paris, 3 vols., 1874-1878), vol. i, p. 258.

Illustration on opposite page

Page from the parish register of Saint-Jean-Baptiste de Montaigu, 1753, recording Revelliere-lépeaux's birth and baptism, reproduced with the permission of M. Maxime Delahet, mayor of Montaigu. M. Delahet was so kind as to take the register from Montaigu to Paris to be photographed. This birth registration is probably in the handwriting of Revelliere-lépeaux's own father, whereas the duplicate kept in the Archives de la Vendée, though contemporary, is a copy.

le vingt cinq davril mil sept cent cinquante trois
a ete baptisé louis marie fils de noble [...] jean
baptiste de la revelliere licencié ès loix conseiller du roy lieuternal juge au siege royal
de montaigu et de damoiselle marie anne
maillocheau son epouse né le jour precedant
ont ete parin noble homme jean baptiste
joseph brunel docteur en medecine de
la paroisse de nostre dame de beaupreau
en anjou et marainne damoiselle louise angelique
maillocheau de la sainte vie de cette paroisse
les quons soubsignez avec le pere dudit enfant
la marge ses soubsigneront damoiselle
approuve louise laxonerie maillochau
[...] jeanne thibauneau

magdelaine pavageau augustin maillocheau
revelliere [...] douteau curé de montaigu

its deformity and that he might never enjoy normal good
health, while rounded shoulders and a chest squeezed into a
painfully small space might render him increasingly subject
to lung trouble.

Along with this fragility of health Louis-Marie developed
a very highly strung imagination and a dismaying super-
sensitiveness to ridicule. He would frequently burst into tears
at the slightest provocation or fall into spells of brooding.
When he was walking at dusk, he might see, at the end of a
long alley of trees, figures that his companions knew surely
did not exist. The forthright manner of the mayor with his
son and the unfailing affection of the entire family for the
boy prevented him from becoming morbid, but all the combined efforts did not succeed in dispelling his tendency to
periodic melancholy, an indisposition, it must be added, from
which the mayor himself suffered.[1]

At the age of thirteen Louis-Marie was sent to join his
brother at Beaupréau for the second half of the academic year.
This first experience away from home proved both happy and
successful. The companionship of his elder brother, of whom
he was very fond, and the fact that his godfather Doctor
Brunet lived at Beaupréau compensated for the inevitable
pangs of separation from his parents. The interests of a new
life were probably even more important. The academy of
Beaupréau was directed by the very competent Abbé René
Darondeau, who was responsible in large measure for the
school's excellent reputation during the latter part of the
eighteenth century. The seven-year curriculum included a final
year of rhetoric but did not offer the various branches of philosophy, which in schools of the time habitually completed
preparation for the baccalaureate. The daily schedule was
strict, with rising hour at a quarter before six o'clock (half

[1] MLL, vol. i, pp. 9-14; of course modern medical opinion points out that
hunchback is due to tuberculosis, a disease that would have been aggravated
by the treatment Revelliere-lépeaux received, and what is known of his
physical history bears out such a diagnosis.

an hour later in winter) and bedtime at nine o'clock. In addition to two hours of class each morning and afternoon, there were several periods of carefully supervised study and recreation. Because the school was sponsored by the congregation of Sulpicians, and because it was regarded as a recruiting ground for the clergy, particular attention was paid to religious instruction and to daily prayers. At Beaupréau, Louis-Marie entered class three [1] and, even though he labored under the handicap of coming in at the middle of the year, ranked first of his class in Latin translation and second in composition, when prizes were distributed at the end of the term.[2]

Since his elder brother had finished the course of study offered at Beaupréau the year Louis-Marie joined him, both boys were sent the following autumn to Angers, then a city of about thirty thousand inhabitants.[3] Young men of the region of lower Poitou who went away to school customarily chose Poitiers for the last years of their formal education, but the mayor of Montaigu preferred Angers for his sons. He himself was a native of Anjou; he had studied at the University of Angers and had continued to live in the provincial capital before his marriage; furthermore, he had property in the commune of Rochefort-sur-Loire, only sixteen kilometers southwest of Angers, necessitating annual visits of inspection; these trips had made it possible for him to keep in touch with friends and acquaintances in and about his favorite city. Jean-Baptiste and Louis-Marie, consequently, entered the College of

[1] In eighteenth-century French schools, as today, the classes were numbered in descending order, class one being the highest and then two, three, and on down, in contrast to the American system of designating the lowest grade as class one and the others in ascending order.

[2] B. Bois, *La Vie scolaire et les créations intellectuelles en Anjou pendant la Révolution (1789-99)* (Paris, 1928), pp. 12, 21-24; Port, *op. cit.*, vol. i, p. 257; Abbé F. Uzureau, *Le Collège de Beaupréau en 1763-1764* (Angers, 1898), reprinted from *Mémoires de la Société nationale d'agriculture, sciences et arts* (Angers, 1897) ; Abbé F. Uzureau, *Un Collège de province au XVIIIe siècle, Beaupréau* (Angers, 1900).

[3] Port, *op. cit.*, vol. i, p. 34.

the Oratory in November, 1767, while their elder sister Marie-Charlotte was placed in a boarding school for girls in the same city.[1] This action proved to be the first step in the return of the Revelliere family from Poitou to Anjou, for both sons completed their academic training at Angers, Jean-Baptiste in five years and Louis-Marie in eight, and they eventually made the capital of Anjou their home.

The College of Anjou[2] had existed at Angers since 1509, but instruction had been discontinued late in the sixteenth century, and the buildings were falling into ruin when, in 1624, the congregation of Oratorians undertook to re-establish the school. In 1629 their *collège* was given royal sanction. By the middle of the eighteenth century it had earned a notable standing among provincial schools, not only for Latin and rhetoric but also for the two subsequent years of philosophy, which Jean-Baptiste de la Revelliere was beginning in 1767. The Oratorians had been deeply influenced by the Jansenist movement, and there were still evidences of strong Jansenist tendencies among them. It is also to be remarked that a number of the professors were freemasons, members of the lodge *Tendre Accueil*.[3]

---

[1] MLL, vol. i, pp. 14-15, 17.

[2] *Ibid.*, vol. i, pp. 15-17; Bois, *op. cit.*, pp. 3, 8, 46-49; Emile Gabory, *La Révolution et la Vendée* (Paris, 3 vols., 1925-1928), vol. i, p. 13; Port, *op. cit.*, vol. i, pp. 77-78; Abbé E. Rondeau, *Les Fêtes scolaires au Collège d'Anjou* (Angers, 1908), reprinted from the *Revue des Facultés de l'Ouest*, pp. 2-6.

[3] BA, MS SM 78, *Manuscrit de la loge du Tendre Accueil, Angers, 18e siècle*. This volume, containing the minutes of meetings from 1774 to 1785, leaves no doubt as to the membership of a number of professors from the *Collège de l'Oratoire*. The late G. Dufour, in his *Essai sur J. B. Leclerc, sa vie et ses oeuvres*, pp. 32-33, makes the comment: " La loge du Tendre accueil dans la Doutre d'Angers était une association de bienfaisance avec peut-être quelque goût philosophique et libéral; elle rachetait les captifs chez les Deys d'Algérie ou les empereurs du Maroc et cette façon d'aimer la liberté pour les autres à la manière de M. Vincent n'était point encore révolutionnaire. Avoir les listes de ces maçons des années 1770-80, il semble que le collège de l'Oratoire recrutât pour le Tendre Accueil. On y rencontre

In the decades of 1760 and 1770 the College of the Oratory formed the minds of the Angevin contingent of revolutionaries—and reactionaries—of the decade of 1790. It is difficult to estimate how much or how little fervor for a new régime the Oratorians taught their pupils, but contemporary accounts of subject matter and methods suggest a strict adherence to a formal classical curriculum, followed by courses in logic, metaphysics, and ethics; lessons in natural history, taught under the heading of physics, made a possible exception in favor of modernism. In the selection of its pupils, the school was theoretically democratic; it offered instruction in 1770 to all social classes, from the son of a syndic of nobility to the sons of doctors and lawyers and down to the son of a local baker, who was too poor to afford clothing suitable for appearance in the final exercises of the year even though he merited more than one first prize. The majority of the pupils, however, came from non-noble but well-to-do families. Fourteen-year-old Louis-Marie regretted leaving Beaupréau. In class two at the College of the Oratory he found the lessons too long and his professor hard-hearted. As a result, he did so badly that he was forced to repeat the class.

The next year was happier. Another professor proved more understanding. Louis-Marie began to take pride in what he was doing, and then, almost as if in compensation for the disappointment and chagrin of having failed, he found in these very repeated courses a comrade, Jean-Baptiste Leclerc, who soon became a warm friend. Another school friend of the same period, Urbain Pilastre, should be mentioned with the young Leclerc. He also was studying at the College of the Oratory, although he and Louis-Marie de la Revelliere met first through their sisters who were both at a neighboring

ensemble tous les maîtres des humanités, les professeurs de 3ᵉ, de 2ᵉ, de rhétorique et de philosophie, avec le vicaire-général du diocèse, nombre de prêtres,..." This manuscript, completed by M. Dufour in February, 1924, but never published, was made available to the author at Angers, in December, 1935, through the courtesy of Madame Dufour.

boarding school. Leclerc, Pilastre, and the younger Revelliere were tremendously pleased with each other, and for many years afterward they remained in close intellectual companionship.

The third year at the College of the Oratory brought Louis-Marie to the study of rhetoric, the last stage in the curriculum preparatory to courses in philosophy. On Monday, August 13, 1770, at the close of the year, as was the annual custom, the school held public commencement exercises in the auditorium that with the classrooms occupied the building today serving as the city hall of Angers. Eleven young men were graduated; the name of "Marin Boylesve de la Maurouziere," son of the syndic of the nobility, headed the list; among the others came "Louis de La Revelliere" and "Jean-Baptiste Le Clerc"; the baker's son did not appear on the program. The ceremonies opened at half-past one o'clock with music by the band of the cavalry corps stationed at Angers. Then followed the academic exercise in which the young students, " Messieurs les Rhétoriciens," responded with all due formality to questions of their professors concerning arrangement, narration, refutation, elocution, and figures of speech. The program was concluded by a three-act pastoral drama entitled *Lindor ou La Force de la Nature*, with Boylesve de la Maurouziere reciting the prologue and taking the chief rôle; "Jean-Baptiste Leclerc " and " Louis-Marie de La Revelliere de L'Epaux " played only minor parts. The session closed with the distribution of prizes.[1]

It is worth noticing that the words *de L'Epaux* complete the name *Louis-Marie de La Revelliere* in the printed cast of

[1] MLL, vol. i, pp. 17-18; Rondeau, *op. cit.*, pp. 7-11. BA, H 3804, *Recueil des pièces relatives à divers collèges de l'Anjou*, includes the printed program of the fête given on August 13, 1770, at the close of the academic year. Abbé F. Uzureau, in his *Anciens collèges de la province d'Anjou, les exercices publics et les distributions des prix à la fin du XVIIIe siècle* (Angers, 1901, reprinted from *L'Anjou historique*), describes ceremonies from 1773 to 1789, the period immediately following the years Revelliere-lépeaux spent at the *Collège de l'Oratoire*.

characters for the play. It was often the custom to add the
name of a piece of property owned by a family to the name
of one of the sons, usually the younger. To distinguish him
from his elder brother the name was given to Louis-Marie.
L'Epaux, or *L'Epeaud,* or *Lepaux,* or *Lépeaux,* for it was
spelled in as many fashions as the imagination might choose,
was the name of a small holding of the Revelliere family near
Montaigu,[1] today in the commune of Treize-Septiers.

Two years of philosophy at the College of the Oratory followed by three years of law at the University of Angers, relieved by pleasant vacations with parents and relatives in the
Vendée, brought Revelliere-lépeaux to the completion of his
education in liberal arts and in law at the age of twenty-two.
The smooth progression of one year after another is deceiving.
The young man, faced with choosing a profession at the age
of nineteen, did not feel an irrevocable calling toward law.
True, his father and grandfather and a maternal great-grandfather had been lawyers, and his elder brother was already
bachelier and *licencié ès lois.* Still, the prospect of a legal
career stirred no enthusiasm in Revelliere-lépeaux. He felt
more drawn toward medicine, and family tradition was not
lacking for that profession; his mother's brother, Augustin
Maillocheau, was a doctor, and his own godfather was Doctor
Brunet, of Beaupréau. Yet from childhood he had been preju-
diced by hearing his father and uncle exchange pleasantries at
the expense of the medical profession. It is entirely possible
that for the time being he would have preferred no profession
at all, but idleness or even well-spent leisure was out of the
question for the sons of a father and mother of moderate
means who had nearly exhausted their small fortune in edu-

---

[1] The property *Lépaux* had belonged to the Maillocheau family at least
since the decade of 1670, when "noble Jean Maillocheau, Sieur de Lépaux,
étudiant aux Pères de l'Oratoire, à Nantes," maternal great-grandfather of
Revelliere-lépeaux, was named godfather of Jean de Laon, son of Jean de
Laon and Jacquette Porteau. *Cf. Rapport de l'Archiviste du département
de la Vendée* (La Roche-sur-Yon, 1912), p. 247.

cating their children. Rather because he was obliged to pursue a definite course than because of any personal bent, Revelliere-lépeaux began to study law in the autumn of 1772 at the same University of Angers from which his father had received his training and from which his brother had just been graduated.[1]

Records of the university have not survived to certify how well or badly Revelliere-lépeaux passed his three years of law. In later life, when he recalled these years, he did not claim for himself a brilliant showing, but he insisted hotly that he had always done his own work, never stooping to use the made-to-order briefs and examination questions and answers sold by dishonest professors to lazy students. In 1774 he was graduated *bachelier ès lois* and in 1775 *licencié ès lois*. Leclerc, two years younger, was in the same class.[2]

His brother Jean-Baptiste had gone to Paris in 1774 to enter the law office of the *procureur* Potel, the brother of P.-J. Potel, curé at Montaigu;[3] Potel was so delighted with the work of the mayor's elder son that he readily consented to receive the younger Revelliere as well. Plans were made ac-

---

[1] MLL, vol. i, pp. 18-20. The *Registre des inscriptions de la Faculté des Droits 1769-1792, Université d'Angers* (AML, D 23, fol 8 r.) shows that on May 27, 1771, "Ludovicus Joannes Baptista Revellière" paid a fee of 63 livres "pro Baccalaureatu" less 37 livres and 10 sous already paid for six registrations (each academic year being divided into three terms). On May 4, 1772, he paid 77 livres, 18 sous, 8 deniers "pro Licentia" (*ibid.*, fol. 12 r.).

[2] MLL, vol. i, p. 20. The *Registre des inscriptions*, fol. 18 r., records the payment of 73 livres less 37 livres 10 sous in 1774 by "Revellière incertin [sic]"; the reference is doubtless to Revelliere-lépeaux's payment of fees for the baccalaureate. The payment on May 16, 1775, for the *licence* is clearly marked "Ludovicus Maria De la Revelliere" (*ibid.*, fol. 22 r., v.). For Pilastre, *cf. ibid.*, fol. 15 v. For Leclerc, *cf. ibid.*, fol. 18 v. and Dufour, *op. cit.*, p. 11.

[3] Mignen, *op. cit.*, pp. 82, 117-118. Pierre-Jean Potel, native of Candé in Anjou, in 1768 left his place as *directeur des religieuses de Clisson* to become curé of the parish Saint-Jean-Baptiste of Montaigu. He signed for the first time as curé at Montaigu on October 10, 1768, and for the last time on July 15, 1790. He died at Montaigu on September 17, 1790, at the age of fifty-eight.

cordingly for Revelliere-lépeaux to begin his career as a law clerk in Paris shortly after he had finished his training at the University of Angers.[1]

During the long years at school the two sons of Mayor de la Revelliere looked forward to vacations in the Vendée, where September and October were especially pleasant for a country holiday. They often went to see Madame Maillot de l'Offraire and her daughters, distant cousins of the Maillocheau family, who lived at Mouchamps, a village thirty-two kilometers southeast from Montaigu. Revelliere-lépeaux was very fond of the second daughter, Charlotte, who was three years older than he. Charlotte Maillot, also called Mademoiselle de la Bastière, was not beautiful, but she was amiable, kind, and intelligent, and to the young man on vacation from law school she seemed perfect. In his own mind he became sure of his intentions, but he said nothing, because financially he was not in a position to propose marriage. In September, 1775, Charlotte Maillot's elder sister was married and went to live at La Guimenière, her husband's property not far from Mouchamps. Friends and relatives were invited for a week and more of merry-making at Mouchamps and La Guimenière. It was very gay for Revelliere-lépeaux, who had just been graduated in law and saw himself soon married to Mademoiselle de la Bastière. Shortly afterward, however, Pierre-Paul Clemenceau, a young neighbor, came back to the Vendée from Montpellier, where he had completed his studies in medicine, and Revelliere-lépeaux learned that Mademoiselle de la Bastière had been promised in marriage to the young doctor. When their wedding was celebrated at Mouchamps on September 3, 1776, Revelliere-lépeaux had been in Paris with his brother for nearly a year.[2]

[1] MLL, vol. i, p. 20.

[2] MLL, vol. i, pp. 20-27. *Cf.* AV, PR, Mouchamps, 1776, record of the wedding of Pierre-Paul Clemenceau and Charlotte Maillot de la Bastière. Charlotte Maillot, born in 1750 (AV, PR, Mouchamps, 1750), died in 1819 (information from M. Gustave Pilastre); her husband lived until 1825 (*Etat civil de Montaigu, 1823-1827*, fol. 19 v.).

Despite his genuine disappointment at losing Mademoiselle de la Bastière,

In Paris, although registered as an *avocat au Parlement* and working in Potel's office beside his brother, he found no relish for law and regretted increasingly that he had not studied medicine. Potel kept him, nevertheless, partly out of generosity, partly in deference to his father, but largely because Jean-Baptiste de la Revelliere made up the work his brother left unfinished. Gradually Revelliere-lépeaux spent more and more time as he pleased, learning Italian, picking up a smattering of science from former schoolmates who had come to Paris to study medicine, and going to the theatre as often as he could afford it.[1] Eight or nine months after his arrival in Paris, he was joined by Leclerc who also entered a law office and contrived to give up working almost before he had started. Leclerc was passionately fond of music and had studied harmony and composition. The two saw their first opera together, Gluck's *Iphigenia in Aulis*. In the current controversy between the admirers of Gluck and of Piccini they became ardent Gluckists. In return for lessons in musical composition, Revelliere-lépeaux taught Leclerc Italian. The two were soon inseparable. They went together to theatres and expositions. They studied philosophy and discussed governments. While they were reading and talking of the new liberty that must surely come, the War of Independence broke out in North America. It was unthinkable not to help in such a struggle for freedom; Revelliere-lépeaux found a place as sub-lieutenant in a company of dragoons; he was overjoyed at the thought

Revelliere-lépeaux remained on the best terms with his cousin and her husband. Many years later, Doctor Clemenceau wrote underneath an engraved portrait of his one-time rival the lines "Digne fils..." reproduced at the beginning of this chapter. This portrait is now at L'Aubraie, near Réorthe, Vendée, château of M. Paul Clemenceau, brother of the late Georges Clemenceau and great-grandson of Doctor Pierre-Paul Clemenceau.

[1] MLL, vol. i, pp. 27-29. Each year, in the *Almanach royal*, Potel figures in the list of *Procureurs au Parlement*. From 1775 to 1777, his address is given as "rue des Marmouzets en la Cité" (1775, p. 603; 1776, p. 344; 1777, p. 342). In the *Almanach* of 1778 (p. 342) and of 1779 (p. 342), the address is "rue du Figuier, près Saint-Paul."

of leaving all the boredom of a law desk for adventure in the new world. Nevertheless the company was not actually formed. With regret he tried once more settling down to the routine of a clerk.[1]

At that, life was not too tiresome. His brother Jean-Baptiste gave him money to amuse himself with Leclerc and sometimes brought Thomas-Louis Boileau, one of his close friends and former schoolmates from Angers, to make a quartet. Potel invited Leclerc and Boileau to his house as freely as the Revelliere brothers, so that the four young men came and went as they chose. Potel, a widower, had two young and attractive sisters-in-law, Adelaide and Julie Sellier, whom Revellierelépeaux and Leclerc found entirely charming. The idea of marrying sisters pleased the bosom friends, and the two young couples were beginning to build Spanish castles in the Vendée when Leclerc's family called him home.[2]

Without Leclerc, and with an ever-increasing distaste for law, Revelliere-lépeaux found no reason to stay in Paris. In September, 1778, the mayor's younger son went back to Montaigu, stopping on the way at Chalonnes, near Angers, where Leclerc's family had a country house, long enough to persuade his friend to come with him to the Vendée for a visit.[3] Revelliere-lépeaux spent a year with his father and mother at Montaigu. He went often to La Bougonnière, his sister's home since her marriage in February, 1777, to François-Frédéric-Hardouin Bellouard, Sieur de la Bougonnière.[4] He also visited

[1] MLL, vol. i, pp. 29-33; Dufour, op. cit., pp. 15-16.

[2] MLL, vol. i, pp. 33-36. The MS of the memoirs (BN, MSS fr., Nouvelles Acquisitions, 21562, p. 45) gives a somewhat fuller account of Leclerc's proposal of marriage than the printed text. Dufour (op. cit., p. 19) ignores the incident: "En 1778, les études de J. B. Leclerc étaient considérées comme terminées; il revint à Angers et à Chalonnes."

[3] MLL, vol. i, pp. 36, 40.

[4] Mairie de Montaigu, PR, Saint-Jean-Baptiste, 1777, fol. 2 r., v. La Bougonnière is in the present-day commune of Saint-Hilaire-de-Loulay, canton of Montaigu, department of the Vendée.

his cousins at Mouchamps and La Guimenière. Leclerc came
to Montaigu for all his own vacations, and together they made
short trips to the seaside, and to Nantes, La Rochelle, and
Rochefort. During one of Leclerc's visits, in March, 1779,
the lawyer Potel came from Paris to spend a few days with
his brother the curé and brought with him Jean-Baptiste de la
Revelliere.

In contrast to Revelliere-lépeaux's later reputation for anti-
clericalism, an incident of this epoch is illuminating. A distant
cousin of the Revelliere family, Mademoiselle Gouraud de la
Bonnelière, had entered the convent of the Fontevrists, not far
from Montaigu; on March 21, 1779, in the little convent
chapel crowded to overflowing, Revelliere-lépeaux, Leclerc,
and an ecclesiastic from Nantes, friend of the Potel brothers,
sang a trio to help celebrate the fête of Saint Benedict, patron
of the convent.[1]

Leclerc returned to Angers, Potel and Jean-Baptiste to
Paris, and Revelliere-lépeaux to everyday life at Montaigu.
The mayor and his wife were far from content with their
younger son. He was twenty-six years old. He was not, they
had to admit, a disgrace to them, but he showed not the
least inclination to establish himself professionally. When his
brother Jean-Baptiste was working and succeeding, it was dis-
appointing to see Louis-Marie apparently without purpose or
ambition. If there had been a fortune the problem would have
seemed less acute, but there was not. Finally it was decided
that he should return to Angers to find a serious occupation;
but at Angers he found Leclerc again, and all the time passed
in reading, in music, and in excursions. It was Paris once
more within the limitations of Angers.[2]

Thomas-Louis Boileau, back from his years in Paris to
begin his career as *conseiller au présidial*[3] at Angers, was
often with Revelliere-lépeaux and Leclerc during the winter

[1] MLL, vol. i, pp. 40-44.   [2] *Ibid.*, vol. i, pp. 46-48.

[3] The *présidial* was a court of first instance with civil and criminal
jurisdiction.

of 1779-1780. Early in the spring, his sister Mademoiselle Boileau, usually called Mademoiselle de Chandoiseau from the name of the property where she lived with her parents in the parish of Faveraye twenty-five kilometers south of Angers, came to visit him. Mademoiselle Boileau had learned a great deal about plants from one of her neighbors, Doctor Burolleau, a charter member of the Société des Botanophiles founded at Angers in March, 1777.[1] She had even been admitted as a corresponding member of the association. Revelliere-lépeaux's interest in natural science deepened immediately upon meeting her; he eagerly joined her and her brother on their walks in the country about Angers.

A year later, on February 13, 1781, in the chapel of Chandoiseau, Jeanne-Marie-Melanie-Victoire Boileau was married to Louis-Marie de la Revelliere de L'Epeaux, great-grandson of the doctor, the lawyer, the merchant, and the country gentleman.[2] For a short time they stayed at Chandoiseau, but when the fine weather came Revelliere-lépeaux took his bride to his parents' home in Montaigu. That autumn he removed to Nantes where, without exercising any profession, he and his wife lived quietly on their combined incomes. The winter at Nantes was saddened by mourning for three members of their immediate families. Maître Louis Boileau, the father of Madame Revelliere-lépeaux, died at Chandoiseau in October, 1781; Mayor de la Revelliere at Montaigu in February, 1782, followed by Hardouin de la Bougonnière, Revelliere-lépeaux's brother-in-law.[3] The spring began more auspiciously when,

[1] BA, MS 1035, *Livre des conclusions*, fol. 2 r. This bound manuscript of thirty-six folios is the society's book of minutes, or the duplicate, from March, 1777, to January 7, 1793. A concise history of the Société des Botanophiles is given by A. Boreau in his " Le Jardin des Plantes d'Anjou et les progrès de la botanique en Anjou," *Revue d'Anjou*, 1852, tome ii, pp. 37-76.

[2] Mairie de Faveraye, PR, Faveraye, 1781; AML, PR, Faveraye, 1781, fols. 2 v., 3 r.; AV, PR, Saint-Jean-Baptiste de Montaigu, 1781, fol. 2 r.

[3] AML, PR, Faveraye, 1781; AV, PR, Saint-Jean-Baptiste de Montaigu, 1782, fol. 4 r.; MLL, vol. i, pp. 50-51.

on March 14, a daughter was born to Revelliere-lépeaux and Jeanne Boileau. The child was named Clémentine.[1] Having gone out very little through the winter, the young couple were happy to find a new friend in Doctor Bonamy, who was called for special consultation after the birth of Clémentine. Doctor Bonamy was so pleased to discover someone who shared his interest in botany that he treated Madame Revelliere-lépeaux as his daughter, refused all payment, and concluded by presenting her with a key to his splendid natural history library and urging her and her husband to use his books as their own. They in turn were glad to offer Doctor Bonamy plants and fossils from the neighborhood of Chandoiseau for his collection.[2]

The residence at Nantes was cut short by Madame Boileau's decision to divide her late husband's estate among her children. It became necessary to return to Anjou where Revelliere-lépeaux could manage his wife's inheritance. Her share included vineyards and other pieces of land in the adjoining parishes of Faye and Chavagne, twenty kilometers south of Angers, and the right to a tithe of a thousand francs a year.[3] Since they enjoyed country life, they rebuilt an old house in the hamlet of Sablons, very near the village of Faye. It was little more than a hut, which had been used at grape-gathering time; but after it had been remade they found it very pleasant, so pleasant that they chose to live nearly the entire year at Sablons in the midst of their flowers, their vegetable garden, and their fruit trees, and to spend only three or four months of each winter at Angers in a house in the rue Toussaint. At

---

[1] ALI, Série E, Etat civil, Nantes, PR, Saint-Saturnin. Clémentine de la Revelliere was baptized on March 16 at the church of Saint-Saturnin in Nantes, with her great-uncle Doctor Augustin Maillocheau for godfather and her aunt Louise-Marie Boileau for godmother.

[2] MLL, vol. i, p. 51; J. P. Guépin, *Flore de Maine-et-Loire* (Paris, Angers, 1845), p. xii.

[3] MLL, vol. i, p. 52. M. Eveillard, notary at Thouarcé, Maine-et-Loire, whose papers include many eighteenth-century transactions of the parish of Faveraye, believes that this estate was settled orally, without recourse to a notary.

Angers they paid a capitation tax of forty livres a year, and three livres additional tax for a servant.[1] Thanks to his wife's inheritance, Revelliere-lépeaux was freed from the necessity of earning a livelihood. In 1785 their second daughter, Angèle, was born.[2]

About this time Jean-Baptiste de la Revelliere left Paris to settle at Angers, where he bought the office of *conseiller au siège présidial*. On August 31, 1784, he was married to Victoire-Marie Berger, daughter of Doctor Berger, professor in the Faculty of Medicine of the University of Angers,[3] and took a house in the rue Saint-Michel.[4] When Madame de la Revelliere, the widow of the mayor of Montaigu, saw her two sons established at Angers, she decided to remove from Montaigu to Angers in order to be near them. Marie-Charlotte Revelliere de la Bougonnière came with her mother, bringing her own son [5] and her two stepchildren. The family of Jean

[1] The amount of tax is high, falling within the upper ranges of the list of taxpayers. This fact, together with the mention of one servant, suggests a comfortable though hardly a luxurious standard of living. BA, Archives anciennes de la Mairie d'Angers, *Registres de la Capitation*: CC 169, p. 187; CC 170, p. 188; CC 171, p. 194. This series of registers indicates that Revelliere-lépeaux's residence in the rue Toussaint did not antedate 1786, since his presence at the address is noted for the first time in the assessment of 1787. A list of members of the Société des Botanophiles (BA, MS 1036), undated but probably of 1789, gives his address as at the Porte Toussaint.

[2] This date of birth is fixed by the record of interment, on August 5, 1792, when Angèle was seven years old. Mairie de Faye, PR, Faye, 1792.

[3] Mairie de Montaigu, PR, 1784, fol. 7 r.; AML, PR, Trinité d'Angers, fols. 69 v., 70 r.

[4] BA, Archives anciennes de la Mairie d'Angers, *Registres de la Capitation*: CC 167, p. 17; CC 168, p. 17; CC 169, p. 16; CC 170, p. 17; CC 171, p. 18. Jean-Baptiste de la Revelliere was assessed 24 livres a year, plus 3 livres for a servant. Since his name occurs, rue Saint-Michel, for the first time in the list for 1785, it is to be concluded that his residence at that address began in 1784 or 1785.

[5] MLL, vol. i, p. 53; Jean-Frédéric Bellouard had been born in February 13, 1778 (AV, PR, Saint-Jean-Baptiste de Montaigu, 1778, fol. 2 r.); Marie-Sophie Bellouard, born on February 28, 1779 (*ibid.*, 1779, fol. 4 v.), had died on February 5, 1782 (*ibid.*, 1782, fol. 2 v.).

Revelliere, merchant of Le May-sur-Evre, was Angevin once more.

The regret of Revelliere-lépeaux and his wife at being separated from Doctor Bonamy of Nantes was counteracted in part by the pleasure of finding old friends at Angers more interested than ever in botanical projects. On July 20, 1781, Leclerc had been elected a member of the Société des Botanophiles.[1] Doctor Burolleau *fils*, the son of the former neighbor and tutor of Jeanne Boileau, after serving as secretary of the society became its director, succeeding Baron de la Richerie, who died in the autumn of 1783.[2] On May 7, 1784, " M. de la Revelliere de L'Epaux " was proposed for membership, and at the following meeting on May 14, 1784, he was unanimously elected.[3] Two years later, April 28, 1786, " M. M. Burolleau et De La Révéliere de L'Épaux " proposed the name of " Mr. De La Brardiere " who was accepted as a member at the next meeting, on June 9.[4] He was none other than Urbain Pilastre, boyhood friend of Louis-Marie de la Revelliere, whose name, several generations earlier, had been lengthened by that of a family property *Brardière* as *L'Epeaux* had been added more recently to Revelliere. Pilastre had just returned to Angers from a long sojourn abroad, chiefly in Switzerland and Italy.[5]

Although the three former schoolmates worked side by side to develop public interest in botany and were in many other

[1] *Livre des conclusions,* fol. 7 r.

[2] *Ibid.,* fol. 8 v.

[3] *Ibid.,* fol. 9 r.

[4] *Ibid.,* fols. 12 v., 13 r.

[5] *L'Anjou historique,* vol. xiv, pp. 124-129 (Septembre-Octobre, 1913) ; this article, " M. Pilastre député de Maine-et-Loire (1752-1830)," was reprinted from the notice concerning Urbain Pilastre which appeared in the *Journal de Maine-et-Loire* at the time of his death in April, 1830. Blordier-Langlois, *Angers et le département de Maine-et-Loire de 1787 à 1830* (Paris, 1837), vol. ii, p. 264; M. Bougler, *Mouvement provincial en 1789, Biographie des députés de l'Anjou depuis l'Assemblée Constituante jusqu'en 1815* (Paris, 2 vols., 1865), vol. i, p. 296; Port, *op. cit.,* vol. iii, p. 94.

ways very close to each other, there is no evidence to indicate that either Pilastre or Revelliere-lépeaux followed Leclerc's example with regard to joining the freemasons. Leclerc's signature appears several times in the book of minutes of the lodge *Tendre Accueil*, but there is no record of either of his friends in the register.[1]

The death of Doctor Burolleau *fils*, on September 3, 1787, left the Société des Botanophiles without a director, and it was arranged to choose a new director after Christmas. The votes cast on February 25, 1788, were in favor of " Mr. De L'Epaux."[2] Revelliere-lépeaux's first problem in his new position was to find suitable grounds for the society's garden; the grounds originally chosen had been declared unsatisfactory as early as May, 1784, but the lease which expired in 1786 had been renewed for three years, after a struggle that nearly split the association of botanists.[3] The new director began by appointing a committee of three members, one of them Pilastre, to resift the entire problem and make recommendations. One solution after another was proposed, none feasible. In July, 1788, on behalf of the Botanophiles, Revelliere-lépeaux himself appealed without success to the city of Angers to buy land for the society. At the beginning of 1789, when the lease was about to expire and there was no hope of procuring money for a desirable site, Pilastre came to the rescue. Leasing a piece of land in his own name from the local Benedictine monastery of Saint-Serge, he offered it to the Société des Botanophiles with the one stipulation that they pay to the Benedictines the very small annual rent which was due in addition to the amount charged for the lease. At the meeting of February 20, 1789, the offer was accepted, and on March 5 the society thanked Pilastre formally for his gift and recognized *Les Bassins* in the parish Saint-Samson as their

[1] BA, MS SM 78; Leclerc signed the minutes of the meetings of July 5 and July 21, 1785; *Cf.* Dufour, *op. cit.*, p. 32.

[2] *Livre des conclusions*, fol. 15 r., v.

[3] *Ibid.*, fols. 9 r., v., 10 r., 11 r., v., 12 r.

permanent garden.[1] The former director, M. Burolleau, had for several years been giving a course of lectures in practical botany, primarily for the benefit of medical students of the University of Angers. Revelliere-lépeaux, by virtue of his new office, succeeded to the task. With some hesitation he accepted the charge, and after several months of energetic study opened his course in the late spring of 1788. He was a facile speaker, and he was not averse to romanticizing the systems of Linneus and Tournefort. When he described the acanthus, he related it to architecture through reference to the Corinthian capital; the mulberry tree was enlivened by the story of Pyramus and Thisbe; and the classification of the hemlock was coupled with the inevitable Socrates. His method was so popular that the audience grew rapidly through the four months' duration of the course. After the final lecture there was a burst of applause, and he was accompanied to his home in triumph by a group of friends and admirers. Revelliere-lépeaux had at last found an occupation to his taste. Gladly he promised to continue his course the next year.[2] The next year, however, was 1789.

[1] *Ibid.*, fols. 15 v.–18 v. The site chosen is the same occupied by the present-day *Jardin des Plantes* at Angers. A copy of the agreement to the lease is to be found in a bound volume of miscellaneous papers of the Société des Botanophiles (BA, MS 1036). An autograph manuscript of Urbain Pilastre, *Notes concernant le jardin des plantes d'Angers*, is in the collection of M. Gustave Pilastre at Salidieu, Mareuil-sur-Lay, Vendée.

[2] MLL, vol. i, pp. 54-59.
Livre des conclusions, June 28, 1781, fol. 7 r.: "Mr. Le Secretaire a annoncé un cours de botanique qui commencera lundy prochain a cinq heures et demie du soir."
Ibid., July 4, 1785, fol. 8 r. : "M. le Secretaire veut bien commencer lundi prochain un cour public de Botanique, il commensera [sic] ses leçons a sept heures du matin."
Ibid., June 9, 1786, fol. 12 v.: "On a accordé à Mr. Le Directeur la permission De Donner Dans Le jardin Des Leçons de Botanique à messieurs Les Étudiants en Médecine."
Ibid., May 3, 1788, fol. 16 v.: "M. le directeur prié et sollicité par M. M. les Étudiants en médecine, et par plusieurs amateurs de leur donner des

While he had been laying out a botanical garden at Angers and making his début as a professor, the first Assembly of Notables had met at Versailles in response to Louis XVI's summons. The disillusioning encounter of the Notables with their monarch had done little to rescue the government from its financial embarrassment, but before they were dismissed on May 25, 1787, they had approved the organization of provincial assemblies. The measure was registered by the Parlement, and in the autumn of 1787 the new provincial assembly of Anjou was convened. One of the aims of this body was to raise the qualifications of local officials, make them responsible spokesmen instead of the last links in the chain of the central government's authority over the people, and if possible at the same time draw them away from complete subservience to the king's intendants. The *syndics de paroisse*,[1] administrative officers of the smallest villages, had customarily been chosen by the local parish assemblies or appointed by the intendant or one of his subordinates. Since neither formal education nor legal training had been demanded, a syndic could be a peasant, even illiterate, as long as he was able to collect taxes, help allot the corvée, and arrange the levy and quartering of troops when necessary. With the intention of regenerating the *syndics de paroisse*, the provincial assembly renamed them *syndics municipaux* and confided their supervision to the *commission intermédiaire*, a committee of administrators whose duty it was to direct affairs when the general provincial assembly was not in session. Among the new *syndics*

Leçons de Botanique, a demandé à M :M : les associés la permission d'établir et de suivre son cours dans le jardin de La société ; L'assemblée en applaudissant à la bonne volonté et au zèle de Mr le directeur lui a accordé sa demande d'une voix unanime."

[1] Pierre-Jean-Jacques-Guillaume Guyot, *Répertoire universel et raisonné de jurisprudence civile, criminelle, canonique et bénéficiale, ouvrages de plusieurs jurisconsultes* (Paris, 17 vols., 1784-1785), vol. xvi, article " Syndic "; M. Marion, *op. cit.*, pp. 523-524.

municipaux of Anjou was Revelliere-lépeaux, chosen for his parish of Faye.[1] It was his first political office.

By the time Revelliere-lépeaux had concluded his botanical lectures at Angers, in the autumn of 1788, and had resumed his duties as resident syndic of Faye, Louis XVI had run through his series of transient ministers, Necker had been re-called, and the re-establishment of the Estates General was conceded. The second Assembly of Notables met in November, 1788, and was dissolved in December. Necker sent out his "New Year's Gift," the *Résultat du Conseil du Roi,* with his own preface, on December 27, 1788. On January 24, 1789, Louis XVI issued to the governors of the provinces letters convoking the Estates General at Versailles the following May 5.

The question uppermost in Anjou throughout February and March was the election of the province's quota of deputies to the Estates General. Regulations accompanying the letters of the king authorized practically universal suffrage for native-born and naturalized Frenchmen who were twenty-five years of age. The suffrage of the third estate, however, was indirect by several degrees. In Angers primary assemblies represent-ing the corporations of crafts and professions chose delegates to a *bailliage* assembly. In the country the customary parish or communal assemblies met for the corresponding first step of election under the presidency of their syndic or before a judge. The *bailliage* assembly then chose one-fourth of its own members, who formed the true electoral assembly em-powered to vote for the panel of deputies.[2] The mood of exultation induced by the prospect of sending deputies to

[1] MLL, vol. i, p. 60; AML, C 192, autograph manuscript, report of Revelliere-lépeaux as syndic of Faye in answer to the request for infor-mation sent out by the *commission intermédiaire* of Anjou concerning the state of the roads, shows him in full exercise of his authority as syndic in March, 1788.

[2] Guillaume Bodinier, *Les Elections et les représentants de Maine-et-Loire depuis 1789* (Angers, 1888), pp. 3-9.

Versailles was overshadowed for a time by the intense antagonism that the electoral campaign aroused and uncovered. Anjou did not come to the point of hand-to-hand fighting, as did Brittany, but feeling ran very high. Nobles were accused of attempting to manipulate the vote of the town-dwelling laborer and the peasant. The non-noble professional class was firmly convinced that it must struggle vigorously, if leadership of the third estate was to be kept from slipping into the hands of the second estate. A heated controversy followed, led for the nobles by Count Walsh de Serrant and by Chasseboeuf de Volney[1] for the commoners. Both sides used personal persuasion as far as it would reach, but first-hand influence was constantly reinforced by pamphlets, both signed and anonymous.[2]

Pilastre, Leclerc, and both Revelliere brothers, following the leadership of Volney, threw themselves into the contest. Revelliere-lépeaux entered the lists on February 28 with his eleven-page *Lettre à un seigneur d'Anjou accusé de tromper le peuple*. The *Lettre*, signed " Les associés pour la défense du peuple, et l'instruction des paysans," was in reply to Count Walsh de Serrant's skillful *Avis au Tiers Etat* which had attempted to split the third estate by stirring up enmity between town and country in the hope of winning peasant support for candidates who might be controlled by the nobility. The tone of the *Lettre* is ironic; the " Associés," posing as the friends of " Monsieur le Comte," inform him of tales which are defaming his good name; they are deeply shocked at the insidious *Avis* which is—falsely, without doubt—attrib-

---

[1] Constantin-François Chasseboeuf, 1757-1820, whose self-adopted pseudonym was *Volney*, was already known as a traveler and author. His *Voyage en Egypte et en Syrie* (Paris, 2 vols., 1787) and his *Considérations sur la guerre des Turcs et de la Russie* (London, 1788) were adding to his prestige in 1789.

[2] Albert Meynier, in *Un Représentant de la bourgeoisie angevine à l'Assemblée Nationale Constituante et à la Convention Nationale, L.-M. La Revellière-Lépeaux (1753-1795)* (Paris, 1905), pp. 89-120, depicts the background of the electoral struggle in Anjou.

uted to him; they profess their love and admiration for Monsieur le Comte as he really is, and then urge him to disclaim the *Avis* and re-establish the good reputation his own true character deserves.[1]

In the course of the controversy, Revelliere-lépeaux published another pamphlet of about the same length, *Adresse à la noblesse et au clergé*.[2] In this pamphlet he first called attention to the false sense of security induced by a moment of calm that was interrupting the storm of the electoral struggle. Then he launched quickly into a more theoretical analysis of the situation, concluding with a critique of Montesquieu's classification of governments. Even though politely recognizing Montesquieu's pre-eminence in the field of political thought, Revelliere-lépeaux took exception to several of his conclusions. Since the *Adresse* was written with special reference to the nobility, Revelliere-lépeaux chose the occasion to criticize Montesquieu's insistence upon an established aristocracy as a necessary support to the monarchical form of government. Revelliere-lépeaux did not urge the abolition of the titles of aristocracy, but he contended firmly that the truest support of any throne lay in the loyalty of the mass of subjects and that, if monarchy in France was to meet the problems at hand, special privilege for aristocrats must disappear. From that point he went on to find fault with Montesquieu's scheme of classifying governments. Whereas Montesquieu assumed three kinds of governments, republics, monarchies, and despotisms, Revelliere-lépeaux distinguished only two, republics and despotisms, monarchy falling to a secondary place as a kind of republic or a mixture of republic and despotism. Revelliere-

[1] BN, Lb³⁹ 7242; BA, H 1562, 1.

[2] BA, H 2025, *Correspondance de MM les députés des communes de la province d'Anjou* (Angers, 10 vols., 1789-1791), vol. i. The pamphlet is purposely anonymous, as a short preliminary *Avis* declares. The copy of the BA, however, has the words " M de L'espeaux " inscribed under its printed title. Meynier, *op. cit.*, pp. 112-114, recognizes Revelliere-lépeaux as the author.

lépeaux attacked Montesquieu on his own ground, referring to his definition of monarchy as a government in which one person rules by fixed and established laws in contrast with despotism in which one person rules according to his own will. He went on to show that if the laws were made by the monarch himself the resulting government was a despotism, but that if the laws were made by the people or by a part of the people the resulting government was a republic. In order to settle the issue even more precisely to his satisfaction, Revelliere-lépeaux added his own definition of monarchy as a government in which one person is charged with executing the will of all. The *Adresse* ended with a reiteration of the importance of the whole people and the futility of a privileged nobility. The clergy, Revelliere-lépeaux concluded, should limit their efforts, politically speaking, to the delicate labors of conciliating the other two orders.

The primary assemblies about to meet in town and country faced yet another problem only second in importance to the choice of delegates to the *bailliage assembly*. The cahiers, which the provincial delegations were to bring to the Estates General, were subject to the same indirect process as the election of deputies. Each primary assembly was expected to fortify its representatives to the *bailliage* assembly with criticisms and recommendations to be considered in making up the final cahier that would be carried to the Estates General.

Revelliere-lépeaux had a hand in writing at least two of the model cahiers that were widely circulated in Anjou during those months before the drafting of the provincial cahier. His collaborators for *Plaintes et désirs des communes tant de ville que de campagnes* may have been Pilastre and Leclerc;[1]

---

[1] BN, Lb^{39} 1600. BA, H 2025; this copy follows immediately the *Adresse à la noblesse et au clergé* in vol. i of the *Correspondance de MM les députés*...; hence, the inscription "idem Les 3 amis" refers to "M de L'espeaux" and two of his friends, probably Leclerc and Pilastre; Meynier, *op. cit.*, p. 141, accepts this triple authorship; Bougler, *op. cit.*, vol. i, pp. 130-131, takes for granted that Revelliere-lépeaux was the sole author.

for *Doléances et pétitions pour les représentants des paroisses de . . . aux assemblées de la nation pour les états généraux, rédigés par un Laboureur, un Syndic & un Bailli de Campagne,* tradition has it that *Laboureur* is to be interpreted as Pilastre, *Syndic* as Revelliere-lépeaux, and *Bailli de Campagne* as Jean-Baptiste de la Revelliere.[1] The *Plaintes et désirs des communes* were a simple list of thirty-two proposals for reorganizing the national and local government of France. The *Doléances et pétitions* developed these basic ideas into a fuller political program of sixty-four articles classified under three headings, constitution, finance, and legislation, and offered the whole as an example to any and every commune in a quandary as to the best way of drawing up its recommendations to the *bailliage* assembly for the provincial cahier.

If these two pamphlets truly reflected the political philosophy of Revelliere-lépeaux in 1789, he must be put down as a loyal subject of Louis XVI, eager for reforms to be wrought under the patronage of the king. The *Doléances et pétitions* proposed bestowing the name of " Louis the Liberator and the Regenerator " on "this good king, this tender father, this

[1] BN, Lb³⁹ 1547 carries the inscription "MM Lepeaux et Reveillere freres," while the copy BA, H 2025 has the name "Brardiere" written directly above *Laboureur*, "L'espeau" above *Syndic* and "de La Reveilliere*" above *Bailli de Campagne*. Meynier, *op. cit.*, p. 142, accepts this distribution of authorship without question. In Revelliere-lépeaux's memoirs, however, vol. i, p. 61, occurs the statement: "A cette époque, le docteur Tessié, mon frère et moi, nous rédigeâmes un projet de cahier, qui fut imprimé et qui servit de base à celui qu'adopta l'assemblée bailliagère." This sentence in the printed memoirs follows the manuscript version (BN, MSS fr., Nouvelles Acquisitions 21562, 69-70) exactly, save for the difference in spelling the name *Tessier*. Doctor Tessier was a co-worker with Revelliere-lépeaux in the Société des Botanophiles, and he may well have collaborated in writing this pamphlet; or, Revelliere-lépeaux's memory may have betrayed him in this instance. A third interpretation of *Laboureur, Syndic,* and *Bailli* is advanced by the Chanoine Uzureau, of Angers, who names "La Révellière-Lépeaux, Pilastre et Leclerc" as co-authors in his " La Révellière et le ' cahier ' de Faye (1789)," *L'Anjou historique,* vol. xxix (1929), p. 221.

excellent prince " [1] for his generous and wise dealing with his people. The king's status as hereditary chief executive should be subject, however, to his acceptance of a contract with the nation. The contract should be contingent, first of all, upon acquiescence in vesting all legislative power in a general assembly freely elected by the nation. The national Estates General, meeting at least once every five years, should legislate for the country, levy taxes, and call the ministers of the king to account for their stewardship. The body should include at least as many representatives of the third estate as of the clergy and nobility combined. Votes should always be taken individually, never by estate, and each deputy should declare his vote aloud. To assure a fair and competent local administration, intendants should be replaced by provincial estates organized along the same lines as the national Estates General. In order to remedy evils that had grown up, certain administrative changes would be necessary: all existing taxes should be abolished, both local and national, and new taxes apportioned among provinces and levied upon real property such as fields, prairies, woods, vines, châteaux, and houses, irrespective of the social status of the owners; the debt already accumulated by the state should be recognized and paid by issuing national bonds that in turn should be redeemed by the state as the years passed; a reorganized system of courts, with chief centers in the leading provincial cities, should guarantee prompt justice within each province and judgment of every accused person by his peers; in religious matters the power of Rome over the church should be weakened and disproportionate privileges of higher clergy reduced, while the possibility of allowing clergy to marry should be considered; there should be freedom of the press and freedom from arbitrary arrest; hunting and other seigneurial prerogatives should be abolished, whereas tithes and other customary dues should be redeemable upon reasonable payment.

[1] *Doléances et pétitions*, p. 6, article 2.

When Revelliere-lépeaux, as syndic of his parish, called and presided over the primary assembly of Faye on March 1, 1789, he was named one of the three delegates to the *bailliage* assembly at Angers, and his *Doléances et pétitions* was adopted with only two modifications as the cahier of Faye.[1]

Revelliere-lépeaux was one of more than eight hundred men representing the third estate of the city of Angers and the adjoining country districts who met in the church of the abbey of Saint-Aubin at Angers on Monday and Tuesday, March 9 and 10, 1789. After celebration of Mass the assembly listened to an address by its president, Marie-Joseph Milscent, and then set about immediately to select that quarter of its number which, together with supplementary deputations from the districts of Beaugé, Beaufort, Châteaugontier, and La Flèche, would form the ultimate electoral body of the third estate of Anjou. Revelliere-lépeaux was named one of the two hundred and seven members of the Angers contingent and member of the committee of twenty-six to draft the cahier that the Angevin deputation of the third estate would carry to Versailles.[2]

---

[1] MLL, vol. i, pp. 60-61. The Chanoine Uzureau had the good fortune to see the original manuscript of the *Cahier de plaintes et remontrances de la paroisse de Faye, pour être présenté à l'assemblée générale de la province indiquée au 9 mars prochain* before it was sold, in April, 1929, by the Librairie Simon Kra, Paris. Cf. *L'Anjou historique*, vol. xxix, p. 222. His description (*ibid.*, pp. 222-223) of the two variations of the document of Faye from the *Doléances, voeux et pétitions* must serve instead of first-hand verification unless the manuscript is some day resold or given to a public collection:

" Voici l'article ajouté au texte par les habitants de Faye: 'Le *tirage de la milice* sera supprimé dès à présent, à moins que le besoin le plus indispensable de l'Etat ne l'exige. Cette opération porte l'effroi dans les familles, occasionne des dépenses inutiles à toute la jeunesse du Tiers-Etat, et fait perdre aux habitants des campagnes un temps très considérable et très précieux pour l'agriculture.'

" Quant à l'article supprimé dans le texte imprimé, il est non moins significatif. Le voici: 'Pour attacher encore plus particulièrement le peuple à son pasteur par les noeuds les plus chers à l'humanité, les Etats Généraux aviseront aux moyens de faire accorder au clergé la liberté du mariage.'"

[2] BA, H 2025, *Procès-Verbal*, p. 45; Bodinier, *op. cit.*, pp. 8, 18.

At eight o'clock on Monday morning, March 16, the electors
of Anjou—clergy, nobles, and third estate—met in the large
assembly room of the Palais-Royal. From there they adjourned
to the cathedral for the celebration of Mass. Before they separated, each order to select its deputies, they joined in taking
the oath " to proceed faithfully to the composition of the general cahier and to the election of deputies " as prescribed by
the royal letters of January 24, 1789.[1]

The third estate was the first to conclude its cahier and
name its deputies. Meeting on March 18, at the Hôtel-de-Ville,
it worked with such dispatch that on March 22 the chairman
Milscent could write to Barentin, Keeper of the Seals:

Monseigneur, all my work is finished; our cahiers drawn up and
signed, our eight deputies named, the minutes written, approved,
and signed and our electors on the way to their homes. The clergy
and the nobility cannot understand the rapidity of our procedure,
and, although our eight deputies are chosen, they have not dreamed
of beginning their deliberations.[2]

The clergy met at the convent of the Cordeliers from March
23 until March 27; the nobility at the abbey of Saint-Aubin
from March 31 until April 6.[3]

There is no evidence that Revelliere-lépeaux played a dominant part on the assembly to prepare the cahier for consideration by the assembly of the third estate at the beginning of
its electoral sessions. It is easy to find resemblances between
his *Doléances et pétitions* and the provincial cahier; the idea
of contract, for example, persisted in the final cahier, along
with emphasis upon sessions of the national Estates General
at regular intervals and the privilege of buying freedom once

---

[1] Bodinier, *op. cit.*, p. 11; Armand Brette, *Recueil de documents relatifs
à la convocation des Etats Généraux de 1789* (Paris, 4 vols., 1894-1915),
vol. i, pp. 82-83.

[2] AN, B^a 13; Bodinier, *op. cit.*, p. 21.

[3] Bodinier, *op. cit.*, pp. 12-13, 16-17.

and for all from feudal dues. Proof is lacking, however, to show that Revelliere-lépeaux was responsible more than any other member of the committee for incorporating these ideas in the provincial cahier.[1]

"Louis Marie de La Revelliere de l'epeaux, *Bourgeois*" was the third deputy to be elected by the third estate of Anjou. He had neither formal training nor experience in political administration. His reputation as a successful professor of botany, his recent activities as syndic of his own commune, and his air of assurance in speaking and writing of political affairs had won his election. The other deputies of the third estate in Anjou could claim little more political training or experience. The first two, elected before Revelliere-lépeaux, were Milscent, presiding officer of the electoral assembly, and Volney, the publicist. Of the other five deputies, three were lawyers, one a doctor, and one a merchant. Urbain-René Pilastre de la Brardière and Jean-Baptiste Leclerc were the first two of the four alternates to be named.[2]

With the opening of the Estates General only a few weeks away, there remained little time for preparation before the deputies were off to the capital. They did not expect the excursion to keep them away from Anjou very long. At the meeting of the Société des Botanophiles on April 3, 1789, when their approaching absence was announced, it was not considered necessary to choose a new director; instead of Revelliere-lépeaux's resigning his position, the Benedictine Dom Brault was named to replace him only temporarily.[3] At the end of April, Revelliere-lépeaux, taking leave of his wife and two daughters, set out for Versailles, traveling with

---

[1] Bougler, *op. cit.*, vol. i, p. 176; MLL, vol. i, p. 61.

[2] BA, H 2025, *Procès-Verbal*, p. 51; Revelliere-lépeaux is given the title of *proprietaire* in this list of deputies. Bodinier, *op. cit.*, p. 19.

[3] *Livre des conclusions*, fol. 20 v.

Leclerc, Pilastre, and Volney.[1] Eleven years earlier he had left Paris, full of enthusiasm for music and the theatre and Italian, uncertain about his profession, certain only that fate had never meant him to be a lawyer. Now he was returning as one of the hundreds of deputies called to help Louis XVI deal with the state's financial problems.

[1] MLL, vol. i, p. 65.

CHAPTER II
DEPUTY FROM ANGERS

Qu'est-ce qu'une monarchie? D'après ce principe universellement avoué, que dans tout gouvernement légitime, l'expression de la volonté générale est la loi, la définition est simple: c'est un gouvernement où un seul est chargé de faire exécuter la volonté de tous; et la seule différence de ce gouvernement et du gouvernement républicain, c'est que dans le premier, le prince ou chef du pouvoir exécutif est un individu, et dans le second c'est un être collectif.

Revelliere-lépeaux
Opinion sur la sanction royale
2 septembre, 1789

INDUBITABLY Revelliere-lépeaux read both Montesquieu and Rousseau, and, when he composed his first pamphlets for publication, he was already imbued with the ideas of liberty and plans of social reorganization that were abroad among educated people toward the end of the eighteenth century. It is obvious, however, that Rousseau was Revelliere-lépeaux's guide through the early days of his career in the Constituent Assembly. In his *Opinion sur la sanction royale*, of September, 1789, Revelliere-lépeaux's definition of law as an expression of the General Will, and of government as the General Will's agent, was quite in the spirit of the *Contrat social*, as well as his classification of governments according to the number of magistrates engaged in administering each type. Nearly six years later, in his *Discours sur les relations extérieures* (pp. 6-7), he was still calling the author of the *Contrat social* " that immortal man whose political maxims and moral principles will always cause him to be regarded as the true apostle of liberty and of virtue, in spite of all those who belittle him."

From 1789 to 1797 Revelliere-lépeaux, like many other earnest souls, was wrestling to conciliate the exigencies of administration with his idea of the political verities. In 1789 he was a hopeful subject of Louis XVI; in 1791, still a confirmed monarchist. By 1793 he had become a dogmatic regicide; that same year and the next he wandered and hid, a fugitive from the Convention, threatened with death if discovered. Then in 1795, after the storm, he helped write the constitution that set France upon what proposed to be a normally republican basis. The six years altered his fundamental convictions very much less than this shift of allegiance from monarchy to republic might seem to indicate. His faith was so anchored in the mystical, all-pervading General Will, with which he believed society endowed by the very fact of its collective existence, that he was not to be shaken by the untoward end of any form of government that happened to be serving as its instrument. Only later, when he labeled a particular type of republican government as the one possible expression of the sovereign General Will, was he unable to countenance further change in the form of government. This fixation of loyalties brought him ultimately to political suicide—not, however, until 1799.

His respect for the General Will was founded in his belief that human nature was innately sensitive to truth and could be trusted to apply truth successfully to a political situation. This confidence depended upon his acceptance of the hypothesis that truth as a unity did exist and in a condition applicable to the solution of human problems. To Revelliere-lépeaux, interpreting unity literally, existence of one truth excluded the possibility of rival truths; the General Will, interpreter of truth, was to be trusted so long as it was uncorrupted, but deviations could be only the work of evil forces and were to be repressed without pity.

From his conception of the indivisibility of truth came Revelliere-lépeaux's unfailing distrust, throughout his entire political career, of parties and factions. He was unable to entertain for a moment the presumption that more than one honest political party could exist. The period from 1789 to 1795 served to define his general distrust of factions in terms of specific enmity toward the political groups that detached

themselves in the round of changes. In 1789 he took with him
to Versailles a dislike of aristocracy. At the Constituent Assembly he formed the habit of lumping the principles he disapproved under the headings of *tyranny* and *anarchy*, but until
1792 he did not attach the idea of tyranny to monarchy; with
the opening of the Convention, royalty was doomed. To his
mind kings took their place definitely beside aristocrats in the
category of tyrants, and he voted for the death of Louis XVI.
The swift march of events brought him to add a third kind
of tyrant to his list by the middle of February, 1793: a possible dictator, a French Cromwell.

Revelliere-lépeaux enjoyed looking forward to the time when
every man could take his turn as lawmaker and then, resuming
private life, give way quietly to his successor. Believing thus
in universal popular genius for expressing the General Will,
he was nevertheless suspicious of turbulent and unordered
masses with their threats of anarchy. He was ready to worship the spontaneous good nature and common sense of individuals from the simplest walks of life, but in crowds people
were not neat enough for him. He was more inclined to picture the man in the street as someone deceived and betrayed
than as a person inherently bad. Yet, when his own narrow
escape from death forced him to consider the basic necessity
of security for members of governing bodies, he was ready
to limit the active prerogatives of the mass, relegating it to the
rôle of a passive channel for truth.

Thus Revelliere-lépeaux arrived at the year 1795 with four
major political hatreds growing out of his conception of the
aristocrat, the king, the dictator, and the mob as tyrants and
traitors. He had rejected each form of government in turn,
until he reached the idea of a republic based upon suffrage
limited to men of approximately his own milieu. He himself
found his solution of the problem entirely logical, entirely
reasonable, above any suspicion of party persuasion—in short,
the solution the General Will had been trying to force upon
the consciousness of man since the beginning of time.

Not without realizing the difficulties of governing, but strong and secure in his failure to appreciate the paradox of his non-partisan advocacy of a limited republic, Revelliere-lépeaux was to enter courageously upon the era of the Directory.

I

Milscent, on completing his duties as presiding officer of the Angevin electoral assembly, described Revelliere-lépeaux as "the most perfectly honest man, but a little obstinate in his ideas and preoccupied with the great system of equality among all men." [1] Revelliere-lépeaux was insistent upon formal and theoretical equality as he entered national politics, even from the first day of assemblage at Versailles, when he marched in the ranks of the third estate heading the procession from the church of Notre-Dame to the church Saint-Louis. Finding, upon arrival at Saint-Louis, that places allotted to the third estate were less well situated than those of clergy and nobility, Revelliere-lépeaux became the spokesman of a little flurry of opposition that momentarily threatened to upset the Marquis de Brézé's carefully arranged plans following traditional precedents in seating arrangements. He had only time enough, however, to announce categorically to the master of ceremonies that he would never dishonor his rôle as representative of the French nation by accepting so inferior a place before he was swept on into one of the lateral wings of the transept by pressure of the mass of deputies entering the church.[2] The incident was apparently closed but not in Revelliere-lépeaux's mind. As a further protest against the political recognition of social distinctions, he habitually wore colored costumes, reserved to members of the second estate by the king's edict regulating the dress of the Estates General; he called the sober black suits intended for the third estate more

[1] AN, B^a, 13; Bodinier, *op. cit.*, p. 22; Brette, *op. cit.*, vol. ii, p. 113, note 2.
[2] MLL, vol. i, pp. 66-69.

fit for Orgon in *Tartufe* than for any representative of the sovereign people.[1]

These first claims for equality presaged Revelliere-lépeaux's continuous and unvarying attitude toward form and etiquette. Although he made it a point always to maintain an extreme simplicity in his own mode of living, for himself and the members of his family, he appreciated deeply every courtesy or honor that came to him in official capacity, at the same time resenting any real or imagined slight he could construe as a slur upon his patriotic honor and hence upon the honor of the country at large. The presumption of his wish to be reverenced as if he were the mystical personification of the French nation before long won him a reputation for pompousness and conceit entirely at odds with his private character. Intimate friends seldom misinterpreted his motives, but more than one casual acquaintance was ruffled by his assuming the rôle of high priest. His most intimate friends continued to be Leclerc and Pilastre, who assiduously observed everything that went on, although they remained only substitute deputies, with no legal voice in affairs for many months after the opening of the Estates General. The three lived in the same house at Versailles, 66, rue de la Paroisse.[2] Free from the heavier responsibilities of members of the National Assembly, Pilastre and Leclerc nevertheless attended the sessions daily and devoted themselves to sending the Angevin electorate a meticulous account of what was happening. This *Correspondance de MM. les députés des communes d'Anjou avec leurs commettants,*[3] eagerly received at Angers and printed there, remains one of the most accurate of contemporary attempts by deputies to keep their constituents politically informed. Pilastre, in November, 1789, and Leclerc, the following October, were rewarded for their faithfulness when they became deputies in the

---

[1] *Ibid.*, vol. i, pp. 70-72.

[2] Brette, *op. cit.*, vol. ii, p. 113; MLL, vol. i, p. 79.

[3] *Cf. supra*, p. 43, note 2.

places left vacant by resignation of two of the Angevin contingent.[1] The Angevin deputation rather soon fell into the
habit of visiting their provincial neighbors, the representatives
from Brittany, and with them constituted the most influential
elements in the Breton Club, where ideas were mulled over
and where the Duc d'Aiguillon was to make his plans for
dealing with the question of feudal dues.

Within ten days after the Estates General's formal opening
sessions, all three estates realized that at least a play of compromise would be necessary before business could be undertaken, and some members of each estate understood that more
than a feint would be required. On May 13, the clergy and
nobility had announced the appointment of their respective
commissions to discuss with the third estate the question of
uniting the three orders. On May 16, the commoners were
still debating what measures to take, not yet able to reach a
decision. Some were advocating the election of sixteen commissioners to meet with the clerical and noble delegations;
others were pointing out the advantages of impressing the first
and second estates by solemn deputations, headed by orators,
which would appear before plenary sessions of the two higher
orders instead of arguing in private committee.[2]

When the turn of the Angevin deputies came to express
their opinions, Revelliere-lépeaux favored the method of persuasion and conciliation through meetings of committees of
the three orders. The form of conciliation was of less concern

[1] Pilastre replaced Laurent-François Rabin, curé of Notre-Dame of
Cholet. *Correspondance de MM. les députés...*, vol. iii, p. 130; Bodinier,
op. cit., pp. 12, 27.

Leclerc replaced Milscent, third estate deputy. AML, L 152-153, *Correspondance avec la députation de Maine-et-Loire 1789—An VIII*: Milscent
to the administrators of Maine-et-Loire, 31 juillet 1790; "L. M. Larevel-
liere" and nine other deputies to the administrators of Maine-et-Loire, 18
8bre 1790; Bodinier, *op. cit.*, pp. 19, 27; *Correspondance de MM. les députés
...*, vol. vi, p. 680; M. Saché, *Les Principes de la constitution, une lettre
des députés de Maine-et-Loire (1790)* (Angers, 1908).

[2] *Correspondance de MM. les députés...*, vol. i, pp. 37-38, 42-45.

to him, however, than a rider which one group of deputies
was trying to have voted along with the general resolution.
This more conservative group wished to make a formal declaration that the third estate intended to respect the property
and the honorary prerogatives of the clergy and the nobility.
Revelliere-lépeaux observed that, before being legally constituted, the "assembly of the communes" could make no declaration whatsoever concerning legislation; it was unworthy
of the national body to disclaim before representatives of two
of its branches the odious charge of wishing to attack legiti-
mate property, whereas it was unthinkable that a vague promise
not to attack property would overcome the opposition of the
two privileged orders, unless it should be taken in a sense
favorable to all their pretensions. Furthermore, he continued,
the declaration of willingness to preserve honorary prerogatives of clergy and nobility might easily be turned into an
argument for refusing the vote by head. Finally, it would be
impossible to admit the existence of distinctions and pretensions without endangering the unity and activity essential to
the Estates General.[1] These opinions Revelliere-lépeaux shared
with the majority of his colleagues. The following Monday,
May 18, the third estate voted to limit the conversations of
the commissioners to the question of verification of powers in
common and to require that written minutes of their meetings
be kept. All conferences and half-measures proved fruitless,
and, with his colleagues, he took the Tennis Court Oath a
month later, signing on the same page with Mirabeau and
Robespierre.[2]

This first publicly expressed opinion, though unpretentious
as a début, clearly indicated Revelliere-lépeaux's firm intention
to champion the popular cause against every presumption on
the part of the nobility or of the clergy. The historic days of

[1] *Ibid.*, vol. i, pp. 42-43; MLL, vol. i, p. 75.

[2] At this epoch he signed *L. M. Delarevelliere Delépeaux*; *cf.* Musée des
Archives Nationales, *Registre des procès-verbaux des séances des députés,*
p. 78.

1789 failed to distinguish him particularly from his fellow deputies. The night of July 13, before the fall of the Bastille, he spent with Pilastre and Leclerc at his side in the assembly's permanent session in spite of warnings by their friendly land-lord that orders had been issued to the troops to fire upon the nation's representatives.[1] He professed never to have understood the reasons for bringing Louis XVI from Ver-sailles to Paris on October 6, perhaps because he had hard work reconciling the menace of a mob with his idea of the General Will as an agent of truth; years later, while admitting his inability to explain what happened, he offered the Duc d'Orléans and his intrigues as a possible explanation of the riddle.[2]

After the National Assembly had followed Louis XVI to Paris, Revelliere-lépeaux helped found the Jacobin Club, which claimed most of the former members of the extinct Breton Club, whether or not it is to be considered as a positive re-incarnation of the earlier group. Despite his initial bent toward club affiliations, he was soon alarmed by the Jacobins' grow-ing domination over the political situation; he was one of the first to brand them as party-minded and factionist, and in July, 1791, withdrew definitively.[3]

Outside the Angevin circle, he had made few close friend-ships, but these struck deep roots and absorbed more and more of his leisure time as his attendance at the Jacobins waned. One of the most satisfying of the new associations was the companionship of André Thouin and his clan at the Jardin du Roi, soon to become the Jardin des Plantes. André Thouin, the son of a gardener and himself a gardener from childhood, had grown up with his brothers and sisters in the Jardin du Roi under the benevolent tutelage of Buffon. In his genera-tion the Thouin family passed from the status of day laborers

[1] MLL, vol. i, pp. 79-81.
[2] Ibid., vol. i, pp. 79-81, 263-297.
[3] Ibid., vol. i, pp. 85-86; Meynier, op. cit., p. 185.

to that of botanists engaged in horticulture. Each of the brothers found a specialty to his liking. André himself, head gardener since his father's death, was to become professor of botany in 1793 in the Museum of Natural History, Jacques the Museum's head secretary, and Jean its gardener-in-chief, while Gabriel chose landscaping and supervision of the nurseries. The elder sister, Madame Guillebert, and her husband, a former tutor of Buffon's son, lived with the Thouin brothers and their families in a patriarchal group, and with them the younger sister Louise and cousin Gorelli, whom they treated as one of their own family. The late eighteenth century vogue for the beauties of nature had brought numerous prominent men to visit the gardens and to rest by the fireside. The kitchen of the king's gardeners had become the salon of Rousseau and a symbol of the sophisticated simplicity that was to regenerate society. Without abandoning the plain ways of men close to the soil, the Thouin brothers acquired cultivation by talking with philosophers.

Revelliere-lépeaux was introduced into this extraordinary household by an errand on behalf of the Société des Botanophiles of Angers. His reception was so cordial, and his own delight at the courtesy which distinguished the philosophical botanists so genuine, that he willingly accepted their first invitation to dinner and, soon becoming an habitual guest, spent a part of nearly every Sunday in the kitchen, where Rousseau had held court, or, in fine weather, on the terraces in front of the hothouses. André Thouin gratified the wishes of the Angevin botanophiles with shipments of desirable plants and shrubs from his garden and seconded the efforts of Revellierelépeaux, Leclerc, and Pilastre to keep their friends in touch with the latest botanical developments of the capital. In May, 1790, when it became apparent that the National Assembly's sessions were likely to continue many months longer, and it seemed best that Revelliere-lépeaux's wife join him in Paris, bringing their daughters Clémentine and Angèle, they were all received enthusiastically at the Jardin des Plantes.[1]

The same spring of 1790, Pincepré de Buire, deputy from Péronne, in the extreme north of France, also urged his wife to come to Paris. Revelliere-lépeaux had noticed with admiration from the very beginning of the Estates General this tall and venerable gentleman of simple tastes and, feeling an irresistible attraction toward him, had taken the initiative in speaking first, although Pincepré de Buire was older than he by more than twenty years. The spontaneous feeling of sympathy had proved to be mutual, and in a very short time there was made a friendship, which a few years later was to save Revelliere-lépeaux from the guillotine. Fortunately, the wives of the two deputies found as much in common as their husbands, and the household of Pincepré de Buire took its place with the Thouin kitchen in the pattern of everyday life and holiday excursions of Revelliere-lépeaux and his family.[2]

So the two years passed. From the opening of the Estates General in May, 1789, until the closing of the National Assembly in September, 1791, Revelliere-lépeaux's name appeared upon the official records of the body some forty times.[3] On July 17, 1789, he was named one of a committee of thirty to consider the question of making a constitution.[4] Although he was not prominent enough to be considered seriously for the more important Committee of Eight appointed on August 14 to draft the constitution, he had a great many ideas as to how the document should be composed and was impatient whenever

[1] MLL, vol. i, pp. 72-75; *Livre des conclusions*, fols. 23 r., v., 26 r., 28 r. During 1790 and 1791 Revelliere-lépeaux and his family lived in the Hôtel de Picardie, rue des Orties-Saint-Roch, butte des Moulins (MLL, vol. i, p. 88; Brette, *op. cit.*, vol. ii, p. 113).

[2] MLL, vol. i, pp. 72, 184.

[3] This reckoning is based upon the following sources: *Archives parlementaires, Correspondance de MM. les députés..., Le Moniteur, Procès-Verbaux de l'Assemblée constituante,* and *Réimpression de l'Ancien Moniteur.*

[4] *Réimpression de l'Ancien Moniteur*, vol. i, p. 129.

the committee appeared to take its responsibilities lightly or to lack perseverance and dispatch.[1] His most important speeches and memoirs of the two years, notably an opinion against granting veto powers to the king in September, 1789, an opinion against royal investiture of judges in May, 1790, and an opinion against the re-election of deputies in May, 1791, were called forth by debates over the constitution. Membership on the Committee on Pensions, created on January 14, 1790, kept him occupied many hours and gave him the valuable practice of making two long reports to the National Assembly in the name of the committee.[2] In April, 1790, he accepted election as secretary of the assembly, although he had once refused the office earlier in the session at Versailles.[3]

Little by little his preconceived political theories received the impact of parliamentary experience, but his speeches plainly showed that his theories would be able to hold their own with his experiences. He believed that practice, given half a chance, would normally coincide with reason, but if they contradicted each other he put his faith unblushingly in reason.

His *Opinion sur la sanction royale*[4] combined a practical

---

[1] MLL, vol. i, pp. 81-82, 84-85.

[2] *Ibid.*, vol. i, pp. 75, 77; *Procès-Verbal de l'Assemblée nationale constituante, 14 janvier, 1790*, p. 9. His first report, on July 31, 1790, had to do with pensions for men of letters (*Moniteur*, 1790, no. 214; *Archives parlementaires*, vol. xvii, pp. 444-445; *Réimpression de l'Ancien Moniteur*, vol. v, pp. 278-279), while the second, on February 21, 1791, advocated helping the poverty-stricken Acadian refugees (*Archives parlementaires*, vol. xxiii, pp. 378-380; *Correspondance de MM. les députés...*, vol. viii, pp. 208-213; *Moniteur*, 1791, no. 53; *Réimpression de l'Ancien Moniteur*, vol. vii, p. 440).

[3] MLL, vol. i, p. 77. He served as one of the four secretaries for the normal term of two weeks, from April 9 to April 24, 1790 (*Archives parlementaires*, vol. xv, p. 285; *Procès-Verbal de l'Assemblée nationale constituante, 24 avril, 1790*, p. 30).

[4] There is a difference of opinion as to whether or not this entire discourse was delivered in the assembly. In the *Correspondance de MM. les députés...*, vol. ii, pp. 333-340, the title is given as *Opinion sur la sanction royale, prononcée dans la séance du 2 septembre 1789, par M. Delarevelliere*

objection, namely that an unlimited veto would lead to royal tyranny, with the theoretical impediment of sovereignty's inherent indivisibility. His argument was that sovereignty belonged to the people naturally and could not be alienated, even at their express desire, whereas to allow the king unlimited veto would mean that the people were giving away a part of their sovereignty. The king, as a member of society, had a right to his opinion, but he ought never, according to the dictates of reason, to set himself against all the rest of society by an absolute veto. Revelliere-lépeaux thus reached the conclusion of the undesirability and impossibility of unlimited veto for the king. On the other hand, where was there any assurance of protection from the betrayal of faith on the part of the legislature? His answer to his own question was that such a contingency was less probable than royal presumption, and that an emergency would best be met by a suspensive veto that would return the matter to the discretion of the real sovereign, the people, at the subsequent elections. Then he concluded his discourse with the sober reminder that even should the veto eventually be found an ideal expedient there was always time to confer it upon the monarch, inasmuch as history had shown it a great deal easier to give away prerogatives than to recapture one of them.

This discourse is important for its indication of Revelliere-lépeaux's attitude toward the British government as well as his persuasion against the royal veto. He profoundly admired the genius of the English people and their political accomplishments, he explained, but he would be the last to advocate adopting any device simply because it came from England. The people of that country, because they loved independence, had found successful methods of safeguarding their liberties; these improvements had come almost inadvertently in the course of events, without the benefit of a conscious and wide-

Delépeaux. The *Archives parlementaires*, vol. ix, p. 65, Index vol. xxxiii, p. 448, records it as " son opinion, non prononcée, sur la sanction royale."

spread overhauling that might have ironed out the inconsis-
tencies. As a result, pernicious evils continued to exist side by
side with enlightened practices; hence, the fact that the king
of England had a veto or any other power did not justify
giving a corresponding prerogative to the king of France.
Rather, now that the French people were risking that difficult
expedient, revolution, for the sake of being free to rearrange
their entire political framework, they should consider each
question in the light of reason and not adopt thoughtlessly the
current mode of another country, however praiseworthy the
foreign nation might be.

Eight months later, when the National Assembly was discussing the investiture of judges, Revelliere-lépeaux gave another opinion [1] that won him applause. It had been voted to
make the office of judge elective, but after approving so startling an innovation many deputies were quite willing to leave
the honor of installing judges to the king. Revelliere-lépeaux
burst forth with warnings that investiture was only one step
toward gathering judicial power back into royal hands. As
usual, he justified his position by appealing to the reason of
the situation; reason, in this case, involved an interpretation
of the doctrine of separation of powers. He began by reiter-
ating the basic principle that government was an attribute of
the people's sovereignty; sovereignty itself was indivisible but
was best served by differentiated agents. The people should
carry out every part of the government of which it was physi-
cally and morally capable, leaving to its law-making and law-
enforcing agents only what could not be achieved directly; in
particular, it was much better to keep the administration of
justice under the supervision of the electorate than to delegate
it to either the legislature or the king, because one of the two
might gradually absorb the judiciary, thus leading to an undue
concentration of power that could raise one of the people's

[1] *Archives parlementaires*, vol. xv, pp. 390-391; *Correspondance de MM.
les députés...*, vol. v, pp. 85-90; *Moniteur*, 1790, no. 126; *Réimpression de
l'Ancien Moniteur*, vol. iv, p. 289.

agents higher than the people itself. The people might cease to be sovereign.

His official expression of trust in the people suffered no diminution during the following year. He was constantly eager to subordinate the legislature as well as the king to the sovereign electorate. In May, 1791, when the National Constituent Assembly voted that its members would not be eligible to the following Legislative Assembly, he seized that occasion to press the matter of inserting in the constitution a permanent prohibition against re-election of deputies.[1] He was willing to admit their being seated in alternate legislatures, but he was indefatigably opposed to consecutive candidacies. He pointed out the wisdom of bringing every representative of the people to a sense of the temporary character of his mandate. Emphasizing each deputy's temporary elevation would, he believed, enhance the dignity of the estate of the simple citizen. Any advantage accruing from uninterrupted experience on the part of legislators would be more than counteracted by the evil cliques and corruption that an overweening sense of security might induce. There should be no gratuitous fear of the scarcity of suitable legislative candidates, because the incoming régime of liberty would automatically prepare citizens for political responsibility. He urged France to witness Great Britain, where " all men endowed by nature with a certain aptitude, and so situated as to receive a careful education, take the trouble to study political matters and render themselves capable of the management of public affairs." [2] This confidence in the abundance of capable men to be brought forth under a régime of liberty sounds democratic in the extreme. On the other hand, reference to a selected group of the British public as able to govern, namely, those who possessed " a certain aptitude " and " a careful education " suggests a

[1] *Archives parlementaires,* vol. xxvi, pp. 200-201 ; *Correspondance de MM. les députés...*, vol. ix, pp. 161-166; *Moniteur,* 1791, no. 140; *Réimpression de l'Ancien Moniteur,* vol. viii, pp. 435-436.

[2] *Correspondance de MM. les députés...*, vol. ix, p. 165.

reserve that somehow gives the lie to his concluding assertion that " . . . every superiority, even that of talents, is disquieting for liberty . . ." He was firm in his conviction that he was founding a state upon the will of the whole people, but already his definition of the people was being limited.

In view of Revelliere-lépeaux's traditional reputation for hostility toward organized Christianity, it is of interest to note that in April, 1790, he expressed himself strongly against recognizing the Catholic Church as the one state church.[1] Yet he believed in state regulation of the Catholic Church. In June, 1791, he advocated state investiture of ecclesiastics and supported the Civil Constitution of the Clergy. His parliamentary record during the Constituent Assembly did not, it must be remarked, foreshadow his subsequent devotion to the cult of Theophilanthropy. If deism was already absorbing his personal attention, he gave no sign of it in his public addresses.

His concern about finance found expression chiefly in respect to Angevin affairs. Early in the Constituent Assembly he protested against Necker's plan to keep the *gabelle,* for the salt tax was particularly despised in Anjou.[2] On the other hand, when it was proposed to issue the first Revolutionary paper money, Revelliere-lépeaux asserted (September, 1790) that in spite of rumors to the contrary Anjou was willing to support the assignat as far as lay in its power.[3]

Finally, then, on the last day of September, 1791, Louis XVI closed the National Constituent Assembly with pomp and ceremony, and Revelliere-lépeaux, in accordance with his own cherished principles, returned to the status of simple citizen. He was proud of having given France a constitution and determined to support that constitution with every ounce

---

[1] Meynier, *op. cit.,* p. 177; *Correspondance de MM. les députés . . .,* vol. iv, pp. 525 *et seq.*

[2] MLL, vol. i, pp. 75-77.

[3] *Moniteur,* 1790, no. 269; *Archives parlementaires,* vol. xix, p. 194.

of energy he possessed. The same final day he had mounted the tribune in defense of the people's rights. To be sure, it was only a matter of form. The day before, the king had sent a short note, peremptory in tone, to the president of the assembly: " I propose, Monsieur, to close the assembly tomorrow; I authorize you to announce my visit; I shall arrive at three o'clock. Signed: Louis." Revelliere-lépeaux was offended by the terms of the note, when it was read in its entirety in the minutes to be ratified on the last day; Louis XVI appeared to take no cognizance of the fact that he was King of the French by the grace of God *and the constitutional law of the state*. Without, however, making an issue of this particular communication as an offense against the dignity of the assembly, Revelliere-lépeaux asked that a formula of correspondence between the legislative body and the king be drawn up and established by the following assembly, which would know how to " maintain the consideration due to the national majesty in the person of its representatives charged directly by the nation to express its will." [1] The assembly saw fit to adopt this last-minute tribute to the General Will.

II

The Revolution was over, many Frenchmen then believed, but it was not yet understood or accepted. Revelliere-lépeaux, returning to Angers with his wife and daughters, devoted himself to explaining and persuading, patiently at first and then with a desperate tenacity urging devotion to the new régime. Taking up the life of a simple citizen did not mean for him cultivating his garden at Faye, while the world passed by. He accepted election to the board of administrators for the department of Maine-et-Loire. He joined the National Guards. When he was approached about his possible candidacy for the office of mayor of Angers, he declined the honor in order to throw his influence to Pilastre, who did become

---

[1] *Archives parlementaires*, vol. xxxi, p. 675.

mayor.[1] He busied himself for the most part in and about
Angers, but from May to August, 1792, he was at Orléans on
call for jury duty in the national high court.[2] Twice during
those three months he went to Paris for short stays. Then,
less than twelve months after the close of the Constituent
Assembly, the whole political question was reopened. Revelliere-lépeaux was elected deputy to the Convention and went
to Paris again. Again he was faced with the task of making
a constitution, this second time for a government without a
king.

Although the period of the Legislative Assembly has settled
into history as an interim, a space of somewhat labored breath-
ing between the Constituent Assembly and the Convention, the
year's essential significance to Revelliere-lépeaux, on the contrary, lay precisely in his unawareness of the temporary nature
of the régime. He was troubled by the Legislative Assembly's
lack of success in dealing with the political situation in general and with the state of Paris in particular; he was first
puzzled and then resentful in his attitude toward the opponents
of the constitutional monarchy. Not until the very end of the
year did he reluctantly admit that his work of constitution-
making was all to do over again, and even then he thought
that the Legislative Assembly was criminally negligent in de-
posing the king without having some constructive plan of its
own ready to meet the situation.[3] In the process of expound-
ing as permanent what proved to be temporary, he nevertheless added to his political experience. He had been recognized
as a facile and self-assured speaker since the days of his botany
lectures. Several of his addresses at the Constituent Assembly
had brought more applause and favorable comment than simple

---

[1] MLL, vol. i, pp. 88-89; "La Municipalité d'Angers pendant la Révolution," *L'Anjou historique*, Mars 1904, pp. 476-489; "M. Pilastre,
député de Maine-et-Loire (1752-1830)," *L'Anjou historique*, Septembre-
Octobre 1913, p. 126.

[2] MLL, vol. i, pp. 112-113.

[3] *Ibid.*, vol. i, p. 117.

politeness required. Once more in Angers, with the prestige of having served two years and a half as deputy and with the confidence of having set the government upon the right track, he welcomed every occasion to speak in public. The routine of his duties as departmental administrator gave less play to his developing oratorical powers than did his membership in the flourishing and exclusive society of the Friends of the Constitution,[1] which had been founded at Angers in the spring of 1790 and where both national and local problems were proudly watched over and zealously discussed. The tone of the society was on the whole loyal to the new régime, and when occasionally a daring soul ventured to suggest that the reform was only half accomplished or that the king's actions were treasonable such untoward allusions were usually hushed. Especially was this loyalty to the constitution the rule during the six months from November, 1791, to April, 1792, the period of Revelliere-lépeaux's active membership in the society. Later, while he was away at Orléans, the wave of questioning grew stronger, gradually undermining the society's allegiance to the Constitution of 1791.

The society of the Friends of the Constitution at the time of its organization was intensely missionary in spirit, and Revelliere-lépeaux's undeviating convictions were in tune with its proselytizing fervor. The rural sections near Angers, where both peasants and nobles, and certain of the bourgeois as well, uncompromisingly refused to accept the constitutional monarchy, offered a public most decidedly in need of conversion. Had it not been for the question of taxes, the objectors might have been left to adapt themselves little by little to the situation, but without taxes the new government could not go on. Revelliere-lépeaux, his colleagues in the departmental administration, and his fellow Friends of the Constitution all believed that forcing payments by National Guard bayonets

[1] MLL, vol. i, p. 89. An admirable concise history of the political clubs of Angers at this epoch is given in Meynier, op. cit., Chapter VII.

would not help matters. There remained the way of personal persuasion, which the departmental administration tried first by sending out a delegation on a three-week circular tour, in January and February, 1792, passing through the districts of Saint-Florent, Cholet, and Vihiers. The Friends of the Constitution followed the official example by sending out an expedition on their own account, toward the end of March, into the country spoken of as the Mauges, passing by Chalonnes and Beaupréau. They sponsored a second expedition, the Monday after Easter, to Chemillé. Revelliere-lépeaux was appointed head of both official and unofficial missionary delegations, and in each instance he acted as chief orator. He and his friends attempted to bring together the citizenry in these several towns, to commemorate the day by some such ceremony as planting a tree of liberty, to harangue the crowd, and then to close with a joyous fête. The receptions varied, from cold official tolerance at Beaupréau, where the expedition was considered entirely gratuitous if not a little silly, and where Revellierelépeaux was reproached bitterly by his own godfather, to the hearty welcome at Chemillé, where the program was carried out with enthusiastic good will. Revelliere-lépeaux, although encouraged by the signs of approval, was forced to admit that the permanent results of itinerant preaching were extremely unsatisfying, whereas the countryside for the most part resented him and his band of constitution purveyors as a set of Don Quixotes or as more serious intruders who ought to be punished for disturbing the peace.[1]

Certain incidents of these patriotic excursions made an indelible impression upon Revelliere-lépeaux, who, with all his devotion to general principles, was extremely personal in his reactions. These impressions changed his positive beliefs very little. His mind was too well made up for that. Nevertheless,

[1] MLL, vol. i, pp. 93-107; Meynier, *op. cit.*, Chapter VIII; *Rapport du voyage des commissaires de la Société des Amis de la Constitution d'Angers, au club ambulant établi dans les Mauges, fait à la séance du 1er Avril, l'an IV de la liberté; par Louis Marie Larevelliere-Lepeaux*, 8 pp.

they defined his enemies and classified his decisions about what he could not tolerate in the future.

The expedition of four members of the society of the Friends of the Constitution to Beaupréau at the end of March, with Revelliere-lépeaux as leader, was swelled at Chalonnes by the addition of a contingent of like-minded apostles, among them Leclerc. On the way from Chalonnes to Beaupréau, the handful of envoys were obliged to pass by Saint-Laurent, where the church had been closed after the refusal of the priest to take the oath of allegiance to the new régime, and the rumor had spread abroad that the white Virgin had miraculously flown out to a neighboring oak tree for refuge. By the time Revelliere-lépeaux and his comrades came to Saint-Laurent, nearly two thousand people had gathered to worship before the oak tree. The roads and paths of the entire vicinity were congested; it was difficult to push through even on horseback; and for a time the crowd was in a threatening mood toward the newcomers who showed no desire to reverence the apparition of the Virgin. Finally they managed to argue and push their way through without suffering any harm. On their return journey, three days later, they found the crowd dispersed. Thinking to destroy at its root what they considered superstitious veneration, they cut down the offending oak tree, but they had hardly reached Angers before they heard the news that their lesson to the misguided faithful had only caused the Virgin to take up a new abiding place in a nearby bush.[1] Obstruction of public roads by religious processions and pilgrimages grew upon Revelliere-lépeaux as a symbol of the church's opposition to the new political régime.

Revelliere-lépeaux's pre-Revolutionary desires to reform the Catholic Church, by allowing the clergy to marry and parishioners to choose their own clergy, had not seemed to him sufficient reason for breaking with the church. His drifting away from Catholicism had not gone so far as to prevent his

[1] MLL, vol. i, p. 101.

daughters' baptism in the church or his own friendship with several curés. During the Constituent Assembly, in spite of the fact that he had favored the Civil Constitution of the Clergy, he had not made himself conspicuous by his anti-clerical attitude. Many years later, in his memoirs, he reflected that it had been a mistake to arouse the opposition of the Catholic Church by demanding a civic oath that offended the conscience 'of the clergy. Although there is no evidence to indicate that he reached this conclusion in the early days of the Revolution, he did say in December, 1791, that if recalcitrant priests had merely refused to take an oath no one would have disturbed their liberty of conscience.[1] Personal observations in Anjou during the year 1791-1792, after the Constituent Assembly and before the Convention, did a great deal to convince Revelliere-lépeaux that the influence of the Catholic Church was being thrown against the newly established constitutional monarchy. He made up his mind that the Catholic Church was menacing political liberty. Gradually he became convinced that reform in the church would not help the situation, and eventually he reached the belief that an unrestricted church and a free state could not live together. The foundations of his later unrelenting hostility to the Catholic Church were thus laid before the Convention began. Even so, he in no way interfered with the pious beliefs of his sister, nor did he betray her when she offered refuge to non-juring priests.[2]

His two visits to Paris during his sojourn at Orléans, for the celebration of the capture of the Bastille and again a short time afterward, filled him with still other anxieties and strengthened other distrusts that were already haunting him. While he was marching with the batallion of the Jardin du Roi, to the Champ-de-Mars for the celebration of the fourteenth of July, according to his memoirs written a quarter of a century

---

[1] *Département de Mayenne et Loire...Roi des Français* (Angers, le 14 décembre, l'an trois de la liberté française), 2 pp.; MLL, vol. i, p. 108.

[2] Godard Faultrier, *Le Champs des Martyrs* (Angers, 1899), pp. 12-15.

later, he was struck by the fact that everybody was shouting for this or that popular hero, whereas no one seemed to think of crying " Vive la nation " or " Vive la liberté " or " Vive la constitution." He was very indignant and expressed his feelings so vehemently to the group around him that at least in his immediate vicinity the cries of enthusiasm no longer rose for one man or another but for the whole nation.[1] On the occasion of his second visit, the memoirs continue, his fears of impending demagoguery were fed by his meeting Robespierre at the house of Duplay. He had lunched with Robespierre once during the Constituent Assembly and had shared his views on many subjects; in particular, he had voted as did Robespierre against the re-election of deputies. Robespierre in 1792, however, as a beautifully powdered household divinity, though not yet the Robespierre of 1793, was too pretentious and distant for Revelliere-lépeaux, who disliked him on the spot, or, it might better be said, believed years later that he had disliked him on the spot.[2]

Leaving Orléans about the middle of August, Revelliere-lépeaux set out once more for Angers, totally discouraged. His three-months' separation from his family had netted the cause of liberty only one jury service on an unimportant case and had cost him a great deal of painful loneliness, especially toward the end when news reached him that his younger daughter Angèle was seriously ill. He was politically disillusioned. The king, whom he had trusted and defended, even when in his heart he was beginning to suspect royal treason, was no longer in a position to protect and carry out the constitution, and the constitution itself had come to a most unenviable pass. Shortly before his arrival at Angers, while he was struggling against this mood of general despondency, he received word that Angèle had died.[3]

[1] MLL, vol. i, pp. 113-114.
[2] Ibid., vol. i, pp. 114-115.
[3] Ibid., p. 116; cf. supra, p. 36, note 2.

At the end of August, 1792, primary assemblies met again all over France, much in the manner of March, 1789. In the course of the subsequent electoral assembly of Maine-et-Loire, Revelliere-lépeaux was the fourth deputy elected, but he received next to the highest number of votes among the entire delegation. On the morning of September 5, with Pilastre and Leclerc he was given his new mandate.[1] The first attempt to create a new government to express the General Will had miscarried. The three bosom friends, with their eight fellow deputies from Maine-et-Loire, set out for Paris once more, this time intending to draw up a constitution for a government without a king.

III

> ... on convoqua une Convention, qui, de quelque manière qu'on la juge, fera toujours l'étonnement de la postérité.[2]

For Revelliere-lépeaux and for many of his colleagues, the Convention fell, in retrospect, into three periods: pre-Terror, Terror, and post-Terror or pre-hiding, hiding, and post-hiding. In his memory and theirs survived the indelible impression of danger, strong enough to be remembered as the axis of preceding and subsequent experiences, as people today speak of " before the War " and " after the War." This overwhelming danger was sandwiched in between two less tragic eras, the first eight months of the Convention, September, 1792, to May, 1793, when Revelliere-lépeaux was bold though puzzled, and the closing fifteen months, August, 1794, to October, 1795, which found him weary but still trusting his middle-of-the-road republican principles.

The early pre-Terror stage of the Convention actually lasted several months longer for Revelliere-lépeaux than for many of his colleagues. He was excluded from the Convention, not in May but in August, 1793. His first period of active parlia-

---

[1] Bodinier, op. cit., p. 48; MLL, vol. i, pp. 117-118.
[2] MLL, vol. i, p. 117.

mentary service as a member of the Convention continued, therefore, about ten months. During this time he tried hard to be uncompromisingly republican but as non-partisan as possible. His bewilderment over the outcome of the Constitution of 1791 had somewhat cleared by the time he was elected to the Convention, so that he was able to vote for the republic with an untroubled conscience. The shift from monarchy to republic was less upsetting for him than for certain of his colleagues, since removing a public agent from his position for unworthy behavior is not so critical an adjustment as tumbling a divinely appointed king from his throne; and he had, at the outset, seen the king only in the rôle of executor of the General Will. On the other hand, although his political turn of mind made this adjustment easy once he was convinced of the king's fault, he had been slower than some of his friends to reach the conclusion of republicanism, because the General Will had allowed the king to be sanctified by incorporation into the constitution. That constitution had been his hope of salvation for the French and for mankind. When he at last admitted that it had slipped from under his feet, Revelliere-lépeaux's one desire was to provide his country with another constitution, one in which no mistake would be made, and to surround the second and final promulgation of the General Will with all the trappings of reverence and awe in order to make it increasingly respected as generation after generation lived under its beneficent aegis.[1] He never stopped urging a constitution as the solution for all ills, and, whatever happened, he held doggedly to that idea.

Until the trial of Louis XVI, Revelliere-lépeaux came into the limelight only once, on November 19, 1792, when he served as the mouthpiece of those missionary-spirited Conventionals who were bent upon saving all the tyranny-ridden peoples of the earth:[2]

[1] MLL, vol. i, p. 227; *Réimpression de l'Ancien Moniteur*, vol. xxv, p. 492.

[2] *Moniteur*, 1792, no. 325. On September 25 he had spoken briefly against concurrent exercise of judicial and legislative powers by the same individual.

The National Convention declares, in the name of the French nation, that it will confer fraternity and aid upon all peoples who shall wish to recover their liberty and charges the executive power with giving to the generals the orders necessary to carry aid to these peoples and to defend the citizens who may have been or who may be afflicted for the cause of liberty.

This first propaganda decree, as it has been called, seemed no more presumptuous to Revelliere-lépeaux than his proselytizing excursions into the country lying about Angers; nor did the infinitesimal harvests from his provincial plantings discourage him in the slightest from attempting the same procedure on an international scale. The idea that his kind of salvation might not be welcome did not occur to him. His way was true and reasonable; therefore the reaction to its appeal could not be other than spontaneously and permanently favorable. His policy of establishing a bevy of sister republics as buffer states all along the borders of France during the Directory was to be the logical conclusion of this optimistic earlier persuasion.

He saw that he could not make recommendations to sister nations without first putting his own house in order. Due judgment and execution of Louis XVI might be a trying and in some ways a regrettable necessity, but the monarch had set himself up against his own people and against the dictates of reason as expressed by the constitution. In becoming a traitor Louis XVI had forfeited at the same time his right to the throne and his right to live; his continued existence threatened the republic. Accordingly, Revelliere-lépeaux spent the months of December and January in a state of preoccupation with the fate of the king who had formerly been his " tender father " and " excellent prince." [1] The execution of Louis XVI was the sacrifice which the future safety of the people required, so that a republic could be constructed without fear. To this end, Revelliere-lépeaux composed two pamphlets; [2] and to this end

---

[1] *Doléances, voeux et pétitions . . . par un laboureur, un syndic & un bailli de campagne*, p. 6.

[2] *Opinion de L. M. La Revellière-Lépeaux . . . sur la question de savoir*

he voted, first, against referring the fate of the monarch to the people, in the second place, in favor of the death penalty, and, finally, against delay in carrying out the execution.[1] His position was clear and unhesitating, and he suffered no regrets.

He never again swung as far to the left as when he voted to execute the king. After that measure had been taken, he confidently expected to establish in France a moderate republican government. Already on January 7, in his *Opinion . . . sur la question de l'appel au peuple*, he had discoursed at length upon the dangers of popular tyranny and had not hesitated to attack specifically the Commune of Paris, stout Angevin that he was with his firmly grounded sense of justice and equal rights for the entire people. A month later, February 11, his article " Le Cromwellisme " appeared in the *Chronique de Paris*, putting him irretrievably on the other side of the fence from the Mountain. Without mincing words he insisted that unleashed popular control was the surest path to anarchy, which in turn invited dictatorship.[2] These were unmistakably Girondin sentiments; but, although Revelliere-lépeaux was content to remain the friend of the Girondins, he never actually entered their ring. Since 1789 he had urged that as much local government as possible be left in the hands of locally chosen officials, but in his advocacy of decentralized administration he did not demand a referendum upon matters of strictly national im-

si Louis XVI peut être mis en jugement (1er décembre, 1792). In sending a copy of the pamphlet to a friend at Nantes, on December 10, 1792, Revelliere-lépeaux made the comment: "... independently of purely political arguments, I have tried to bring in moral considerations, as you will see, ... only too happy to put in a favorable light some of the truths which men should never forget if they are to be good, free and happy." (BMN, MSS 661, no. 139). *Opinion de L.-M. Revelliere-Lépeaux . . . sur la question de l'appel au peuple* (7 janvier, 1793).

[1] MLL, vol. i, pp. 125-131; Meynier, *op. cit.*, pp. 322-329; *Réimpression de l'Ancien Moniteur*, vol. xv, p. 193; *Supplément au No. 121 du Journal des débats et des décrets*, p. 5.

[2] MLL, vol. iii, pp. 3-6.

port.[1] On grounds of impracticability he had voted against referring Louis XVI's fate to popular decision throughout France;[2] his vote was interpreted as willingness to disregard the provinces and saved him in Jacobin eyes. It is true that in March he took his place courageously in the tribune and by his arguments contributed to the defeat of Danton's proposal that ministers might be chosen from among members of the Convention.[3] In April he spoke in favor of bringing Marat to judgment.[4] Nevertheless, in the Convention's purging at the end of May and the beginning of June, he was neither put out nor threatened, although he missed no occasion to champion the cause of his arrested colleagues. Not until August, after making himself continually a nuisance to the Mountain, was he finally attacked in full session and obliged to retire. He managed to escape into hiding, as did Pilastre and Leclerc, and shortly afterward the Committee of General Security ordered the three put under arrest.[5]

---

[1] MLL, vol. i, pp. 136-145, presents a thought-over version of his ideas on federalism and local government. In 1789 his fervor for decentralization seems to have grown from his belief in popular sovereignty and in the wisdom of an arrangement whereby each individual might exercise every political right of which he was capable. His was a positive program, including a plan for provincial assemblies, local assessment and collection of taxes, a system of local courts, and even a reconstitution of the national army on the basis of provincially-supported units (see *Plaintes et désirs*, p. 5, and *Doléances, voeux et pétitions*, pp. 7, 11, 12, 16). As the Revolution progressed he opposed the growing power of Paris over the Convention on the ground that such a domination was the tyranny of the few over the many and hence an abandonment of the principle of popular sovereignty. For local affairs, it is clear, he continued to prefer decentralization, but in matters of national import he seems rather to have objected to the exclusion of the greater part of France from any voice in affairs than to have decried a centralized system of management (except as it might lend itself to despotic exploitation).

[2] Cf. *Opinion ... sur la question de l'appel au peuple.*

[3] MLL, vol. i, pp. 133-135; *Moniteur*, 1793, nos. 73, 82.

[4] *Moniteur*, 1793, no. 107.

[5] AN, F7, 4774, 9; MLL, vol. i, pp. 150-160; *Moniteur*, 1793, no. 156.

Then the period of hiding began. Revelliere-lépeaux had already been deprived of the comfort of seeing his wife and daughter before the committee's decree put him beyond normal legal protection. When times had been troubled in the spring, he had sent them, for greater security, to live at Montmorency near Paris, where he saw them only occasionally on Sunday. His anxiety had deepened when Clémentine fell dangerously ill with smallpox, and she was scarcely well when circumstances attending the expulsion of deputies at the end of May caused him to take the further precaution of dispatching her and her mother to Angers, where there was reason to suppose they would be safe.[1] When the order for his arrest was issued, he was living on the quai d'Ecole, a lodging he soon left to join Pilastre and Leclerc in the rue Copeau,[2] where they were less well known and might hope to escape detection. There could be no question of Revelliere-lépeaux's returning to Angers, for there, as well as in Paris, the Jacobins had taken full possession and were delighting to bring traitors and federalists to justice. Jean-Baptiste de la Revelliere had been put in

[1] MLL, vol. i, pp. 145-146, 150.

[2] The rue Copeau of 1793 is today the rue Lacépède; MLL, vol. i, pp. 155, 157.

Illustrations on opposite page

Priory of Saint Radegonde in the forest of Montmorency, near Paris, where Revelliere-lépeaux was in hiding for several weeks in the spring of 1794. Here, also, the manuscript of the memoirs of Madame Roland was secreted before its publication. The house was reduced to a pile of stones at some time between November, 1932, and March, 1933. Curiously, it was classed as a public monument at about the same period, and in May, 1933, photographs of the building, taken when it was still intact, appeared in daily papers of Paris (*Le Journal, Jeudi* 25 Mai 1933). The photograph (A. Tennyson Beals, New York) reproduced here was made from a heliogravure published as the frontispiece of Auguste Rey's *Le Naturaliste Bosc et les Girondins à Saint-Prix* (Paris, 1882).

prison,[1] and Revelliere-lépeaux's wife and daughter were subjected to unpleasant and threatening comments. To go home
would have been nothing short of suicide.

The three friends stayed on in the rue Copeau, absenting
themselves more and more from their rooms as the probability
of discovery seemed more and more imminent. They formed
the habit of going often to spend the night at the home of first
one friend and then another, so that their whereabouts would
be fairly uncertain at any given moment. Leclerc returned
home once too often and was arrested. Revelliere-lépeaux was
beside himself, and save for the intervention of friends would
have gone back to the rue Copeau to be found and sent off to
prison with Leclerc.[2] Still in a state of despair, he met the
naturalist Bosc at the home of the Thouin family. Bosc himself was under suspicion, owing to his very close friendship
with the former minister of interior Roland, Madame Roland,
and their coterie, but he was able to ward off serious consequences by living and botanizing on the property Sainte-Radegonde, near Montmorency, which he was looking after on behalf of Bancal des Issarts.[3] Loath to incriminate his friends,
Revelliere-lépeaux was nevertheless brought to accept Bosc's
offer of hospitality and was smuggled out of Paris at the end
of February, hunchbacked and easily recognizable though he
was, to hide quietly in what was left of the buildings of the old
priory. If any questions were asked in the immediate neighborhood, Bosc let it be understood that his guest was someone very
ill, come to profit by a sojourn in the country air.[4] That excuse
began to wear thin, however, and after three weeks at Sainte-
Radegonde Revelliere-lépeaux decided to accept the pressing
invitation of Pincepré de Buire to take refuge with him at

[1] MLL, vol. i, p. 158.

[2] *Ibid.*, p. 163.

[3] Auguste Rey, *Le Naturaliste Bosc, un Girondin herborisant* (Paris,
1901), pp. 22-23.

[4] *Ibid.*, pp. 32-35; MLL, vol. i, pp. 163-168.

Péronne. Revelliere-lépeaux loved the forest of Montmorency as a botanist, and he had sentimental remembrances of his explorations of the preceding spring with his wife and daughter. For hours after Bosc started him on his way and turned back to welcome another fugitive, who was taking the place left vacant at Sainte-Radegonde, Revelliere-lépeaux wandered about the wood, saying good-bye to familiar landmarks. Then he began the long tramp northward, by devious paths and long roads which taxed his waning strength. He left Sainte-Radegonde on March 18, and only eleven interminable days later, with scarcely a sou in his pocket and hardly the strength to put one foot in front of the other, he finally was received with open arms by his friends at Buire.[1]

Not even at that distance from Paris could he enjoy a sense of security. A comfortable bed, good food, and fresh air did wonders for the failing health he had mentioned in a letter to the administrators of Maine-et-Loire as the reason for his resignation from the Convention.[2] Still, every morning when he woke up, he knew that for him to live through the day was one more risk for his hosts as well as for himself. Fortunately, the officials of the neighborhood closed their eyes more or less to the presence of the sick botanist who spent his days roaming about the fields and was reputed to be gathering specimens for a herbarium such as had never before been seen in that part of the country. Fortunately, also, the personal friends of Pincepré de Buire did not ask too many questions when they came to visit or tell too many tales when they went away. News trickled through slowly, especially that censorable news which would give information about relatives and close friends. Occasional letters from the Thouin establishment told what they could in an enigmatic way, but Revelliere-lépeaux did not hear of his

[1] MLL, vol. i, pp. 168-179.

[2] AML, L 152-153, *Correspondance avec la Députation de Maine-de-Loire*, Letter, autograph and signed (these words to be abbreviated hereafter as *a.* and *s.*), " L. M. Revelliere-lépeaux " to " Les citoyens administrateurs du dept. de Maine et Loire," 15 août l'an 2.

brother's execution, following a summary trial before the revolutionary tribunal,[1] until after the reign of the Commune was over. April, May, June, and July passed pleasantly. Sunshine and nourishing food and the distractions of scientific pursuits wrought a marked improvement in his health. Yet he and his friends continued to live under the threat of discovery and death.

At the end of July, 1794, with Robespierre's death, there was relief. The White Terror had its victims, to be sure, but the focus of action shifted, and the discomfort of fearful expectancy moved toward the left. Revelliere-lépeaux, with tears of gratitude to his fearless hosts left Buire and Péronne for Paris. There he found Leclerc, safe after cramped months in prison where he had been kept, so the story went, until his two friends should be ferreted out in order to make the punishment more severe by sending all three to the same guillotine the same day. Pilastre, too, had escaped, after a prolonged wandering, beginning at Angers and ending at Montmorency, where he worked as a carpenter. Toward the end of the Terror he had managed infrequent secret meetings with Bosc near an overgrown pond which Bosc, disguised as a peasant, indicated by singing " A la mare, aux canards "[2] as he walked by the workshop, where Pilastre heard without seeming to pay any attention. Taking advantage of their new freedom, Leclerc was married on November 9, 1794, to Louise Thouin, and Pilastre on the same day to Adelaide Lejay, niece of two artists, Monnet and Geoffroy. Revelliere-lépeaux was present at both weddings.[3]

All the happiness and gaiety of release from fear and tension, however, could not change the fact that Revelliere-lépeaux

---

[1] F. Uzureau, *Deux Fédéralistes angevins guillotinés à Paris*, reprinted from the *Revue historique de la Révolution et de l'Empire*, Juillet-Décembre, 1916.

[2] Rey, *op. cit.*, pp. 40-41.

[3] *Ibid.*, p. 43; MLL, vol. i, p. 199; Collection Pilastre, Archives de Soudon, Marriage contract of Urbain Pilastre and Adelaide Marie Lejay.

was penniless. His comfortable, though modest, income from his own and his wife's property was cut off by the ravages of war in the west of France, where his house, so carefully built and so sentimentally cherished at Faye, had been looted, burned, and razed to the ground. By frugal living in the days of the Constituent Assembly, he had been able to put aside something from his salary as a deputy, but this had been sunk long before in buying a piece of property out of the lands that had been confiscated and resold by the nation. This property, though it might in the end turn into a good investment, was making no immediate returns.[1] Because there was no money for traveling and because affairs in Anjou needed attention, his wife and daughter were unable to join him in Paris; and he returned to the hospitable Buire to spend the winter of 1794–1795 without having seen Madame Revelliere-lépeaux and Clémentine. The following March, after a separation of nearly two years, his family was reunited in Paris, where they took a tiny apartment near the Jardin des Plantes and were managing to scrape along with the minimum of food and comfort when his salary as reinstated deputy to the Convention relieved them from fear of the misery that is one step beyond poverty.[2]

The question of his reinstatement had been first brought before the Convention as early as December, 1794, but the final decision was not made until March, 1795.[3] His standing rose from day to day through the seven remaining months of the Convention, not in any spectacular fashion but solidly and in a way to attract confidence. His argument in favor of secret treaties, delivered eight days after his return to the Convention, won marked applause and earned his election, a few days

---

[1] AN, C, 353, 1838ᵛ; *Annales historiques de la Révolution française,* Janvier-Février 1928, pp. 67-68: "Compte rendu par L.-M. Révellière-Lépeaux, député de Maine-et-Loire, en vertu du décret de la Convention nationale du 4 vendémiaire an IV de la République."

[2] MLL, vol. i, pp. 199-201.

[3] *Ibid.,* vol. i, p. 201; *Moniteur,* An III, nos. 81, 171.

later, to the place of secretary.[1] In April he was appointed one of the Committee of Eleven to prepare still another constitution.[2] Toward the end of July he was raised to the presidency of the Convention and filled his two weeks' term of office successfully.[3] Then, for the last two months of the session, September and October, he was a member of the Committee of Public Safety, whose business was less grim than during the Terror but still quite serious in carrying its full share of the executive burden of the government.

Revelliere-lépeaux did not hold grudges against his own persecutors and sought no reprisal against the deputies who had brought about his brother's death. That attitude won him friends among those deputies who felt uneasy after the turn affairs had finally taken.[4] Yet, although he was willing to forgive individuals, Revelliere-lépeaux opposed what he called the spirit of anarchy that had made such a state of affairs possible. The Constitution of 1793 was anathema to him, and he bent every effort, in his attempts to give France the constitution she had been needing since 1792, to protect the General Will from being betrayed by either king or people.[5] This position held against all comers, together with his insistence that the financial affairs of the nation be put straight,[6] won him the confi-

[1] *Moniteur*, An III, no. 188.

[2] *Ibid.*, An III, no. 217; MLL, vol. i, pp. 227-245; *Rapport et projet de décret concernant l'ordre des délibérations et la police du Corps législatif, présentés à la Convention nationale au nom de la Commission des Onze, par L.-M. Revellière-Lépeaux. Imprimés par ordre de la Convention nationale* (Paris, An III), 28 pp.

[3] *Moniteur*, An III, nos. 306, 318.

[4] *Moniteur*, An III, no. 247, demonstrates his leniency with regard to Collot-d'Herbois, Barère, and Billaud.

[5] In favoring a moderate property qualification for admission to electoral assemblies, he argued: "... il importe de favoriser dans les élections les hommes d'une fortune médiocre; au-dessus du besoin, ils ne sont pas à vendre; au-dessous d'une grande opulence, ils ne songent pas à acheter, car ils n'en ont pas les moyens." (*Réimpression de l'Ancien Moniteur,* vol. xxv, pp. 307-308.)

[6] *Discours sur les relations extérieures, prononcé dans la séance du 26 Ventôse*, p. 1.

dence of property holders. His reputation for hard work and honesty, his habit of speaking logically and without hesitation when the occasion presented itself, and the fact that he had fewer enemies than most of his colleagues, raised his chances relatively higher than might have been expected, when the moment arrived to choose the five Directors who would put into execution the Constitution of the Year III.

Returned to the national legislature as deputy from Maine-et-Loire, Revelliere-lépeaux at the age of forty-two passed into the Council of Ancients, where on October 28 he was elected president of that body at the same time his friend Daunou was chosen president of the Council of Five Hundred. A few days later, when the Council of Five Hundred sent to the Council of Ancients its fifty candidates for the places of Executive Directors, Revelliere-lépeaux's name was at the head of the list, with seventy votes more than Reubell, his closest competitor. On the first day of November, 1795, the Council of Ancients, balloting constitutionally to designate the five Directors, marked Revelliere-lépeaux unquestionably as its favorite. He received two hundred and sixteen of the Council's two hundred and eighteen votes. His own vote and that of his friend Pilastre, cast negatively at Revelliere-lépeaux's insistent request, were the only dissenting voices in the wave of approval with which the Council of Ancients bestowed upon him one of the five highest governmental positions within the gift of the republic.[1]

[1] MLL, vol. i, pp. 309-315; *Moniteur*, An IV, nos. 44, 45; *Procès-Verbaux des séances du Conseil des Cinq Cents*, 8-9 Brumaire An IV; *Procès-Verbaux des séances du Conseil des Anciens*, 4-10 Brumaire An IV.

10 Brumaire

N° 7

L.M. Reveillère-lepeaux

Au conseil des 500.

Citoyens,

Réduit a un très grand épuisement par une longue suite de maux et de fatigues, ne pouvant par conséquent me livrer que difficilement au travail, ayant de plus une extreme répugnance pour tout ce qui m'arrache a la vie privée, j'avois pris la ferme résolution de refuser ma nomination au directoire executif au cas que j'y fusses porté, et je m'en étois expliqué avec tous mes collegues.

Cependant les deux conseils m'ont honoré de leurs suffrages et les hommes auxquels je dois le plus de confiance m'ont vivement pressé d'accepter. je ne me crois pas plus sage que le corps legislatif et tant d'hommes qui ont toute mon estime. j'accepte donc. j'yrai jusqu'à l'extinction de mes forces. heureux! si mes foibles moyens peuvent concourir avec la sagesse du corps legislatif et les genereux efforts de mes nouveaux collegues à consolider la republique, a affermir la constitution a dejouer touts les complots, amortir toutes les haines, éteindre la soif de toutes les vengeances, a cicatriser toutes les plaies et à ramener enfin parmi nous la confiance, la concorde la paix et l'abondance. salut et respect.

L.M. Reveillère lepeaux

CHAPTER III
FIRST EXECUTIVE DIRECTORY

> Me voici arrivé à l'époque la plus remarquable de ma vie,
> puisqu'elle se lie d'une manière bien plus particulière aux évène-
> ments politiques et à l'existence de la république; car il n'y a eu
> de république, suivant moi, que pendant le gouvernement direc-
> torial. Avant, ce ne fut qu'anarchie et confusion; après, il n'y
> eut que le despotisme d'un seul, sous le nom de premier consul.
>
> Revelliere-lépeaux
> *Mémoires*, vol. i, pp. 297-298

REUBELL used exactly seven words to inform the Council of Five Hundred that he accepted his election to the Executive Directory. Barras wrote a scant five lines with six adjectives and pronouns in the first person singular: " My respect for the decisions of the two councils, my zeal, my courage, and my devotion to the republic determine me to accept my nomination to the Executive Directory." Le Tourneur sent a formal half-page answer. Revelliere-lépeaux, however, filled a whole sheet of paper, explaining how his sense of duty, his love for the re-public, and the advice of his most cherished friends had brought him to accept a place in the Directory in spite of the uncertain state of his health and his extreme aversion to giving up the life of a private citizen.[1] Sieyès was the only one of the five who refused the honor.

---

[1] *Réimpression de l'Ancien Moniteur*, vol. xxvi, pp. 362, 364. The originals of these four letters and of Carnot's subsequent note of acceptance are on display at the Musée des Archives Nationales in Paris.

Illustration on opposite page

Autograph signed letter of Revelliere-lépeaux to the Council of Five Hundred, dated November 1, 1795 (10 Brumaire An IV), accepting his election to the Executive Directory. This letter is reproduced from a photostat made with the permission of the Archives Nationales at Paris from the original in that collection.

Between nine and ten o'clock on the morning of November 2, 1795 (11 Brumaire Year IV), Reubell, Barras, Le Tourneur, and Revelliere-lépeaux met at the former headquarters of the Committee of Public Safety. Having pocketed a box of quill pens and a sheaf of writing paper from the committee's left-over supply, the four men rode in their carriage to the Palace of the Luxembourg. They were accompanied, as the constitution provided, by a guard of more than two hundred, but the uniforms of the foot soldiers were in a sorry state, and the men on horseback had no riding boots.

The Directors found the palace unheated and without furniture. The concierge bestirred himself and presently offered them chairs around a rickety table beside a fire of borrowed wood. They began by reading the minutes of the meeting of the Council of Ancients at which their election had taken place. Next, they agreed that Reubell should preside during the first term of three months. Four messengers of state were chosen, all of them former members of the Convention. Charles-Joseph Trouvé, editor of the *Moniteur* and protégé of Revelliere-lépeaux, was named secretary-general of the Directory.[1] Before this initial session adjourned, the four men attacked the problem of appointing ministers; the portfolio of foreign affairs, it was decided, would go to Sieyès, war to Carnot, and justice to Merlin de Douai.[2]

Merlin accepted the ministry of justice, but Sieyès was no more willing to be minister than Director. Carnot, refusing the portfolio of war, was elected by the councils as the fifth member of the Executive Directory to fill the place first given to Sieyès. He joined Reubell, Barras, Le Tourneur, and Revelliere-lépeaux at the Luxembourg on November 4 (13 Brumaire Year IV), the third day of their meetings. Together the five

[1] AN, AF III, 21D, 75. A. Debidour, *Recueil des actes du Directoire exécutif* (Paris, 4 vols., 1910-1917), vol. i, pp. 23-24, gives the account of Trouvé's resignation a few days later and of the appointment of Lagarde to succeed him.

[2] Debidour, *op. cit.*, vol. i, pp. 1-6; MLL, vol. i, pp. 316-317.

men composed an act declaring the Executive Directory duly installed. The note was copied on sheets of paper from the Committee of Public Safety, signed, and sent to the Council of Five Hundred and the Council of Ancients, where it was read the following day. At last the constitutional republic was under way.[1]

For several months the Directors worked ten hours a day, from ten or eleven o'clock in the morning until three or four in the afternoon, and from eight or nine o'clock in the evening until well after midnight.[2] Occasionally one or the other of them was absent, but at least three of their five signatures were necessary to validate any decision, and the days were rare when each Director did not sign his name many times.

Their chief aides in dealing with the crush of affairs were the six ministers appointed in the course of the first meetings: Merlin de Douai for justice; Bénézech, interior; Delacroix, foreign affairs; Aubert-Dubayet, war; Truguet, marine; and Faipoult, finance. Each minister was allowed to establish a secretariat with his own staff. No minister, however, had the right to confer officially with any other minister; each was responsible immediately and entirely to the Executive Directory. The Directory's unrelenting supervision of the ministries resulted in a mountain of work, which necessitated an informal partition of administrative tasks: Reubell took over justice, finance, and foreign affairs; Carnot, war; Le Tourneur, marine and colonies; Barras, police and certain other subdivisions of interior; Revelliere-lépeaux, public instruction, sciences, and the arts.[3]

[1] Debidour, *op. cit.*, vol. i, pp. 11-12; MLL, vol. i, pp. 329-330; *Procès-Verbal des séances du Conseil des Cinq-Cents, Brumaire An IV*, p. 49; *Procès-Verbal des séances du Conseil des Anciens, Brumaire An IV*, p. 35.

[2] AN, AF III, 1. The hours of opening and closing sessions are often recorded in the minutes of the first months, but later the time is given only exceptionally and then, as a rule, only for days of special ceremonies.

[3] This arrangement seems to have resulted from a private agreement or a gradual tacit understanding among the Directors; although taken for granted in contemporary memoirs, it does not figure upon official records.

This division of labor did not lead to a clear-cut separation. The men exchanged views every day. Reubell's precedence in foreign affairs did not prevent Revelliere-lépeaux from placing some of his own candidates in the diplomatic service. Carnot, contrary to the usual belief, had by no means exclusive control of military affairs; an unpublished letter from Bonaparte to Revelliere-lépeaux indicates that he discussed military affairs with other Directors as freely as with Carnot.[1] No more did Revelliere-lépeaux's occupation with public instruction and the arts and sciences lessen Carnot's keen interest in the Institut. Nevertheless, Revelliere-lépeaux did find his chief task in reconstructing institutions and in opening the way to creative talent rather than in the affairs more frequently classed under the head of politics and diplomacy. He was far from despising armies and treaties, but he conceived other methods of social control. He saw himself as official protector of learning and the arts, and he was proud to belong to a government that proposed to enlarge upon the Bourbon tradition of art patronage in good republican fashion. Now that he was converted from monarchy to republic, he believed that art and education could be infinitely more valuable and more honorable in the service of a free people than in the shadow of any court. Kings had catered to talent according to their own whims, but the France of the future, without neglecting special genius, was pledged to the nobler program of perfecting an entire people.

[1] January 28, 1797 (9 Pluviôse An V). Collection Pasquier.

Illustration on opposite page

Autograph postscript and signature of a letter from Bonaparte to Revelliere-lépeaux, dated January 28, 1797 (9 Pluviôse An V). The complete letter, never published, is in the collection of M. l'Abbé Emile Pasquier, who kindly authorized the reproduction of these concluding lines.

I

In 1789, state responsibility for education was as yet a thing untried in France. Although theories had been increasingly bandied about during the eighteenth century, schools had remained for the most part church undertakings. Consequently there were great differences of opinion when it came to mapping out some workable procedure for a governmental system of instruction. Should the state assume complete control of primary, secondary, and professional education for all citizens, or should it concern itself with only the reading, writing, and arithmetic that every person was sure to need? Should there be schools for girls as well as for boys? Should school attendance be compulsory? Should schools be established and financed directly by the state, or might private organizations be recognized and subsidized? Should there be any religious instruction in state schools? If not, what moral instruction might be adopted in its place?

The Constitution of 1791 marked the first legal assumption of public education by the state in a clause providing for primary instruction without charge. During the four years that followed, from September 1791 to September 1795, the former educational régime was paralyzed; universities and the four Academies were suppressed; many primary and secondary schools directed by religious orders were abolished outright, while others were virtually dissolved by the attempt to impose civic oaths upon instructors. Efforts to launch a constructive program during these four years led to countless recommendations and reports, frequent debates, and a succession of laws, each at variance with its predecessor, but with little practical result. Under the Legislative Assembly and the Convention, few schools were opened.

Throughout the Convention, however, the Committee of Public Instruction did not cease wrestling with these problems. Its legacy to the Directory, tempered by unsuccessful experiments in law-making and law-enforcing, was summarized by six short articles in the Constitution of 1795 and elaborated in the organic law of October 25, 1795 (3 Brumaire Year IV). The plan called for three kinds of schools, all state-founded and state-managed: primary schools to teach reading, writing, arithmetic, and republican morality; central schools for pupils from twelve to eighteen with a curriculum of languages, drawing, natural history, mathematics, chemistry and physics, grammar, composition, history and legislation; and special schools for the advanced study of astronomy, geometry and mechanics, natural history, medicine, veterinary science, rural economy, antiquities, political sciences, painting, sculpture, architecture, and music.

It was planned to have at least one primary school in each canton and at least one central school in each department. Although both primary and central schools would be under the ultimate control of the government at Paris, the departmental administrations would carry the burden of ordinary routine. Tuition would be charged, but, if pupils were poor, as many as one-fourth of the total number might attend without paying. Private schools would be permitted as well as state institutions, but they might be subjected to governmental inspection. The number, location, and organization of special schools were left to subsequent legislation.

The primary, central, and special schools were intended to meet the basic needs of public instruction. This triple system was to be supplemented, moreover, by the Institut and a series of national fêtes, thereby extending the field of education beyond schoolroom learning. The Institut de France, replacing the four Academies, was intended to reward the élite. The seven national fêtes, celebrating Youth, Marriage, Gratitude, Agriculture, Liberty, Old Age, and the Founding of the Republic, would belong to everybody.

Such was the blueprint drawn up by the Convention and inherited by the Directory. As the wheels of the republican régime began turning, Pierre-Louis Ginguené [1] was made head of the fifth division of the ministry of interior, called "General Direction of Public Instruction," and was charged with transforming the pattern into a working system.

The Institut was the first part of the general project of public instruction to come to life. While it professed to be something new, it closely resembled the academies that had been suppressed by the law of August 8, 1793. As the reincarnation, if not the lineal descendant, of the academies, it had a background, a personnel, and a sense of stability upon which to build.

Article 298 of the Constitution of 1795 authorized the founding of the Institut by the simple statement:

There is for the whole republic a national Institut charged with assembling discoveries, with perfecting the arts and the sciences.

The organic law of October, 1795, shunning the name Academy, organized the new Institut in three classes: physical and mathematical sciences, moral and political sciences, and literature and fine arts.

The Directory had been installed only a few days when Revelliere-lépeaux wrote the message of November 20 (29 Brumaire Year IV) which formally established the Institut by appointing its first forty-eight members:

The Executive Directory;
Considering that one of its duties is to open speedily all the sources of public well-being;

[1] Pierre-Louis Ginguené, 1748-1816, who had suffered imprisonment during the Terror because of the political implications of one of his poems, was one of the leading figures in the Committee of Public Instruction throughout the later days of the Convention. Shortly before Revelliere-lépeaux re-entered the Convention, Ginguené offered him the position of director general of public instruction which was being left without an incumbent by the resignation of Garat. Revelliere-lépeaux claims to have refused the offer because of excessive modesty (MLL, vol. i, p. 201). In 1795 Ginguené was named a member of the Institut, in the same class of moral and political sciences as Revelliere-lépeaux. Under the Directory, he was first made director of public instruction and later was sent as minister to Turin.

Profoundly convinced that the happiness of the French people is inseparable from the perfection of the sciences and the arts and from the increase of all human knowledge, whose power alone can feed the sacred fire of liberty which has been revealed to the nations, forge new cannon for victory, cover better cultivated fields with more abundant and more useful crops, by purifying the people's ways of living construct new foundations for domestic happiness, guide administrative zeal, enlighten the conscience of the judge, and reveal to the prudence of the legislator the future destinies of peoples mirrored in their virtues and even in their past errors;

Wishing to demonstrate solemnly to France and to all civilized nations its firm resolve to further the progress of enlightenment and to offer a new proof of its respect for the constitution in giving it without delay the reinforcement that it has prescribed itself and that is bound to assure forever to talent its éclat, to genius its immortality, to inventions their permanence, to human learning the achievement of its perfection, to the French people glory, and to virtue its most fitting reward;

Decrees:

The following persons are members of the Institut:

.   .   .   .

The Minister of Interior will notify each citizen whose name appears on the list of his appointment to the national Institut. In addition, he is charged with arranging a meeting place for them in the building of the Louvre, in accordance with the law of the first of Vendémiaire Year IV of the Republic.

Revelliere-lépeaux signed first, and after him Le Tourneur, Reubell (president), Carnot, and Barras.[1]

The original forty-eight members of the Institut were thus named by the Executive Directory. In reality, at least half the number were taken from a list prepared before the end of the Convention by the same Committee of Public Instruction which formulated the October organic law.[2]

[1] AN, AF III, 323, 1313.

[2] *Documents inédits sur l'histoire de France, Procès-Verbaux du comité d'instruction publique de la Convention Nationale*, vol. vi (Paris, 1907), pp. 833-834.

The forty-eight assembled for the first time on Sunday afternoon, December 6, 1795 (15 Frimaire Year IV). The five members of the Directory had been invited, but the pressure of affairs kept them from accepting. They did not fail, however, to send greetings to the newly established body of intellectuals nor to outline the government's expectations:

Today the Executive Directory looks with a very deep satisfaction upon the gathering of men who, according to the constitution's expressed wish, are about to set in motion the forces of the sciences and the arts in support of liberty and of the republican government which guarantees liberty to us. If matters equally important and pressing did not monopolize every moment of its time, it would have appointed one of its members to be present at your first session in order to prove how great a value it attaches to the formation of the national Institut; but if it is prevented by the force of circumstances from being present, in the person of one of its members, among the men most renowned for their talents, it is at least assured that you will never forget the public good as the end toward which all your efforts should be bent; that everything must take on a new character in the new order and that the sciences and the arts formerly too often used for the achievement of despotism or the destruction of men in the excesses fostered by idleness and weakness, must today turn about face so as to enfold all citizens in the love of virtue and inspire in them a deep respect for morality, a sustained enthusiasm for all that is noble, the firm will to maintain liberty and equality even if it costs their last drop of blood, an unchangeable consecration of all their faculties to the enlightenment of their fellow citizens and the progressive development of all the resources of public prosperity.

The Executive Directory will always be eager to further your efforts by all the means it commands; in turn, it counts upon the aid of your knowledge and your various talents. We are also assured the support of the legislature, and this happy co-operation of legislation, government, and learning will raise our fatherland to the highest degree of prosperity.[1]

[1] AN, AF III, 332, 1409.

A time was to come when men wondered whether the Institut's preoccupation with duties as expert advisers to the government left its members leisure or energy for their own researches, but at the beginning of the Directory the need for immediate social reconstruction put a premium on public utilization of the nation's best minds.

The original forty-eight members were obliged by the October law to elect twice their number in order to complete the proposed body of one hundred and forty-four. In the subsequent elections, on December 10, 1795 (19 Frimaire Year IV), three weeks after he wrote the Directory's message establishing the Institut, Revelliere-lépeaux himself was chosen a member of the class of moral and political sciences, section of *Morale*. He protested that he had not expected such an honor, but he accepted the place gladly. During the ten months that remained of the Year IV of the republican calendar (December 1795 to September 1796), the class of moral and political sciences held forty-four meetings. Revelliere-lépeaux was present four times: Tuesday, February 16 (27 Pluviôse), Sunday, February 21 (2 Ventôse), Tuesday, March 22 (2 Germinal), and Sunday, March 27 (7 Germinal).[1]

At the inaugural public appearance of the Institut, held in the Hall of the Caryatids at the Louvre on April 4, 1796, more than fifteen hundred persons were present, among them many leaders of the fashionable as well as of the intellectual world. The five members of the Directory, their official plumes nodding, arrived very precisely at six o'clock, the hour of opening. Revelliere-lépeaux was the only member of the Directory who had been elected to the Institut. Carnot was not named to the class of physical and mathematical sciences until the following

[1] This information regarding the dates of Revelliere-lépeaux's attendance was communicated through the kindness of M. Lyon-Caen, Secrétaire perpétuel de l'Académie des Sciences Morales et Politiques, Institut de France. In support of Revelliere-lépeaux's possible attendance at another session, see his autograph letter to Geoffroy, January 28, 1796 (8 Pluviôse An IV), BMN, MSS Dugast Matifeux, 44-41.

August. At this April meeting, however, Revelliere-lépeaux played no greater rôle than his colleagues. Not he, but Le Tourneur, then president of the Directory, delivered the address which fixed the seal of official approval on the Institut and formulated the hopes and desires of the government.[1]

While the old academies lived again in the Institut, the former universities were purposely left out of the new educational system; they were to be replaced by the special schools, defined by Daunou as "those particularly devoted to the exclusive teaching of a science, an art, or a profession." [2] The conception of a galaxy of advanced and professional schools which would make higher education immediately useful to society proved too ambitious for the powers of the Directory,[3] but if the efforts of four years did not add greatly to the list of special schools already existing and classified by the law of October 25, 1795, these schools were strengthened as well as oriented more definitely toward a patriotic application of their energies.

The list of institutions inherited by the Directory from the Convention under the heading of special schools included the Collège de France, the Muséum d'Histoire Naturelle, the Ecoles de Santé at Paris, Montpellier, and Strasbourg, the Bureau de

[1] A. Aulard, *Paris pendant la réaction thermidorienne et sous le Directoire* (Paris, 5 vols., 1898-1902), vol. iii, pp. 97-98; Debidour, *op. cit.*, vol. ii, pp. 92-93; Franqueville, *Le premier siècle de l'Institut de France* (Paris, 2 vols., 1895), vol. i, p. 23; *Moniteur*, nos. 203-205, 23-25 Germinal An IV (12-14 April, 1796).

[2] C. Hippeau, *L'Instruction publique en France pendant la Révolution, Discours et Rapports de Mirabeau, Talleyrand-Périgord, Condorcet, Lanthenas, Romme, Le Peletier, Saint-Fargeau, Calès, Lakanal, Daunou et Fourcroy* (Paris, 1881), p. 480. This *Rapport sur l'organisation de l'instruction publique*, presented to the Convention by Daunou on October 19, 1795 (27 Vendémiaire An IV), was in support of the plan legalized a few days later by the organic law of October 25.

[3] On June 15, 1796 (27 Prairial An IV), Revelliere-lépeaux annotated the Directory's fruitless message to the Council of Five Hundred, urging the legislators to make laws for executing the constitutional provisions for special schools. AN, AF III, 378, 1910; Debidour, *op. cit.*, vol. ii, p. 619.

Longitudes, the Ecole des Langues Orientales, the Conservatoire Nationale de Musique, and the Ecole Nationale d'Architecture. The schools of public service, whose organization was provided for by the law of October 22, 1795 (30 Vendémiaire Year IV), three days before the general outline of the educational system was voted, were for practical purposes to be considered as a sub-heading of the special schools. The law defined them as schools " to provide training in the various professions devoted exclusively to public service." This education was to center about the Ecole Polytechnique, and accompanying schools for civil, military, mining, and naval engineers.

Among all these foundations for higher and professional learning, the Muséum d'Histoire Naturelle, where André Thouin occupied a professor's chair and the Jardin des Plantes flourished under the direction of the Thouin brothers, appealed most to Revelliere-lépeaux. He knew personally most of the members of its committee of administration, which in 1796 included Van Spaendonck, Desfontaines, Mertrud, Portal, Lamarck, Daubenton, Lacépède, Jussieu, Geoffroy, and Brougniart;[1] and when problems arose they did not hesitate to call upon him for governmental advice or assistance. Late in August, for example, when the professor of natural history at Versailles announced that the orange trees were in grave danger owing to lack of care, the committee forwarded the letter to Revelliere-lépeaux. Early in October the minister of interior reported that the necessary precautions to save the trees had been taken.[2] Revelliere-lépeaux, in turn, did not fail to write the administrators when he had good news, such as the British government's kindness in releasing the captured collections of the traveler La Billardière.[3] Nor did he lack time for sending an occasional gift to enrich the museum, as

[1] BMHN, *Procès-Verbaux des Séances*, vol. ii, p. 182, August 31, 1796 (14 Fructidor An IV).

[2] *Ibid.*, vol. ii, pp. 179-180; vol. iii, p. 4.

[3] *Ibid.*, vol. ii, pp. 187-189, September 10, 1796 (24 Fructidor An IV).

in October, 1796, when he presented it with a particularly interesting shell.[1] He served as go-between in the controversy over the museum's guard in December, 1795,[2] and again in October, 1796, when funds were low, and the contractors who had made repairs were clamoring to be paid.[3] Revellierelépeaux was still a botanist at heart.

The progress of the Institut and the special schools during the first months of the Directory is something measurable and for the most part carefully recorded and already retold and interpreted. It is more difficult to form an accurate idea of the beginnings of the primary and central schools.[4] The most striking feature of these units of the new educational system was their decentralization. If the element of federalism had lost out politically in 1793 and 1794, it had its revenge at the end of 1795, when departmental and local administrations were left to take the initiative in founding and supervising schools. The other most obvious characteristic of the struggle to estab-

[1] *Ibid.*, vol. iii, p. 5, October 5, 1796 (14 Vendémiaire An V).

[2] BMHN, MS 309, fol. 6; MS 1998, vol. ii, p. 203. The administrators of the Muséum d'Histoire Naturelle were alarmed because they understood that the group of competent soldiers who formed the museum's guard were to be replaced by infirm men incapable of active duty. Fearing for the safety of the museum's buildings and grounds, Thouin wrote to Revelliere-lépeaux on December 13, 1795, asking that he use his influence to prevent any changes being made. Revelliere-lépeaux took up the matter with Bonaparte who was then general-in-chief of the army of the interior, and on December 19 wrote to assure Thouin that the museum's guard would be maintained as before, that the proposed change was only a plan to withdraw ten men temporarily. Revelliere-lépeaux protested that he watched constantly over matters pertaining to the museum.

[3] BMHN, *Procès-Verbaux*, vol. iii, pp. 5-6, 17.

[4] Although there is no really satisfactory historical summary of schools for the first year of the Directory, at least none of national scope, a number of careful studies have been made of single schools or of departments. Albert Troux, *L'Ecole centrale de Doubs à Besançon (An IV-An XI)* (Paris, 1926), gives an excellent bibliography of monographic studies of central schools in the various departments. Bois, *op. cit.*, Chapters II-V, and Marcel Reinhard, *Le Département de la Sarthe sous le régime directorial* (Saint-Brieuc, 1936), Chapters XVIII-XX, give valuable information for single departments.

lish state-administered schools lay in their rivalry with private schools, particularly those private schools which made a point of offering religious instruction.

For the first two years of the Directory, until the coup d'état of Fructidor, the Directors, and under their guidance the minister of the interior, acted chiefly in the capacity of advisers to juries of instruction appointed by departmental governing councils. To be sure, programs of study and plans of organization were often sent to the Directory for approval. That necessary gesture, together with the national government's control over buildings available and suitable for housing the new schools, kept the Directors in a certain position of authority; but in practice the programs submitted were usually approved, and the buildings asked for usually granted.[1] Beginning with the spring of 1796 the Directory and the minister of interior did make an effort to have a uniform series of textbooks adopted in all the primary schools of France,[2] but the lack of money and the difficulty of breaking the habits of instructors, many of whom were former priests accustomed to teaching reading and writing from books with a religious import, prevented universal adoption. The influence of the Directory, as far as it could be exerted, was at once anti-clerical and anti-royalist, because it believed that organized religion and love of monarchy were very nearly inseparable and, consequently, that both were incompatible with the republican régime.

[1] *Cf.* for example Debidour, *op. cit.*, vol. i, pp. 781-782, 846; vol. ii, pp. 449-452. Revelliere-lépeaux on June 20, 1796, wrote part of the Directory's message to the Council of Five Hundred (AN, AF III, 380, 1926; Debidour, *op. cit.*, vol. ii, pp. 663-664) asking that the precedent of using buildings of former *collèges* for the new *écoles centrales* be approved by law. This executive request was received favorably, and the law came back to the Directory for final approval and promulgation on July 13 (Debidour, *op. cit.*, vol. iii, pp. 77-78).

[2] In January, 1794, the Convention had offered prizes for ten categories of elementary textbooks. Final judgments upon this competition were not available until May, 1796 (Debidour, *op. cit.*, vol. i, p. 120; vol. ii, p. 327).

In the question of national fêtes the Directory exerted a more immediate influence through the orders sent out all over France for the celebration of each fête and by the example of its official presence at the observance of holidays in Paris. The first months of the Directory passed, however, without notable progress. Beginning with March, 1796, the government took the matter more firmly in hand and in the period from March to September issued instructions for celebrating the seven festivals enumerated by the October law.[1] Three supplementary festivals were added, for January 21, July 14, and August 10, commemorating respectively the execution of Louis XVI, the taking of the Bastille, and the end of monarchy, but these three were not to count seriously in the national schedule until later, in 1798 and 1799.

For all the government's careful instructions, the fêtes did not inspire the hoped-for spontaneous burst of patriotism, but Revelliere-lépeaux and his colleagues did not abandon the program of fêtes. The *Rédacteur*, recognized as the government's mouthpiece, on September 9, 1796 (23 Fructidor Year IV), carried a long explanation of the fête as the regenerator of patriotic fervor and good morals. The government began working through its commissioners in the departments, and on March 7, 1797 (17 Ventôse Year V), at the beginning of what might be called the Directory's second season of fêtes, Bénézech issued detailed instructions to commissioners, outlining the advice they should give to departmental and municipal administrations as they set about organizing celebrations for the spring, summer, and autumn.

During the trials and failures and rare successes of a year and a half, Revelliere-lépeaux pondered over the utility of fêtes and celebrations, and then on May 1, 1797 (12 Floréal Year

[1] *Ibid.*, vol. i, pp. 762-764; vol. ii, pp. 155-156, 322, 343-344, 494-498, 571-573, 712; vol. iii, pp. 13-17, 60, 67, 198-202, 204, 226-228, 312-316, 351-353, 374, 490-491, 668-671. Prosper Poullet, *Les Institutions françaises de 1795 à 1814, Essai sur les origines des institutions belges contemporaines* (Brussels, 1907), pp. 415-417.

V), read a paper on the subject at the meeting of his class of moral and political sciences at the Institut. *Réflexions sur le culte, sur les cérémonies civiles et sur les fêtes nationales* [1] was his contribution to the philosophy of social institutions and his formula for giving life to theories. He began:

> I divide basic institutions into three categories, religious cult, civil ceremonies, and national fêtes; they should all be bound together and, so to speak, modeled according to the same pattern, so that any discordant note may be avoided and so that the whole may move forward with an irresistible force toward the joint purpose: preservation of morality and maintenance of the republic.

Religion, he continued, should deal with ethical problems, teaching man how to love God and his fellow beings. It should make man good by appealing to his heart and sentiments as well as to his mind. Although a few thinking men can dispense with outward forms of religious exercise, the great majority need the stimulus of public worship. For this majority a cult should be established, but it should be kept severely simple in form; as to dogma, it should profess only a two-fold belief in the existence of a deity rewarder of virtue and punisher of evil, and in the immortality of the soul; two principles should then suffice as guides in everyday living: adoration of God and love of one's fellow man. Civil ceremonies, under the direction of the state, should provide a dignified setting, without ostentation or parade, for the three most important events of human existence: birth, marriage, and death. In the national fête, on the contrary, all possible means of pomp and magnificence should be employed to impress the crowds of citizens celebrating simultaneously their devotion to each other, to their fatherland, and to humanity.

Revelliere-lépeaux's scheme of setting up a new framework for society was more than a casual theory to him. In the

[1] The date given in the memoirs as 12 Floréal An VI is an error (MLL, vol. iii, pp. 7-27). Contemporary newspaper accounts and the minutes of the class of moral and political sciences fix the date in the year V, hence 1797.

months preceding the public declaration of his philosophy at the Institut, and throughout the final years of the Directory, he clung to his belief in a sound and attractive pattern of social organization as the basic instrument of creating peace and permanent security. In April, 1796, after the disturbances at Lyons, he wrote the Directory's exhortation to the citizens of Lyons in terms of fêtes and patriotism. Counseling them to overcome all subversive tendencies in their city, he advised them especially to divert their energies from sedition toward constructive industries, using their traditional art of making decorative fabrics to glorify the national celebrations that were to replace the false pomp of kings.

The industrious men who fill your workshops are proud that they no longer make objects of childish luxury or of usurped authority but rather the decorations which are to heighten the pomp and majesty of our national fêtes and the emblems of public power with which to invest the temporary magistrates chosen by the people. Thus, in the bosom of liberty and of the peace being prepared for us by our republican warriors, you will see your former prosperity reborn.

Soon, perhaps, the republic, strengthened by that peace, will summon all her children to a universal fête, where all affections will melt into one, Love of the Fatherland. The Executive Directory expects that, obedient to the voice of your own interest as well as to that of good conduct, you will have forgotten your hatreds and your misfortunes, and that you will bring to that fête only the warm enthusiasm and the generous fraternity which marked the early days of the revolution.[1]

In Paris as well, meantime, there were threats of outbreaks, as Babeuf menaced the government with a threatening popular movement. On April 14, three days before the promulgation of the address to the Lyonnais, the Directory issued a proclamation, composed by Revelliere-lépeaux, to the people of Paris, reminding them of what the new government had already ac-

[1] AN, AF III, 362, 1731.

complished in a few months and asking their support as honest republicans against both royalists and anarchists.[1]

The arrest of Babeuf shortly afterward checked these movements, but it failed to prevent disaffection within the army. The incident of the insurrection of the Camp of Grenelle, which occurred in September, 1796, is a case in point, whether it was a bona fide outbreak or one manufactured by the police to fortify its position against radical groups. Revelliere-lépeaux could never quite make up his mind how the insurrection came about, but he suspected that the other members of the Directory were trying to deceive him. He knew from the officer Grisel, as did his colleagues, what was about to happen, though in his memoirs he disclaims heatedly any intention on the part of the government to use *agents provocateurs*. When the foreseen attack took place during the night of 9-10 September, 1796 (23-24 Fructidor Year IV), he was not awakened until unusual noises roused him to look out of his window in time to see Carnot and Le Tourneur mounted on their horses in the court of the Luxembourg. His pride was particularly wounded because he happened at the time to be president of the Directory. The next morning he wrote with his own hand a note to the Council of Five Hundred, asking permission for the Directory to order domiciliary visits so as to make the arrests necessary to suppress the instigators of the uprising.[2] Although Revelliere-lépeaux believed in the efficacy of national fêtes and addresses to the populace, he did not hesitate to employ stronger measures.

II

The application of the program of public instruction was not without international implications. Each class of the newly inaugurated Institut, for example, was expected to choose eight

---

[1] AN, AF III, 361, 1726.

[2] MLL, vol. i, pp. 421-422; vol. ii, pp. 1-7. AN, AF III, 401, 2168. The first draft is undated, but the Council of Five Hundred acknowledged receipt of the message on 24 Fructidor.

foreign associates, thus admitting in all twenty-four non-French members,[1] who, it was supposed, would keep the Institut informed of the progress of invention and learning all over the world. Such a recognition of the international quality of intellectual enterprise was not surprising; it came naturally at the end of the eighteenth century. The principle of world-wide co-operation in things of the mind was interpreted, however, in terms of the new spirit of republican nationalism. Behind the desire for co-operation was pride in the fact that Paris issued the invitation and the conviction that a free people's Paris was a worthy center for the world's best intellect.

Together with the hope of creating a richer art and literature through intercourse with the outside world grew the ambition to make Paris a storehouse of treasures from the past, and the conception of Paris as the intellectual and artistic center of Europe gave rise to the expectation of enriching the city with treasures of past ages while the Institut was helping to make it the focus of contemporary talent. The eighteenth century idea of world citizenship was experiencing its adaptation to patriotism, but the eighteenth century conscience demanded a righteous explanation of its desires, a reconciliation of its ambitions with its principles. The answer was found in the promise to preserve, repair, and deliver to universal civilization those valuable objects which would otherwise deteriorate and perish through neglect. Such was Revelliere-lépeaux's conception of the rôle of the French nation, and, although not everyone was as naïve as he in this justification, he was not alone in believing that Paris in being glorified would serve mankind. It was a case of trying to reap at one and the same time the benefits of war and peace, on the ground that war was

[1] Léon Aucoc, *L'Institut de France, Lois, Statuts et Règlements concernant les anciennes Académies de l'Institut de 1635 à 1889* (Paris, 1889), p. 6. As a matter of fact, no foreign members were actually elected until after the Directory, the first three, Joseph Banks, Thomas Jefferson, and Joseph·Haydn, being named on December 26, 1801. Franqueville, *op. cit.*, vol. ii, pp. 55-56.

not really war, when it was directed toward the liberation of suppressed peoples.

As things worked out the fruits of war immediately seized the lion's share of attention, while the more tranquil processes of cultural infiltration by such methods as the election of foreign members to the Institut were set in motion very slowly. In March, 1796, the Directory named Napoleon Bonaparte as general-in-chief of the Army of Italy. Revelliere-lépeaux approved the appointment, entertained the young commander at dinner before he left Paris, and rejoiced in the Italian victories that followed quickly. The armistice of Cherasco, April 28, 1796 (9 Floréal Year IV), said nothing about art, but the armistice of May 8 (19 Floréal) obliged the Duke of Parma to give up twenty canvases of Bonaparte's choice. Thereafter in drawing up treaties the young general habitually required the surrender of pictures, sculpture, books, or collections of natural history.[1] In executing the treaties he attempted, in principle at least, to suppress wanton looting of artistic treasures on the part of the armies and to supervise the removal of whatever belonged to him by agreement.

To carry out this policy of taking from Italy whatever would enrich and ornament France, Bonaparte needed expert advice as to what was worth packing and shipping. As early as the first of May he wrote to Faipoult for a list of " pictures, statues, collections, and curiosities to be found at Milan, Parma, Piacenza, Modena, and Bologna." [2] Five days later Bonaparte addressed a letter to the Executive Directory, asking that a committee of well qualified men be sent to Italy to choose from the abundant riches of the country.[3] On May 9,

---

[1] Müntz, "Les Annexions de collections d'art ou de bibliothèques," *Revue d'histoire diplomatique*, vol. ix (1895), p. 384 *et seq.*

[2] *Ibid.*, p. 385. *Correspondance de Napoléon Ier* (Paris, 32 vols., 1858-70), vol. i, p. 213. This Faipoult was probably the friend of Revelliere-lépeaux who had first been named minister of finance and then on January 23, 1796 (3 Pluviôse An IV), transferred to the post of minister plenipotentiary to Genoa (AAE, Correspondance politique, Gênes, 170, 33).

[3] AHG, B *3, *119; *Correspondance de Napoléon Ier*, vol. i, p. 238.

he wrote again to the Directory, repeating the request for a group of connoisseurs and announcing an immediate dispatch to Paris of the twenty paintings taken from the Duke of Parma.[1] Meanwhile the Executive Directory in Paris, encouraged by the reports of Bonaparte's military progress, was contemplating with satisfaction the prospect of treasures from Italy that would surpass those already arriving from Belgium and Holland. In considering the problem of selection the Directors arrived at the same solution as Bonaparte, namely, a committee of experts. With this idea in mind they wrote on May 7, inviting him " to choose one or several artists to search out, gather together, and have transported to Paris the most precious objects. . . ."[2]

The Directory's letter and Bonaparte's crossed en route. It was the Directory, finally, who named the committee. Writing on May 16, 1796 (27 Floréal Year IV), Revelliere-lépeaux announced to Salicetti, one of the commissioners on mission with the Army of Italy, the immediate departure of six men to take charge of sending artistic and scientific treasures back to France:

We have foreseen your wishes as to sending scholars and artists who will bring us pictures, vases, statues, medals, manuscripts, collections of natural history, objects of arts and crafts, altar pieces, et cetera. We are sending my dear and worthy friend Thouin from the Jardin des Plantes, and Labillardière who has just gone around the world with d'Entrecastreaux and has brought back the bread tree which I believe can be grown in Corsica. He is a very good naturalist and zoölogist. Bertholet and Monge are coming with them. A sculptor and painter, very well known, both of whom have traveled and studied a long time in Italy, are also

[1] AHG, B *3, *119. *Correspondance de Napoléon Ier*, vol. i, p. 252. On the same day (20 Floréal An IV) Salicetti wrote to Revelliere-lépeaux (letter in the Collection Pasquier), addressing him as *mon cher ami*, recounting Italy's wealth in paintings and advising that an expert be sent to make a collection for France.

[2] AHG, Correspondance du Directoire exécutif, Register G 2, fol. 43.

on the expedition. We are sending them all by mail coach. The Executive Directory, my dear friend, expects you and the general of the army to help them as far as it lies in your power and to put at their disposal young scholars or artists who will aid them in the prompt and sure execution of all the searches and removals and in making drawings or models of everything that cannot be transported, et cetera.

The Executive Directory counts on giving them only enough funds for the trip. It is confident that you will administer economically the taxes levied in the country, and it expects you to support the six capable men who will join you and to furnish everything necessary for their work. You make a hundred times more money with your bayonets than we can raise with all the laws of finance imaginable. There is our eternal stumbling block. The six scholars and artists whom we are sending are all patriots whose conduct and intelligence can bring only honor to the republic.[1]

Bonaparte, still ignorant that the committee had been appointed, wrote from Milan on May 18, informing Revellierelépeaux that twenty paintings taken from the Duke of Modena would soon be added to the growing collection ready for transportation to France.[2]

With the surrender of Milan to the French it became imperative that the matter of art confiscations be handled immediately by some responsible person. On May 19, 1796, Bonaparte and Salicetti decided that an agent should be appointed " to hunt out and transfer to the territory of the republic the objects of arts, sciences et cetera, which were to be found in the conquered cities, and of which the choice and number would be

[1] Revelliere-lépeaux to Salicetti, autograph signed letter, no. 321 of the Collection Fatio, sold at the Hôtel Drouot in Paris on January 27, 1932 (author's collection). Salicetti's autograph but unsigned response to this letter, written from Milan, dated 4 Prairial An IV, is in the Collection Pasquier. The Directory also wrote officially to Salicetti on May 16 (AHG, B *3, *119, fol. 48).

[2] AHG, B *3, 124; B *3, 125, fol. 35 r. The first draft of Revellierelépeaux's enthusiastic response to Bonaparte's letter, dated 6 Prairial An IV, half written by Revelliere-lépeaux and half by his secretary Vallée, is in the Collection Pasquier, Série B, no. 22.

submitted in advance to the general-in-chief and to the commissioner of the government or to one of them." The next day they appointed Tinet as agent of the arts. He, with the military commissioner Peignon, supervised the work until the arrival of the Directory's committee in June.[1]

Throughout the last half of 1796, when correspondence between Italy and Paris was of necessity brisk, the matter of transporting the new riches occupied its full share of the discussion. The Directory wrote, now to Bonaparte and again to its military commissioners Salicetti and Garrau. Revellierelépeaux exchanged letters with Salicetti and with his friends Thouin and Labillardière. From all reports, the committee of experts was conducting itself with zeal and was gathering an abundant harvest. Everything promised extremely well, but when August arrived without bringing any of the treasures to Paris the Directory began to grow weary of promises. Bonaparte and the commissioners and the group of experts found complaints mingled with praise in letters they received from the Directory. At length rumors came to Paris that the Army of Italy was failing to provide Thouin and his comrades with even the bare necessities for themselves and their work. The Directory became reproachful and was not mollified until in November word from Thouin himself assured the government that Bonaparte was caring for their needs.[2] The fact remained

[1] Müntz, *op. cit.*, pp. 387-388. AHG, B *3, 186, pp. 45-46, 67-68. Salicetti announced the arrival of the six men sent by the Directory in his letter to Revelliere-lépeaux (Collection Pasquier) written from Milan on June 10, 1796 (22 Prairial An IV). On June 30, the Directory expressed its satisfaction in the committee's work (AHG, Correspondance du Directoire exécutif, Register G 2, fol. 72).

[2] For correspondence regarding shipments, see AHG, B *3, 186, pp. 45-46, 67-68; B *3, *119, fols. 72, 86 v.; B *3, 125, pp. 36-37, 48. The Directory's letters began to insist upon prompt shipment in September (AHG, B *3, *119, fols. 92 v., 100 v.). On October 5 the Directory recalled to the commissioners the needs of the learned committee (AHG, B *3, *119, fol. 111 r., v.), and on November 15 expressed pleasure that the reports of neglect were unfounded (AHG, B *3, *119, fol. 131 r.).

Salicetti sent to the Directory on July 13, 1796 (25 Messidor An IV), a

that the Directory did not have the money to enable its committee to act independently of the Army of Italy. Bonaparte was obliged not only to obtain the treasures but also to provide for their transportation. The rich booty, therefore, had to be stored in Italy, awaiting his will and convenience. Winter came, and it was unwise to risk shipping priceless statues and paintings over impassable roads. Revelliere-lépeaux and the other Directors had to stifle their curiosity, forget their sense of their own importance, and postpone their joy in seeing France decorated with the arts of Italy.

A question that seriously troubled neither Bonaparte nor the Directory was that of moral right. Bonaparte counted artistic treasures among the just rewards of military victory. The Directory shared his views and continued to support his policy with its double philosophy of patriotism and service to the world by preserving for future generations what might otherwise be lost. They argued that only a free people had a right to the treasures of the past; the artistic heritage of the Italians was to be rescued from the unclean hands of the aristocrats and princes, properly cared for, and made part of the heritage of France and of all liberty-loving peoples who might visit France.

Such a policy was not launched, however, without protest. There was a difference of opinion among artists themselves. One group objected to the government's high-handed methods on the ground that it was wrong to deprive any people of its own inheritance. Besides, they argued, from a purely utilitarian point of view the results of artistic labor lost their value when they were separated from their own background. Nearly fifty artists went so far as to sign a petition to the Directory, protesting against the removal of treasures from Italy and ask-

complete list of objects soon to be shipped. On July 15 he gave to Revelliere-lépeaux a favorable report of the committee's activities (Collection Pasquier). He had sent a provisional list some weeks earlier (AN, F^{17}, 1279; AN, AF III, 71, Dossier Objets d'art transportés en France, Correspondance des agents français).

ing that a committee from the Institut be appointed to consider the matter before it had gone too far.[1]

The petition was of no avail. It was hardly noticed. Instead, a counter petition, signed by Isabey, Gérard, and others, received great acclaim and was published in the *Moniteur* of October 3, 1796. Its conclusion seconded the government's position:

> The French Republic, by its strength, the superiority of its learning and of its artists, is the only country in the world that can give an inviolable refuge to these masterpieces. All nations must come to receive the fine arts from us with as much eagerness as formerly they imitated our frivolity; and, when we shall have conferred peace upon them, they will hasten here to drink at the springs of wisdom and good taste which these masterpieces will bring forth, and our industries, languishing today, will shine with new luster.

Although the greater part of the pictures and the marbles did not arrive in Paris until the summer of 1798, the government's policy was already defined, and there was to be no further opposition of importance.

Meanwhile, in Holland two living elephants also waited transportation to France. Hans and Marguerite, or Hans and Parkie as they were called affectionately by their keeper, had been born in Ceylon about 1781 and brought by the Dutch East India Company in 1784 as a gift for the statholder. They were fine specimens and reputed to be the only elephants in Europe, aside from one aged animal in the Tower of London. They had been very much admired in the statholder's menagerie at Loo, near The Hague, and the story went that the king of England had once offered a handsome price for the pair. After the victorious French campaign of the winter 1794-1795 and the stat-

---

[1] Antoine Quatremère de Quincy, *Lettres sur le préjudice qu'occasionerait aux arts et à la science le déplacement des monuments de l'art de l'Italie, le démembrement de ses écoles et la spoliation de ses collections, galeries, musées etc.* (Paris, 1796), 76 pp.; Charles Saunier, *Les Conquêtes artistiques de la Révolution et de l'Empire* (Paris, 1902), pp. 49-51.

holder's flight to England, the Dutch republicans had ceded the precious collections of the statholder to France; and in this way the elephants were destined for the Jardin des Plantes at Paris.[1] On February 2, 1795, when Holland had barely been conquered—the formal treaty was not signed until May 16— the administrative council at the museum of natural history asked the Committee of Public Instruction to take steps for the protection of the statholder's collections in case they should be considered property of the French government.[2] As early as April the Committee of Public Safety announced to the council of professors the shipment of two hundred and twenty-six boxes of precious objects and the expected departure of the two elephants.[3] By the end of June the museum was rejoicing over the arrival of the first shipment of packing cases and hurrying to provide temporary quarters for the elephants.[4] Puzzled by the unseemly delay in the elephants' arrival, Lamarck and Jussieu wrote on August 22, 1796, to Ramel, commissioner in Holland, urging him to have the two animals sent to Paris before the difficult winter season set in.[5] Acting on the hypothesis that the slowness might be due in part to the lack of keepers skilled in handling animals, the council sent to Holland Lousardy, an employee from the museum's menagerie.[6]

While the professors continued to arrange and rearrange quarters to receive the elephants, Hans and Marguerite were obliged to stay in Holland, for when plans for the journey had at last been completed it was discovered that the necessary money was lacking. Lousardy wrote to the professors, who in turn took the matter directly to the heads of the government.

[1] *An Historical Description of the Tower of London, and its Curiosities* (London, 1796), p. 16; *Histoire naturelle des deux éléphants du Muséum de Paris* (Paris, 1803).

[2] BMHN, *Procès-Verbaux*, vol. ii, p. 7.

[3] *Ibid.*, vol. ii, p. 39.

[4] *Ibid.*, vol. ii, p. 50.

[5] AN, AA 44, 1336, plaquette 3.

[6] AN, AA 44, 1332, fol. 47; BMHN, *Procès-Verbaux*, vol. ii, p. 68.

On December 26, 1795, Bénézech made a comprehensive report to the Executive Directory. There were no funds at hand to pay for transportation, nor for the animals' food even in case they remained in Holland for the time being. On December 31, the Executive Directory found time to vote money to feed the elephants, and Revelliere-lépeaux wrote the first draft of the order to the minister of finance. Meantime the minister of foreign affairs was asked to notify the ambassador of France to Holland, giving him authority to supervise the expenditure of the allotted funds.[1] The ambassador, Citizen Noël, accepted the charge. Months passed. On October 20, 1796, Revelliere-lépeaux wrote the draft of another letter, this time addressed to Noël himself, asking politely but firmly for explanations. Noël answered with three letters, recounting the hardships and disappointments experienced, when the elephants' cages broke down each time the journey was attempted. He blamed the animal keeper sent by the museum professors, because he had constructed the cages according to a badly conceived plan. Noël asked permission to act without Lousardy. On December 16, Revelliere-lépeaux wrote the Directory's reply, expressing full confidence in Noël and giving him entire responsibility.[2]

So the elephants in Holland, and the marbles in Italy, waited for the New Year.

When philosophers of art try to explain creative effort, they are puzzled by the motives underlying various forms of expression, and they often wonder whether the ferment of art is dependent upon volition or upon accident. Then they ponder over the many uses of the arts and ask themselves whether utility is the stimulus or the effect. Once the idea of utility is reached, it is only a step to the dilemma of genius—whether it is a quality in itself or a superior faculty of adaptation.

---

[1] AN, AF III, 338, 1480; BMHN, *Procès-Verbaux*, vol. ii, p. 96.

[2] AAE, Correspondance politique, Hollande, 590, fols. 155, 240; AN, AF III, 4, 12; AN, AF III, 409, 2252; 420, 2357; Bibliothèque du XVIe arrondissement de Paris à la Mairie, MSS xviii, fol. 139.

Revelliere-lépeaux did not worry too much about the origin or the definition of art. He took genius for granted and was chiefly concerned with its relation to society. He believed that the state, representing society, should encourage talent, but that talent in return should help the state uplift society. He was not alone in the hope of employing the arts as a kind of social yeast, but he was one of the most ardent and singleminded advocates of the policy. He put the test of usefulness to all art, and he believed that whatever served best the program of the Constitution of 1795 was the most worthy.

His utilitarian point of view, illustrated by his eagerness to employ Italian paintings and statues for the perfection of French citizens, is demonstrated even more clearly in his attitude toward the art of the theatre,[1] and particularly in the case of the Odéon. The building of the Odéon, or as it was at that time called the *Théâtre du faubourg Germain* or the *Théâtre du Luxembourg* or the *Ancien Théâtre des Comédiens français*, was at the disposal of the Executive Directory. Almost as soon as the new government was installed the theatrical producer Poupart Dorfeuille asked for a thirty-year lease of the building and equipment. Dorfeuille proposed to establish at his own expense a troupe of actors and a school of dramatic art. He intended to invite the best available French talent to join his company, including even actors who had left France for foreign cities, notably Hamburg. Dorfeuille was not a newcomer to theatrical administration nor to opera; he had made a name for himself at Bordeaux and had directed troupes at the theatres *Ambigu-Comique* and *Variétés Amusantes* in Paris. He promised, if the concession were granted, to manage the Odéon entirely in accord with the wishes of the republican government. Revelliere-lépeaux referred Dorfeuille's request to the minister of interior for consideration. Bénézech investigated, returned a favorable report on December 30 (9 Nivôse Year

---

[1] On January 25, 1796, Revelliere-lépeaux wrote to the minister of interior, on behalf of the Directory, about the possibility of establishing a theatre to inculcate patriotism (AN, AF III, 342, 1524; AN, AF III, *116).

IV), and sketched a resolution to be passed by the Directory.[1] Revelliere-lépeaux two days later asked him for an estimate of the expenditure such a step would involve, and in its session of January 15 (25 Nivôse Year IV), the Directory decided:

> The auditorium of the former *Théâtre français* is hereafter to be used for the establishment of an *Odéon français* or *Théâtre national*. The Citizen Dorfeuille is authorized to found at his expense and to direct this institution in such a way as to render it worthy of its purpose of generating republicanism, devotion to law, respect for morality, and the practice of virtue, and to expand the confines of art; on the condition that he accept those general rules which the government habitually applies to enterprises of this kind.[2]

The expense of certain repairs for the building would be borne by the state, but Dorfeuille would assume all other financial responsibilities. The will of the government was thus unmistakably written down and signed by Carnot as president of the Directory; but the decision remained a dead letter. The Directory went no further than to ask Bénézech for an estimate of expenses.

The matter dragged on for five months until on June 11, 1796 (23 Prairial Year IV), Bénézech made a new report, which Revelliere-lépeaux brought to the Directory's attention. By that time Dorfeuille was willing to assume every expense, even for repairing the building. Bénézech advised that his offer be accepted.[3] Again the proposition was seriously considered. Although at least one long memoir on the subject was addressed to Carnot,[4] Revelliere-lépeaux continued to take the principal responsibility and was recognized as the Director in charge of the negotiations. In spite of the fact that he approved of a national theatre and seemed not averse to Dorfeuille him-

[1] AN, AF III, 387, 2002, 28-29.
[2] AN, AF III, 387, 2002, 27.
[3] AN, AF III, 387, 2002, 34.
[4] AN, AF III, 387, 2002, 26.

self, Revelliere-lépeaux could not believe that the affair would succeed financially. His greatest objection, however, was on another score. He had in mind a truly governmental theatre co-operating freely with other branches of public instruction and including a school of dramatic art as fully under the direction of the state as the teaching of reading and writing and natural history. Accordingly he immediately raised objections to Dorfeuille's proposal. He questioned first the sufficiency of Dorfeuille's resources and, secondly, the probability that any private company would carry out the government's wishes. He suggested finally that it might be wisest for the Directory to take the national theatre under its own supervision.

Dorfeuille answered the objections on June 16 with a long memoir.[1] He pointed out his previous experience as a guarantee of his administrative competence. He reiterated his loyalty to the government and its principles, but he ridiculed the idea of a governmentally run theatre. He insisted that the state enterprise would fail financially because salaried administrators would never make as careful overseers as men with personal interests at stake. Artistically, he continued, governmental management would be fatal because it would look short-sightedly for quick returns in patriotism and would abridge the freedom necessary for the full flowering of dramatic art. At this point he was particularly opposed to Revelliere-lépeaux who maintained that the development of good character—he meant, of course, good republican character—was the purpose of all art worth considering. Dorfeuille was willing to admit and even to urge that the theatre properly directed should help the tone of society and encourage loyalty to the régime, but from his point of view this ultimate service could be expected only as a by-product. The more desirable such a result appeared, the more surely it must be accepted as a gift of circumstances and not as a motive justified in taking precedence over the theatre itself. To be sure Dorfeuille was speaking with his

[1] AN, AF III, 387, 2002: 37, 40.

own interests at heart; he wanted the concession. Nevertheless his opinion was shared by many actors and onlookers who had no personal axe to grind. On June 22 (4 Messidor Year IV), the minister of interior presented to the Directory a résumé of Dorfeuille's answers to the objections and recommended once more that the government accept his offer.[1] On the morning of June 24 (6 Messidor Year IV), Revelliere-lépeaux granted an audience to representatives of Dorfeuille's company; to them he repeated his opinion that the crux of the matter lay in the fact that greater results in patriotism might be expected from governmental than from private management. He urged Dorfeuille to restate his case once more before Bénézech who would sit with the Directory at the time of the final decision, and he promised this final decision within ten days.[2]

The Directory did not give its written approval, as it happened, until July 13 (25 Messidor Year IV), when it decreed:

> The *Théâtre du Luxembourg* is granted for thirty consecutive years according to the following conditions to Citizen Poupart d'Orfeuille and his company to establish a national theatre for French tragedy and comedy and to found a school of dramatics, to the end of regenerating the art.[3]

Dorfeuille had won, and the first draft of the statement was annotated and corrected in Revelliere-lépeaux's own handwriting.

From the first days of its existence, the Directory had ample opportunity to satisfy its pride in the patronage of individual artists and learned men as well as by the establishment of large institutions and the encouragement of group enterprise. Revelliere-lépeaux accepted his share of benevolent responsibilities with alacrity. The most obvious appeals, as might have been ex-

---

[1] AN, AF III, 387, 2002, 39.

[2] AN, AF III, 387, 2002, 35.

[3] AN, AF III, 387, 2002, 23; AN, AF *III, 118, no. 835; Paul Porel et Georges Monval, *L'Odéon: Histoire administrative anecdotique et littéraire du second Théâtre Français* (Paris, 2 vols., 1876, 1882), vol. i, pp. 155-156.

pected, were for money, and his experience on the Committee on Pensions during the Constituent Assembly had given him assurance in deciding the merit of such requests. He was instrumental in obtaining governmental subsidies for a number of applicants with records of distinguished achievement, as in the case of the aged Raynal,[1] author of the *Deux Indes,* or of Adanson, the botanist.[2] Bernardin de St. Pierre was helped, not only in appreciation of what he had already published, but with the intention of giving him leisure to complete other writings he had under way.[3]

Some authors without asking for money were content to seek the Directory's congratulations upon their work, whether it happened to be a poem in praise of the republican calendar,[4] or a new edition of Plutarch's *Lives,* or an exceptionally well composed republican catechism.[5] While less of a drain upon the treasury than requests for pensions, this desire for approval was time-consuming for the Directory and often led in the end to expenditures for aid in publication.

The spring of 1796 brought yet another way of helping men of letters and scientists. The law of May 10 (21 Floréal Year IV), ordering that all foreigners whose residence did not antedate 1789 leave Paris within three days, meant a real hardship for students, authors, and investigators living either temporarily or permanently in Paris. The Executive Directory alone

[1] AN, AF III, 352, 1625. About three weeks before the monetary subsidy was granted, Noël, minister plenipotentiary to the United Provinces, promised to send books desired by Raynal from the collection which had formerly belonged to the Prince of Orange (AAE, Correspondance politique, Hollande, 590, fol. 294).

[2] AN, AF III, 339, 1440; MLL, vol. ii, pp. 466-468.

[3] AN, AF III, 384, 1975. Revelliere-lépeaux had first come to know Bernardin de St. Pierre in the kitchen of the Thouin establishment (MLL, vol. i, p. 74). A letter of November 15, 1795 (British Museum, Additional MS 21513, fol. 162), demonstrates his eagerness to keep in touch with St. Pierre from the very first days of the Directory.

[4] AN, AF III, 351, 1617.

[5] AN, AF III, 412, 2278.

had the authority to grant exceptions, and the desks of the Directory were piled high with requests for extension of sojourn in Paris. The unfortunate persons affected by the law appealed to whichever Director they happened to know even vaguely, but the majority of requests seems to have passed through Revelliere-lépeaux's hands. Benjamin Constant, among others, was able to remain in Paris owing to Revelliere-lépeaux's intervention.[1] Barras was responsible for the permission granted to Thomas Paine.[2]

The problems of looking after the country's students and wise men were not entirely solved by subsidizing Frenchmen and permitting selected foreigners to stay in France. All wise Frenchmen were not content to stay at home. Some of them insisted upon traveling, and they needed the government's help in various ways.

The naturalist Baudin arrived in France in the early summer of 1796, after having been blown out of his course on returning from a two-year voyage to China, India, and Africa. Having been obliged to leave a number of exotic plants and a valuable scientific collection at Trinidad, he called upon the Directory and offered to present his collections to the museum of natural history, if the government would help him organize a return trip to Trinidad to rescue his treasures. The museum warmly supported his project, and the government took the matter under consideration. Truguet, minister of marine, when consulted by Revelliere-lépeaux, approved the expedition and promised his official and personal co-operation, but he warned the Director that international complications might ensue, especially since France was at war with England. He advised sounding the British government regarding its willingness to let Baudin's ship proceed unmolested, on the condition that it engage in no commerce and keep strictly to its scientific objectives. Truguet's advice was heeded; on July 1, 1796, the

[1] AN, AF III, 370, 1812.
[2] AN, AF III, 269, 1805.

Directory voted approval of Baudin's venture and empowered Truguet to undertake necessary negotiations with the Spanish and British governments. The affair was brought to Grenville's attention in London on July 16 and referred to the admiralty on July 17. On July 28 the British government sent a permit to insure Baudin against interruption by the British navy. Having obtained Spanish consent to visit the island of Trinidad, Baudin was able to set out on September 30, 1796.[1]

In the meantime, two French artists, the painter Liger and the architect Moulinier, were planning a trip to Spain, with the intention of reproducing by drawings, paintings, and engravings the wonders of Spain, as other artists had done for Greece and Italy. The Institut had approved the idea and promised to correspond with the two men during their journey. In May, Liger and Moulinier appealed to the government for aid in providing the essential equipment. They wanted political and artistic histories of Spain, maps, field glasses, barometers, and measuring apparatus with instructions in the ways of using the new metric system; they needed, above all, passports and letters of introduction to assure their being able to work unmolested. Bénézech reported their needs to the Directory; Revelliere-lépeaux wrote across the corner of Bénézech's letter that the Directory would be glad to have him submit an estimate of the expense involved. Bénézech answered that at least half the objects included in the estimate would not have to be paid for in money since they could be taken from government stores already in hand and that the entire sum would not reach more than eight hundred or a thousand francs. Revelliere-lépeaux annotated this second letter from Bénézech to the effect that the government was willing to furnish what was needed. On July 16 Bénézech received the Directory's formal order to send Liger and Moulinier on their way.[2]

[1] AN, AF III: 370, 1811; 383, 1962; Public Record Office, London, F. O. 27/48.

[2] AN, AF III: 373, 1848; 387, 2007; AN, AF *III, 118, 840.

III

In attempting to organize the mass of detail and cope with the infinite variety of problems facing them on every hand, the Executive Directory arrived at a geographic division of responsibilities as well as a partition of subject matter into spheres of influence. Carnot, born in the Côte-d'Or and elected deputy from Pas-de-Calais, undertook to supervise the north and north central sections of France; Alsatian Reubell, the northeast; Barras, from the Midi, the southeast; Revelliere-lépeaux, Vendean by birth and deputy from Maine-et-Loire, the southwest; Le Tourneur, native and deputy of the Manche, the extreme west of France and a connected strip of departments running down the center.

The geographic division of influence was applied primarily in the matter of appointments. The constitution allowed a degree of liberty in local affairs by making municipal and departmental administrations elective, but this freedom was counterbalanced by the Executive Directory's appointment of commissioners to inspect the work of local officials, interpret the government's policy to them, and keep the Directory informed by regular reports. This centralizing tendency was further strengthened by the Directory's right to suspend even elected local officials in certain cases.

Legally the appointments of commissioners proceeded from the Directory, and each final appointment sheet was signed by three Directors, but practically it was impossible for five men to know personally all the candidates for the infinite number of posts; they were obliged to depend, for the most part, upon the recommendations of deputies regarding their respective departments. The Directors sometimes asked deputies for suggestions, but very often members of the two councils took the initiative in writing to the Directory or one of its members, or to the minister of interior or the minister of justice. As the process of appointments fell into a routine, the appropriate minister habitually formed lists of candidates based upon vari-

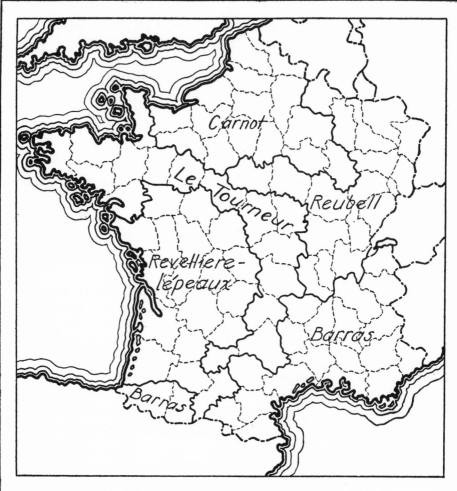

France - 1795

drawn by Marian E. Toy, after "La France
divisée en 88 Départements", frontispiece of _La République Française_,
_Dictionnaire géographique et méthod-
ique_ (Paris, An III de la République)
to show five regional divisions. Each
division included a number of departments in which one of the five Executive Directors was responsible for the
appointment of commissioners.

ous recommendations and his own opinions. Each list was presented to the member of the Directory under whose jurisdiction fell the department in question, and he signed or refused to sign as he saw fit. Barring insistent objection of the other Directors, the lists so signed decided the final appointments. As time went on, recommendations continued to be offered by deputies from the councils, but when the agents of local government had begun to occupy their places they often put in their word, and the commissioners already at work sometimes expressed their opinions about candidates for nearby unoccupied posts.[1]

Revelliere-lépeaux was responsible for eighteen departments : Maine-et-Loire, Indre-et-Loire, Indre, Vienne, Deux-Sèvres, Vendée, Charente-Inférieure, Charente, Haute-Vienne, Creuse, Corrèze, Dordogne, Gironde, Landes, Gers, Lot, Lot-et-Garonne, and Haute-Garonne.[2] Like all the Directors he had more or less influence on appointments for the city of Paris and the department of the Seine. In addition, there is evidence that he was consulted frequently regarding commissioners for the departments of Loire-Inférieure, Morbihan, Sarthe, Loiret, Seine-et-Oise, Marne, Pas-de-Calais, and Jura,[3] occasionally for Ille-et-Vilaine, Loir-et-Cher, Calvados, Seine-Inférieure,

---

[1] These conclusions are based upon the author's study of nominations and appointments in the series AF III, cartons 314 to 637, at the Archives Nationales. These cartons offer interesting material for a study of patronage under the Directory. Unfortunately there is as yet no monographic treatment of this aspect of Directorial appointments.

[2] AN, AF III, 324, 1327. After the first few months, the Directors exercised a slightly less strict supervision over their respective areas of appointment. It is incorrect, however, to say that this evidence of geographical partition was only transient. Although Revelliere-lépeaux seems to have relaxed his control over appointments in Charente, Dordogne, Haute-Garonne, Lot, and Lot-et-Garonne toward the end of 1796, he continued into 1797 with Charente-Inférieure, Corrèze, Creuse, Deux-Sèvres, Gers, and Gironde, into 1798 with Haute-Vienne, Indre, Landes, Vendée, and Vienne, and up until his resignation from the Directory with Indre-et-Loire and Maine-et-Loire (old spelling, Mayenne et Loire). Cf. Appendix B, infra, pp. 275-276.

[3] Cf. Appendix B, infra, p. 276.

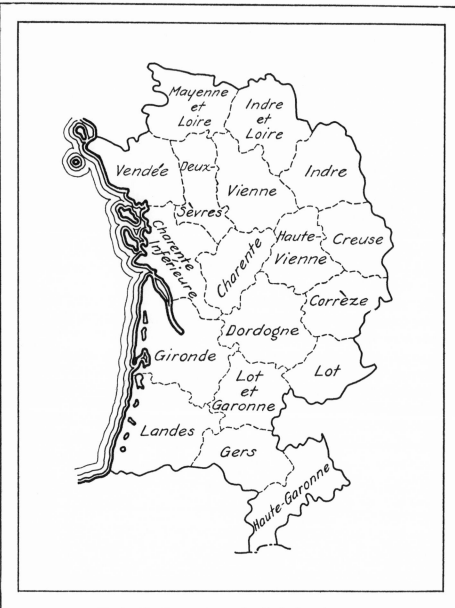

Detail of regional division supervised by Revelliere-lépeaux, comprising eighteen departments.

Aisne, Meuse, Côte-d'Or, and Yonne, and at least once for each of sixteen other departments.[1] On the contrary, in the departments of Orne, Sambre-et-Meuse, Haut-Rhin, and Hautes-Alpes, there are instances in which candidates whom he particularly recommended were not named.[2]

While Revelliere-lépeaux was using his intimate knowledge of the west of France in directing appointments, the graver problem of civil insurrection in the Vendée and neighboring departments weighed heavily upon him. The outbreaks of 1793 had fanned into flame a stubborn opposition to the revolutionary government which the treaties of La Jaunaie (February 15, 1795) with Charette, of Saint-Florent (May 2, 1795) with Stofflet, and of La Mabilais (April 20, 1795) with the Bretons had only temporarily smothered. Trouble was stirring again before the end of 1795, and General Hoche was obliged to recommence his double policy of military operations and peaceful overtures. The Vendée was the particular fatherland of Revelliere-lépeaux, whose skill lay in words rather than war. He liked to write, and, if his colleagues sometimes found him platitudinous and opinionated, they nevertheless trusted him to compose the series of messages by which they tried to aid Hoche win the west of France to support of the republican government.

In February, 1796, while Hoche was nearing the end of his campaign against Charette, Revelliere-lépeaux was concluding an address: *The Executive Directory to the Inhabitants of the Departments of the West.*

Already you were feeling the charm of peace, your fields were being turned once more to raising crops, industries were springing up, trade was enlivening your fairs and markets; confidence was being re-established among men whom dissenting opinions had estranged; houses were being rebuilt, and the increased number of weddings since the pacification was about to fill them with

---

[1] *Cf.* Appendix B, *infra*, pp. 276-277.

[2] *Cf.* Appendix B, *infra*, p. 277.

happy and useful families; finally a sheltering constitution, a definitive and stable government guided solely by principles of a wise political economy assured you that this new happiness could only increase from day to day. Then the horrible noise of war made itself heard. After the most frequent protestations of their entire submission to the laws of the Republic and of their sincere love of peace, still devoured by the thirst to command, the treacherous Stofflet and Bernier tried again to push you over the precipice. In the name of a God of peace, they lift up their voices inviting you to raise the flag of civil war ; . . .

. . . The imposters! . . . They are not ignorant that the Republic knows how to distinguish error from crime and a handful of bold chiefs from the misled people whom they make the plaything of their passions. You are still suffering, it is true; but far from wishing to add to your troubles the Executive Directory only longs for the day when it can bestow upon you the blessings of the constitution; its consoling hand will be reached out to you very especially; it will employ all the means capable of making you forget your misfortunes; you yourselves, inhabitants of the Vendée, you are the masters who will set the date of that happy time.

On February 25, the very day Stofflet was executed, the message was sent to the commissioners of eighteen departments with instructions to scatter it broadcast among the inhabitants of the west.[1]

On March 14, 1796, Revelliere-lépeaux wrote the first draft of the Directory's order appointing Baudin special commissioner to the region of the Vendée and those parts of Maine-et-Loire, Loire-Inférieure, and Deux-Sèvres which had revolted.[2] He composed likewise the first draft of the Directory's instructions, dated March 17, 1796, directing Baudin to serve as a special link between the central government and the local administrations and to co-operate with General Hoche and the officers of his staff.[3] Baudin was expected not only to keep the

---

[1] AN, AF III, 350: 1607, 1613.

[2] AN, AF III, 354, 1653.

[3] AN, AF III, 355, 1665; Debidour, *op. cit.*, vol. i, pp. 798, 837-839.

Directory well informed but to make suggestions, based upon his own observation, regarding policies to be followed.

Baudin, however, refused the place, and in his stead the Directory appointed Letellier, chief of bureau of the ministry of interior, and Dumas, an engineer. Since the idea of sharing such a mission with another person did not appeal to Letellier, he declined. The situation was saved by arranging to divide the region of the Vendée into two parts, one for Letellier and the other for Dumas; on April 7, Revelliere-lépeaux wrote the first draft of the order by which each of the two men was named to his post. By the end of April, Letellier was at work at Fontenay-le-Peuple (Vendée) and Dumas at Angers (Maine-et-Loire).[1] In the meantime the backbone of armed resistance in the Vendée had been broken by the execution of Charette on March 29. In Brittany Cadoudal did not submit until the end of June. At that time Frotté, the leader of Norman revolt, fled to England.

Even after this victory all was not easy for Letellier in the Vendée. On May 23 he wrote to the Directors plying them with questions. Revelliere-lépeaux composed the answer, dated June 4, 1796, praising Letellier but exhorting him to use his own initiative. Agreeing with him as to the necessity for speedy organization of peace-time civil administration, the Directory reiterated its own final authority in appointment but promised to ratify any lists of candidates which he should present. As for religious problems, the Directory hoped to deal in a conciliatory fashion with all priests who did not trouble the public peace or try to alienate their parishioners from the republican government. Letellier had seemed especially distressed by the complicated disputes over property in territory overrun during the civil disorders. The Directory's solution, as explained by Revelliere-lépeaux, was to return property in land to its original owners as far as possible but not to take the responsibility for restoring movable property to its former owners. Letellier

[1] AN, AF III, 360, 1712; Debidour, *op. cit.*, vol. ii, pp. 40, 90, 98.

was advised to remind the inhabitants of the Vendée that, although the Directory considered it a duty to alleviate suffering in every way possible, the west of France was territory conquered by force of arms; rather than complain of minor losses, the people would do well to bend all their efforts toward rebuilding the country.[1]

By the middle of July, 1796, the pacification of the west was so far advanced that the Directory was moved to announce the happy state of affairs to the Council of Ancients and the Council of Five Hundred. On July 15 Revelliere-lépeaux wrote the first draft of this letter which invited the councils to express public gratutide to General Hoche and the *Armée des Côtes de l'Océan*.[2] A few days later Carnot drafted the Directory's resolution to congratulate Hoche and reward him for his splendid work.[3]

Official recognition that the country was at peace did not mean, however, that reconstruction was completed. Throughout July and August, Letellier's nominating lists arrived for the Directory's approval.[4] During the same months, both Dumas and Letellier reported dire need among inhabitants of the west for materials to rebuild houses in the sections devastated by war; on July 26 Revelliere-lépeaux wrote the Directory's instructions to the minister of finance to take charge of this matter and report upon it.[5] When the question of property recurred, Revelliere-lépeaux wrote the Directory's response, on August 3, 1796, dictating a policy consistent with the position taken earlier in the year: landed property would revert to its original owners; animals and personal property not already removed from the farms could also be claimed, but whatever was lost, strayed, or stolen could be demanded only when the orig-

[1] AN, AF III, 375, 1875; Debidour, *op. cit.*, vol. ii, pp. 545-547, 551.
[2] AN, AF III, 387, 2007; Debidour, *op. cit.*, vol. iii, pp. 96-98.
[3] AN, AF III, 389, 2021.
[4] AN, AF III: 389, 2022; 392, 2060.
[5] AN, AF III, 390, 2041.

inal possessor could prove that the actual possessor had come by the property without paying for it.[1]

By autumn, 1796, affairs were progressing so smoothly that special commissioners were no longer needed in the Vendée. On September 18 Revelliere-lépeaux, at the time president of the Executive Directory, wrote to the minister of interior, authorizing him in the name of the Directory to congratulate Letellier upon the successful completion of his task.[2] A month later Revelliere-lépeaux jotted down a few lines to serve as a reminder to Secretary-General Lagarde for one more letter to the minister of interior. This time, on October 24, the Directory authorized the recall of Dumas from his post in Maine-et-Loire and the Deux-Sèvres, upon his own statement that his mission there was finished.[3] Officially, the Vendée was not only conquered and at peace but once more capable of self-government.

IV

While the five Directors governed France, they lived at the Luxembourg. Although the palace had been cold and bare when the government was installed, in a very short time it was decorated and furnished luxuriously, and the part known as the Petit Luxembourg was assigned to the Directors for their private residences.

Each of the Directors arranged his social life as he pleased. Revelliere-lépeaux looked askance at the receptions of Barras, which seemed to him questionable in tone, and was often annoyed by the hymn-singing of servants that rose from the apartments of Carnot. He established himself with his wife and daughter Clémentine, who was fourteen years old in 1795, in a fashion he considered appropriate to his governmental station, but he insisted upon keeping his life as simple as possible. He rose early in the morning to work over correspondence with

[1] AN, AF III, 392, 2063.
[2] AN, AF III, 403, 2187.
[3] AN, AF III, 410, 2260.

his secretary and then lunched with his wife and daughter or with a general or minister or close friend with whom he wished to confer. The afternoons were spent in sessions of the Directory or in special audiences or receptions, and the evenings after dinner, with rare exceptions, at the Jardin des Plantes. His wife received and returned calls of the wives of the other Directors and the ministers, but aside from that duty she limited her social life to supervising the household, arranging the dinners her husband gave, and receiving informally the friends she had made in Paris in earlier years.[1]

Usually on the fifth day of the decade Revelliere-lépeaux gave a small dinner of six or eight covers, and often on the tenth day a large dinner of from fifteen to twenty covers. To these affairs he invited his old friends Pilastre and Leclerc and their wives, as many of the Thouin family as could come, perhaps a minister or two or a general who was in Paris, the musical Méhul who gave lessons to Clémentine, the poet Ducis, the painter Gérard, the naturalist Van Spaendonck, and the young journalist Trouvé who had been secretary-general of the Directory for a brief time and was later to be appointed to diplomatic service in Italy. Revelliere-lépeaux's large dinners were described as dignified and a little stiff, with people consciously on their good behavior and no one talking very much, and certainly Revelliere-lépeaux himself recounts that he and his family enjoyed most those tenth-day afternoons when there were no strange visitors but only Pilastre and Leclerc with their wives, one or two of the Thouin brothers, and a few other intimate friends. Then there was no attempt at formality. As Revelliere-lépeaux liked to describe these occasions, the hours passed in a frank gaiety which, he hastened to add, was entirely within the bounds of social decorum. Much conversation, an attempt at a concert, with Clémentine or her master Méhul at the piano and everyone joining in to play other instruments or

[1] MLL, vol. ii, pp. 410-413.

to sing, made the time fly and proved diverting to the Director, when he felt harassed by the cares of statesmanship.[1]

The one diversion that pleased Revelliere-lépeaux even more than receiving at the Luxembourg or walking in the Jardin des Plantes was inviting friends to spend the day at his Château Gaillard, near Jean Jacques Rousseau's forest of Montmorency.[2] There, too, he walked sometimes with the naturalist Bosc, who continued to live at Sainte-Radegonde, where he had offered a refuge to Revelliere-lépeaux during the Terror. Bosc made no attempt to find a position in the first days of the Directory, but, after the rejection of his suit for the hand of the young Eudora Roland, he determined to leave France for the new world and asked Revelliere-lépeaux's aid in obtaining a place as consul in the United States of America. To his friends, Bosc's suffering seemed out of due proportion, and Revelliere-lépeaux, in a letter of May 1, 1796, although promising every possible aid in case Bosc would not let himself be turned from his project, begged him not to leave the country. Nevertheless, Revelliere-lépeaux on June 17 wrote the Directory's order to the minister of foreign affairs for Bosc's passport. There was an understanding that he would be named to the first French consulate to be vacant in the United States. Setting sail from Bordeaux on August 18 and arriving at Charleston, South Carolina, on October 14, Bosc hoped to join his compatriot Michaux who had established a botanical garden there. He was extremely disconcerted to find that Michaux had just left Charleston, but fortunately he was permitted to carry on studies and researches in the garden while, in France, Revelliere-lépeaux was able at last to have him appointed vice-consul at Wilmington.[3]

[1] MLL., vol. ii, pp. 413-414; François-Yves Besnard, *Souvenirs d'un Nonagénaire* (Paris, 2 vols., 1880), vol. ii, pp. 107-112, 119-123.

[2] Rey, *op. cit.*, p. 58. Although he went occasionally to the forest of Montmorency in the early days of the Directory, Revelliere-lépeaux did not purchase the property at Andilly until in the spring of 1798.

[3] Cl. Perroud, *Roman d'un Girondin* (Paris, 1916); Rey, *op. cit.*, pp. 47-55; AN, AF III, 370, 1811; BN, MSS français, Nouvelles Acquisitions:

At the Luxembourg, working away at affairs of state and undertaking to lighten the personal anxieties of his friends, Revelliere-lépeaux found in his secretary Antoine Vallée a second pair of hands and in another close friend, Yves Besnard, a second pair of eyes and ears.[1] Both Vallée and Besnard had been priests before 1789 and both had renounced orders in the course of the Revolution. Both were from Maine-et-Loire and had known Revelliere-lépeaux before the era of the Directory. At one moment, Vallée nearly forfeited the proffered place as secretary because he was very slow in coming to Paris after he had accepted Revelliere-lépeaux's invitation; at that moment, there was a question of Besnard's becoming secretary to the Angevin Director. When Vallée was finally installed at the Luxembourg, Besnard was at the same time given leave to come and go as he wished and invited to dine with the family either privately or at their formal dinners whenever he had time to come. Revelliere-lépeaux depended upon Besnard for summaries of the press and for his impressions of the drift of public opinion.

In such a fashion Revelliere-lépeaux lived through his first year and a half as Citizen Director. The spring of 1797 brought him a joy which he valued above the satisfactions of political power. In April, his only son was born.[2] The child was named Ossian.

9533, 124-125 (Bosc to Revelliere-lépeaux, 24 Novembre An IV) ; 9533, 123 (Bosc to a friend, 16 Fructidor An IV). Collection Pilastre, Letter a. s., Revelliere-lépeaux to Bosc, 12 Floréal An IV. Although Bosc was appointed vice-consul at Wilmington in 1797, and consul at New York in 1798, delay in communications and the increasingly strained relations between France and the United States prevented him from occupying either of these posts. He returned to France late in 1798, after an absence of about two years.

[1] MLL, vol. i, pp. 225-226; vol. ii, p. 346; Besnard, *op. cit.*, p. 112 *et seq.* Vallée remained with Revelliere-lépeaux until his exit from the Directory, but Besnard left Paris in 1797 to take a place in the municipal administration at Le Mans.

[2] Archives départementales de la Seine, *Extrait du registre des actes de naissance, l'An Cinq, treize Germinal, 10ᵉ Mairie.*

Lareveillere Lepaur.

einer der fünf Directoren der franzöſ: Republick iſt zu Montaigne in Poitu
1753. gebohren, und zu Angers erzogen. Er war Advocat zu Paris, ſtudierte
nebenbey Naturgeſchichte, und ward Mitglied der conſtituirenden Geſellſchafft
und wünſchte ſich ſehr Director zu werden. Er iſt ein ſehr rechtſchaffner Mann.

CHAPTER IV

MINISTERS AND MAJORITIES

Le Citoyen Revelliere-Lépeaux a ajouté que lors même quel
[sic] majorité du corps législatif pourroit se constater, . . . ,
il regardoit comme une maxime pernicieuse dans ses conséquences
que l'on dût céder au voeu de cette majorité, . . .

Procès-Verbal du Directoire Exécutif
28 Messidor An V

THE first eighteen months of the Directory had tested the administrative adaptability of the Constitution of 1795. The summer of 1797 was to call in question the constitution's powers of organic adjustment. In spite of all the agitation over royalist plots and Babouvist plots, the vital issue of 1797 did not lie in the attempts of either royalists or the extreme left to wreck the republic. The Executive Directory struck out against public enemies, real and imagined. Babeuf was executed, and Brottier was first imprisoned, later deported. Then, after a troubled spring and summer, the supposed menace of royalist treason or of a combined royalist-jacobin outbreak led three members of the Directory, Revelliere-lépeaux, Barras, and Reubell, to expel their colleagues Carnot and Barthélemy and purge the two councils in the month of September. Not one of these obvious reactions, however, not even the Eighteenth of Fructidor, faced squarely the central problem. The fundamental dilemma was not whether or not a government should use armed force to maintain its principles. The important choice lay between two principles of governing: whether a people should be ruled in accordance with its immediate desires,

---

Illustration on opposite page

Revelliere-lépeaux in his costume as member of the Executive Directory. This German print (artist not indicated) appeared before the end of the Directory, probably in 1798. Author's collection.

or whether its opinion of yesterday has a right to modify and check its opinion of today.

Specifically, the Directorial dispute was fought between the accepted ideal of *separation of powers* and the developing conception of *fusion of powers* in a cabinet responsible to a legislature. The case was tried and judged in the session of the Executive Directory on July 16, 1797 (28 Messidor Year V), at the time when the ministers were changed. The September coup d'état was only an incident in carrying out a policy already determined before the end of July.

The Constitution of 1795 was republican and representative. Theoretically the new form of government was a true expression of the General Will of the people; the presumption was that the prescribed system of suffrage would continue to support and justify a republic. The demand for retention of two-thirds of the Conventionals was, nevertheless, a tacit admission that popular vote based upon property qualifications might not support the new republican form of government. The plebiscite was not overwhelmingly favorable to the constitution and was even grudging toward the Two-Thirds Decree; yet both were admitted by the people's vote. The elections of October, 1795 (Vendémiaire Year IV), returning a freely chosen third of deputies hostile to the new régime, revealed the true feelings of the public then voting. The elections of April, 1797 (Germinal Year V), reasserting the conservative trend, emphasized the widening breach between popular opinion and the official republic. On May 20, 1797, the second hostile third of deputies took their places in the Council of Ancients and the Council of Five Hundred. On May 27, Barthélemy, an aristocrat by birth, education, and political attachment, was elected a member of the Executive Directory to replace Le Tourneur who was retired by the drawing of lots.

The Constitution of 1795, in providing for this annual renewal of the legislative bodies by one-third of their number and of the Executive Directory by only one of its five members, had created a source of friction. The composition of the two councils inevitably reacted to the change in public opinion more rapidly than did the Executive Directory. In the spring of 1797, the divergence of opinion between the legislative and executive branches of the government was greater than the difference between one-third and one-fifth. In 1795 the self-perpetuated two-thirds majority had been in a position to control the choice of all five members of the Executive Directory. In 1797 the new two-thirds majority — in part freshly elected, and in part dating from October 1795—could change only one of the five Directors. Thus, in the councils there remained only a minority of approximately one-third to represent public opinion as it had been expressed by the practically universal suffrage of 1792, while in the Executive Directory a majority of four-fifths (elected in 1795 by the Conventional two-thirds who formed the majority in the Council of Five Hundred and the Council of Ancients) derived its authority from the sanction already five years old. At first glance, the former Conventionals seemed beaten in the councils, two to one, while in the Executive Directory they still held control by four to one.

During the period between the Two-Thirds Decree of 1795 and the elections of 1797, the Executive Directory and the councils often manifested divergences of opinion, but no occasion, up to the spring and summer of 1797, had tested their fundamental tolerance of each other's existence. The shift of power in the spring of 1797 forced both legislators and Directors to take a definite stand.

On the eve of the elections of April, 1797, before the hostile majority in the councils, the conflicting attitudes of the five Directors were thrown into sharp relief. They feared the change in their own midst. Who and of what opinion would their new colleague be, and which one of them would step down and out to leave him a place? If the new Director were anti-republican, their balance would be unsettled and their cause might be lost. Reubell presented an ingenious plan for the resignation of one Director and his replacement before the new legislature should convene.[1] Barras supported him. Carnot and Le Tourneur opposed the move; they preferred to accept the results of the elections, whatever they might be. Revelliere-lépeaux's point of view is not clearly defined in accounts of the episode, but only a few days later he objected strenuously to the council's assumption of the prerogative to control the place and manner of drawing lots to determine which Director would retire.[2]

Already the rôles of the five Directors were cast for the summer of 1797. Carnot was to accept the elections; respecting the new majority as the expression of public opinion, he was to attempt a rapprochement between the councils and the Directory, but if concessions proved necessary he would have them made at the expense of the Executive Directory to the profit of the councils. The new Director, Barthélemy, although he was not Carnot's choice and although he and Carnot did not become intimate friends, was obliged by virtue of his election to support any movement favored by the legislative majority. Carnot and Barthélemy were to become allies, almost in spite of themselves. Reubell, on the other hand, was patently opposed to the Directory's making any concessions. A strategist, he was willing to attempt any means technically within the law in order to keep the Directory supreme. He would not admit that the new elections were a mandate from the people for modifications of the government's program. Revelliere-lépeaux believed that the new legislative majority was dangerous to the republic he was trying to establish under the Constitution of 1795. He was not a person to hesitate at the propriety of ways and means if he was sure he was in the right; he would not draw back from an open rupture with the councils even while he called it regrettable. Yet, up to July 1797, his personal disapproval of Barras and a certain repugnance for Reubell, together with the fact

---

[1] AN, AF III, 6, plaquette 19; *Mémoires de Barras* (Paris, 4 vols., 1895), vol. ii, p. 513.

[2] AN, AF III, 6, plaquette 19 (26-27 Floréal An V); MLL, vol. ii, pp. 42-44.

that the situation was not too clearly outlined in his own mind, kept Revelliere-lépeaux from joining Reubell and Barras to make a frank majority. He professed respect for the ability and moderation of Carnot, and he received Barthélemy with courtesy.

During the first half of the summer, Barras and Revelliere-lépeaux cast the determining votes, and their power lay in the fact that they held the balance. Barras did vote often with Reubell and appeared to adopt republican attitudes, but at the same time he was maintaining relations with royalist sympathizers; his vote each time, consequently, depended upon the state of his own affairs. There was no question as to his willingness to act contrary to the wishes of the legislative majority, if he chose, and from that point of view he sided more consistently with Reubell than with Carnot.

Events leading up to the change of ministers in July crystal-lized Revelliere-lépeaux's fear of the results of leaving the councils free and unchecked. The discovery of some of his own royalist plottings led Barras to deny completely his conservative leanings and threw him unhesitatingly on the side of Reubell. After July, Reubell, Barras, and Revelliere-lépeaux turned solidly against Carnot and Barthélemy and refused to believe in the possibility or advisability of arrangements with the new legislative majority. At the moment of the coup d'état in September, neither Barras nor Revelliere-lépeaux was uncertain; only Reubell was temporarily shaken and unwilling to use force.

The councils, after the elections of 1797, presented a majority frequently united in opposition to the Executive Directory but far from consolidated in favor of any constructive program. There were all degrees of warm and cold royalists, and all shades of republicans. The nearest approach to a continuous, organized attack against the Executive Directory came from the Clichyans who were responsible for naming Barthélemy. The group most favorably disposed toward the Directory centered about the salon of Madame de Staël, with Benjamin Constant, Thibaudeau, and their friends in charge; this group had a large influence on the *Cercle Constitutionnel* which flourished for two months before it was closed by the authority of the councils as violating the article of the constitution which proscribed political clubs.

The legislative majority assumed its right to criticize the policies of the Executive Directory; some deputies undoubtedly went so far as to conceive the councils' rôle as dominant. Was there serious intention on the part of a considerable number of deputies to consider their powers of representation as a mandate to overthrow the Directory and establish another form of government, or was the opposition only intended to curb the Directors and ameliorate their program? Was the free exercise of the representative system about to destroy the republic? The fate of the Constitution of 1795 depended on the answer to these questions, or even more on what the Directors believed was the answer and upon the tactics with which they proposed to meet the situation.

In view of the impending choice, or the supposed impending choice, between a representative and a republican government, it is essential to reconstruct the actual relations between the councils and the Directory from May to July, 1797.

I

Of all the issues that laid bare the widening breach between the councils and the Directory, serving as both reason and excuse for misunderstandings, the question of finance was the most persistent. Monetary instability greatly complicated tax collection and expenditure, rendering budgetary consistency next to impossible. The sinking assignat was finally abandoned and replaced by *mandats territoriaux* in the spring of 1796. The sale of public lands, which had been interrupted temporarily because of the situation of the assignat, was then reopened. Revenues from the new sales, however, did not enrich the government, because the *mandats* began to fall in value very soon after they were first issued, and buyers paid very low prices for properties they purchased. In consequence, the lands belonging to the nation were greatly reduced in extent without adding funds in any corresponding measure to the government's constantly empty treasury. The expedient of a forced loan to tide over the crises had burdened municipal officers with the difficult tasks of apportionment and collection and had thus contributed not a little to developing hostility between the Directory and the local governments, a feeling which, in turn, may have had something to do with the Directory's unpopularity in the election returns. Only through desperate appeal to the unprincipled Dijon Company was the government able to re-establish in some degree metal currency.[1]

When the new legislative third took its place in the Council of Five Hundred and the Council of Ancients on May 20, 1797 (1 Prairial Year V), it was faced by the government's bankruptcy. The Directory issued a succession of demands for action, sometimes imperious in tone, again importunate, and often rather fault-finding. Behind these reports that the ministry of justice, the ministry of interior, or the ministry of marine was about to be entirely disrupted, because salaries long since due were not forthcoming, the legislators could not help looking for the influence of the Dijon Company or hearing the clink of gold in the well-lined pockets of enterprising middlemen, who furnished the army with supplies or satisfied the government's needs in any one of a dozen other ways. It is unnecessary to repeat the story of the Directory's corruption. That tradition was already well established by the spring of 1797, in spite of the fact that Carnot, Revelliere-lépeaux, and Le Tourneur were honest. The flagrant ways of Barras, and the questionable en-

[1] Albert Mathiez, *Le Directoire* (Paris, 1934), p. 110. The government, in return for a stated loan by the Dijon Company, allowed that company to gather in all the *mandats* outstanding in the public treasuries. The government promised then to buy back the *mandats*. The company gathered a number of *mandats* far beyond the government's expectations and claimed remuneration at so high a figure that the government brought suit, which it lost to the company. The expensive operation did, however, relieve the country of the undesirable paper *mandats*.

tourage of Reubell—whether or not he was guilty of building up his personal fortune at the expense of the government is still a moot question—had enough authority in the Directory and enough influence upon public opinion, as Thibaudeau re-marked,[1] to overpower whatever impression or reality of honesty the other three might show.

It was perfectly obvious at the end of May that neither the Directory nor the legislature put much trust in the other's good faith as far as monetary arrangements and the collection and distribution of taxes were concerned. Revelliere-lépeaux con-stantly explained that the councils, by their refusals and nig-gardly day-to-day grants, threw the Directory into the hands of lenders and companies who sold commodities at exhorbitant prices. The councils, needless to say, had other explanations of the predicament.

The most important crises of the two months from May to July was precipitated by the report and recommendations of Gibert-Desmolières, chairman of the committee on finance in the Council of Five Hundred and sworn enemy of the Direc-tory. He attempted to weaken the Directory's control of purse strings by strengthening the legislature's power over the Com-mission of the National Treasury, established by the Constitu-tion of 1795. This commission's five members were empowered by the constitution to collect taxes and to write orders for pay-ments when the legislature, the Directory, and the appropriate minister had agreed upon amounts and recipients. The commis-sion was elected by the Council of Ancients upon the presenta-tion of a triplicate nominating list by the Council of Five Hun-dred, and each year one of the five members was replaced according to the same electoral procedure, so that the legisla-ture was by the nature of the case already in a position to influence the opinion of the commission. This initial control, however, was insufficient in Gibert-Desmolières's eyes. He pro-

---

[1] A. C. Thibaudeau, *Mémoires sur la Convention et le Directoire* (Paris, 2 vols., 1824), vol. ii, p. 37.

posed taking away from the Directory the power of making financial negotiations and giving that power to the Commission of the Treasury.[1] Such an arrangement, if exaggerated, would have been tantamount to removing from the control of the Directory every matter of executive administration in which money played any part; the Directory's hands would have been tied, and, since the legislature felt itself stronger with relation to the Commission of the Treasury than before the Directors whom the Constitution of 1795 had endowed with relatively greater powers, the consequence would inevitably have been to strengthen the councils at the expense of the Directory.

Gibert-Desmolières's proposition, introduced with his report of June 14 (26 Prairial Year V), in spite of opposition was carried four days later. The members of the Council of Five Hundred who favored the Directory, and in particular Jean-Baptiste Leclerc, Revelliere-lépeaux's intimate friend, made a last unsuccessful rally in the council the day after the vote was taken, vainly hoping to reverse the decision. Leclerc attacked the motion of the finance committee as tending to undermine the entire authority of the Directory; he asserted that it was not honestly a measure of finance, but rather the fruit of the struggle in progress between the Directory and the two legislative houses. The Council of Five Hundred remained adamant, but in the Council of Ancients the measure was voted down on June 27 (9 Messidor Year V).[2]

Even while this first measure was being considered by the Council of Ancients, Gibert-Desmolières was hard at work in the Council of Five Hundred winning support for a second motion, one to refuse payment on all orders drawn in favor of the various ministries for either past or future expenses. There were hot debates for three days, until word came that the

---

[1] *Constitution de l'An III*, Articles 315-325; *Procès-Verbal du Conseil des Cinq Cents*, 26-30 Prairial An V.

[2] *Procès-Verbal du Conseil des Cinq Cents*, 1 Messidor An V; *Procès-Verbal du Conseil des Anciens*, 9 Messidor An V.

Ancients had defeated Gibert-Desmoliéres's first measure.[1] In this way the ardor of the group in the council opposed to the Directory was checked for the time being by the more loyal Council of Ancients. In order to meet absolutely essential expenses, it was voted to collect the third fifth of the taxes due for the year,[2] and the nervous tension was temporarily eased.

The existence of a state of hostility between the councils and the Directory was clearly brought out, in the second place, by discussions over the colonial situation, which was absorbing a large share of legislative and executive attention during the two months from May to July. Within this sphere of colonial problems, attention was focused chiefly upon San Domingo, where French responsibility had been enlarged in July, 1795, by Spanish cessions of the Treaty of Bâle. On May 29, 1797, Vaublanc opened the charge in the Council of Five Hundred by criticizing severely the policy of the Directory and the conduct of the Directory's commissioners in San Domingo. Discussions followed nearly every day until on June 4 it was voted to repeal the law of the year before (January 25, 1796) which had authorized the Directory to send agents to San Domingo. The Council of Ancients followed suit in approving the measure.[3] The Directory, realizing that the situation was slipping out of hand, on June 3 had made the conciliatory move of proposing to recall the agents under criticism. They waited nearly a week longer, though, before officially notifying the Council of Five Hundred of the decision and at that same time asked permission to send out new agents.[4] The inference was that the first set of agents had been indiscreet—although the Directory continued to champion their cause—but that the

---

[1] *Procès-Verbal du Conseil des Cinq Cents,* 7-9 Messidor An V.

[2] AN, AF III, 7, plaquette 21 (17 Messidor An V).

[3] AN, AF III, 6, plaquette 20 (24 Prairial An V) ; *Procès-Verbal du Conseil des Cinq Cents,* 10-16 Prairial An V ; *Procès-Verbal du Conseil des Anciens,* 24 Prairial An V.

[4] AN, AF III, 6 plaquette 19 (15-21 Prairial An V).

Directory saw no reason why a temporarily mismanaged situation should be used as a lever to take away its constitutional right of appointing administrative officers for the colonies. The Directory, by giving way in a specific case, hoped to save its general prerogatives. The opposing group in the Council of Five Hundred was hoping, on the contrary, to use the complications of San Domingo for taking away a portion of the executive's basic power.

A motion authorizing the Directory to send out new agents, first presented on June 13, met its strongest opposition a week later, when Boissy d'Anglas argued that to accept such a proposal meant handing over to the Directory almost dictatorial powers, especially since the same ministers were in office (notably Truguet, Minister of Marine) as when the first set of agents was appointed. Thibaudeau, at this point, came to the Directory's defense, saying that, if the five chief executives were to be saddled with the responsibility for managing affairs, they must be allowed come degree of freedom, and, on the other hand, if the councils tampered ever so slightly with the Directory's selection of ministers, they were going far beyond their constitutional prerogatives. It was the Directors' own affair to choose ministers, however much the ministers might influence the conduct of government at home or in the colonies. The next day, after further discussion, the Directory's friends won, and it was decided to allow the Directory to appoint one, two, or three new agents to San Domingo, for a term to exceed eighteen months. On June 25 the Council of Ancients ratified the action of the Council of Five Hundred. The following day the Directory received and promulgated the new law. On July 4 the new agents, Hédouville and Dervillé, were appointed, and the next day, in proud justification of the righteousness of their policies, the Directors took pains to notify the councils that the army of the republic had won signal victories in San Domingo and was apparently well on the way toward finding solutions for the island's difficult problems. The optimistic news was as premature as it was fortunate, but it added to the

Directory's sense of having managed a delicate situation competently.[1]

Debates on conditions in San Domingo had not only disclosed the growing hostility between certain legislators and the five chief executives; they had also suggested that at some not far distant moment another controversy might arise over the Directory's appointment of ministers. The point of antagonism was shifting from incidents of governing to constitutional bases of the régime.

The Directory's position was thus called into question in two instances without being fundamentally weakened. In the case of the financial tangle, the Council of Ancients had saved the five executives from immediate encroachments of the Commission of the Treasury and indirectly from the hostile majority of the Council of Five Hundred. In the case of San Domingo, the Directory by skillfully withdrawing its agents at the critical moment had stolen the thunder from the opposition in the councils so that forces favorable to the Directory were able to carry the vote giving the Directory the right to appoint new agents. Each of these situations was handled so as to reduce the outward manifestations of friction between the executive and legislative powers, but the sources of friction still existed.

Foreign affairs, bound together inextricably with financial and colonial questions, served also to keep both legislative and executive branches of the government on the alert, each attempting to enlarge its power and influence at the expense of the other. Since the constitution gave the initiative in treaty-making to the Executive Directory, the five men could afford to stand somewhat on their dignity, disregarding the councils' objections until the moment of ratification. The councils, though, had other weapons, and, with their power over taxes and hence over supplies for the armies and salaries for diplomatic agents, they could easily make the Directory aware of

[1] AN, AF III, 7, plaquette 21 (8, 16, 17 Messidor An V) ; *Procès-Verbal du Conseil des Cinq Cents*, 25-27 Prairial An V, 2-3 Messidor An V; *Procès-Verbal du Conseil des Anciens*, 7 Messidor An V.

their disapproval. When the armies were eventually able to supply the government with funds, the Directory came to be more independent, and the councils lost their lever of control, and with it the efficacy of criticism. From that time an open contest, with the odds in favor of the Directory, was quite possible.

When the councils convened at the end of May, the public mind was turned toward making peace. Malmesbury's first overtures had failed, but the second British proposals were about to be considered. The armistice of Leoben had been signed with Austria, and Revelliere-lépeaux, whose political principles at the end of the Convention had included a belief in the necessity of keeping some treaty provisions secret from the masses, was given the custody of the secret articles of the armistice.[1] The legislature was thus hardly in a position to criticize the unknown parts of the Leoben negotiations. Bonaparte's dealings with Venice and her neighbors, however, were common knowledge, and the Council of Five Hundred undertook to remonstrate with the Directory upon its conduct of the Italian campaign and upon its negligence in leaving the councils ignorant of vital developments upon the Italian border and in Italian states. Questions were coming up, too, regarding relations with Switzerland.

On June 23 (5 Messidor Year V), a motion by Dumolard brought the anti-Directorial group out into the open. He proposed sending a message to the Directory asking for information as to Bonaparte's policy in Venice, for reasons why the Directory had left the councils uninformed about events in Italy, for explanations about the revolutionary movements in Genoa and the part played by the French government in founding the Genoese republic, and finally for a justification of French relations with Switzerland. Dumolard was strongly supported, but some of the legislators found the step unconstitutional, forcing the Directory to explain what was its own

[1] *Discours sur les relations extérieures, prononcé dans la séance du 26 Ventôse par L. M. Revellière-Lépeaux,* pp. 1-10; AN, AF III, 6, plaquette 19 (14 Prairial An V).

affair. Thibaudeau proposed investigation of the matter by the committee whose business it was to pass upon the application of constitutional articles relative to the rights of the legislative body in respect to diplomatic negotiations. Dumolard conceded the necessity of delaying his motion, and the matter was sent to committee.[1] Temporarily, the conflict was averted, but once more the Directory was aware that opposition was only waiting for the opportunity to break out in full force; and the Directory, theoretically in full possession of its powers, was uncomfortable and annoyed.

II

The councils, too, were uneasy, especially the Council of Five Hundred, where opposition to the Directory was most concentrated. Of what good was supposedly free suffrage, if the representatives elected by the people were not to direct the government? The Executive Directory owed its power to the councils, one legislator said to another. How could it presume to disregard the councils? Little by little, the so-called constitutional group in the Council of Five Hundred became converted to the idea that, if the ministers through whose hands the daily business of government passed could be relied upon to echo the sentiments of the legislature, something might be accomplished toward administering the country in accordance with the results of the last elections.

Several attempts were made to sound the Directors as to their feelings about such a solution.[2] The Directors might thereby save their face, until in the course of time the composition of the Directory itself corresponded more nearly to the composition of the legislature. If the Directors would yield in the

---

[1] *Procès-Verbal du Conseil des Cinq Cents*, 5 Messidor An V.

[2] *Mémoires de Barras*, vol. ii, pp. 435-436; *Mémoires de Barthélemy (1768-1819) publiés par Jacques de Dampierre* (Paris, 1914), pp. 218-219; Lazare Hippolyte Carnot, *Mémoires sur Carnot (1753-1823) par son fils* (Paris, 2 vols., 1869), vol. ii, pp. 115-116; MLL, vol. ii, pp. 86-91; Thibaudeau, *op. cit.*, vol. ii, pp. 207-209.

matter of choosing ministers favorable to the policies of the councils, they could be left without too great anxiety or too great disturbance in the unseemly proportion of four to one against the wishes of the voting public. Reubell and Revellière-lépeaux, it was soon found, would be difficult to move; Reubell did not like the idea of giving way to the councils; with Revellière-lépeaux it was a matter of conscience to do what he thought right no matter what any one said, and, the larger the number of those against him, the more likely he was to feel he was in the right. The rights of the legislative majority carried little weight, therefore, with these two. Carnot, who was inherently less interested in forms of government than in administration, grasped quickly the reasonableness of respecting the legislative majority and did not fear the ultimate outcome of allowing the councils to influence the choice of ministers. Barthélemy, too, could be counted on the side of the councils. Barras remained uncertain.

When leaders of the group who wished to force the issue of changing ministers had by cautious interviews assured themselves that Barras would come over to their side when the question was brought up in the Executive Directory, Carnot, then president of the Directory, was persuaded to introduce the proposition to dismiss those ministers out of favor with the councils and replace them by candidates satisfactory to public opinion. On Sunday, July 16, 1797, accordingly, Carnot pointed out to his fellow Directors in regular session the advisability of changing four ministers, those of justice, finance, foreign affairs, and marine, precisely the departments in which the greatest controversies had arisen in the two preceding months.[1] Carnot based his proposal upon the wish of the majority of the legislative body. Whereupon Reubell commented that he found it impossible to believe that such a wish had been or could be expressed; that, if by misfortune a

[1] The rôle played by each Director is reconstructed here from the minutes for this session (AN, AF III, 7, plaquette 21), which are unusually detailed.

majority of legislators should wish to meddle with appointing and discharging ministers, the republic would by that very fact be in a state of anarchy, since one governing power would have swallowed up the others; that he had too much confidence in the wisdom and patriotism of the greater part of the legislators to allow himself to be persuaded that they would exert the slightest untoward pressure upon the Directory in so important a matter. He asserted, in conclusion, that he could not think of letting four ministers go on the grounds proposed, especially in view of the character of the public opinion stirred up against them by worthless journalists very probably in the employ of England. On the other hand, he would not stand in the way of reconsidering the appointments of the entire list of ministers to determine whether or not they were carrying on their work to the best advantage and ought or ought not to be changed in certain cases. Carnot hastened to declare that he wished neither to cast aspersions upon the ministers whose dismissal he was asking nor to concede the legislative body rights denied by the constitution; but that, deeply convinced that it would be impossible for the constitution to go forward without some understanding between the Directory and the majority of the legislature, he believed he owed this proof of deference to what appeared to be the clearly pronounced opinion of the majority of the two councils.

Revelliere-lépeaux spoke next, reminding his colleagues how often he had repeated in their meetings the same ideas that Reubell had just expressed; since he shared Reubell's point of view, he could not but adopt the same conclusions. He added that no matter what majority might be formed in the legislature he would regard it as a pernicious principle to yield to the wish of that majority; it was possible that the majority might be led by vicious and unpatriotic men, in which case the Directory's duty was to protect the country from its perverted representatives; but, even if the majority was composed of honest patriots, paying heed to its every wish would lead to such rapid and inconsistent changes in policy that anarchy would be the inevitable result. Furthermore, he added, he, for one, would never lose sight of another maxim, that the executive members of the government, more especially than any other citizens, should be guided entirely by their consciences, listening only to the voice of liberty, the voice of the republic. He thought that even under pain of death the governors should struggle against every attempt, open or veiled, to overthrow the constitution, in order to assure the tranquillity and the happiness of France. He concluded by reaffirming his adherence to Reubell's position. Barras saved himself the trouble of a long discourse, observing in very few words that he was impressed by the correctness of the observations of his colleagues Reubell and Revelliere, and that, like them, wishing to safeguard liberty and the republic, he most definitely refused to consider the proposal to dismiss the four ministers in question. He moved that the Executive Directory take its official vote upon the question without delay. There was nothing left for Barthélemy to say. His brief statement, supporting Carnot's attempt to re-establish confidence between the Directory and the legislature, served only to provoke Reubell's ready response that he could not conceive of any way in which the Directory might have deserved losing the councils' confidence. In his eyes, the best way to assure confidence was to deal with each matter of business as it came in as honest a fashion as possible. Therefore he urged going into the matter of the incumbency of each and every ministry without delay. Barthélemy murmured helplessly that Reubell had failed to follow the sense of his remarks, and the order of the day settled down to considering the approval or rejection of each of the seven ministers in spite of Carnot's protest that he was entirely unprepared to pass upon the three ministers not named in his own proposal.

By the series of votes that followed, the ministers of police, interior, and war, whom Carnot had expected to be left untouched, were dropped without hesitation by a three to two vote and replaced. The other four in question were considered in turn; the ministers of justice and of finance whom the councils had hoped to dismiss were retained, and the only concession to Carnot and Barthélemy was the dismissal of the ministers of foreign affairs and of marine. Even this half-yielding was entirely counteracted, however, by installing two candidates whom Carnot and Barthélemy refused to approve. This series of concluding votes only prolonged and arranged the defeat, for the defection of Barras from the side of the legislative majority had decided the day. Reubell had been the principal defender of the Directory's prerogatives. Revellierelépeaux had seconded him with a determination which would have asserted itself even had all the other four Directors been on the opposite side, but the shifting tactics of Barras, which had tempted the councils and Carnot to take the risk, had turned the scale for the Directory.

III

When Barthélemy returned from Switzerland in June, 1797, to become a member of the Executive Directory, he had lived away from France a great many years.[1] In principle, he had accepted the republican régime, and in theory he was ready to offer it his fullest allegiance, but when he saw what manner of men his colleagues were he was astounded at their presuming to rule over France. He wrote afterward: " Carnot alone acted with propriety, dignity, reason, and nearly always with justice ... As to the other three, you could not conceive of the habitual crudeness of Reubell, the profound ignorance of Barras, the boresome metaphysical platitudes of La Revelliere." [2] Although Carnot found more favor in Barthélemy's eyes than the other three Directors—and this favorable approval was to a certain extent mutual—no deep and close understanding grew

[1] In 1768, at the age of twenty-one, François Barthélemy had been named secretary of embassy at Stockholm. Later he was made secretary at Vienna, then chargé d'affaires at London. At the time he was elected to the Executive Directory he had been for five years minister plenipotentiary to Berne, where he had greatly facilitated the arrangement of the treaties of Bâle.

[2] *Mémoires de Barthélemy*, p. 184.

up between the two men. Twice Carnot agreed with his three colleagues in regarding Barthélemy's eagerness for fair treatment to England (in the peace negotiations about to be undertaken at Lille) as open to suspicion, perhaps treasonable, and by any standard lacking in proper republican patriotism.[1] Barthélemy appreciated Carnot's devotion to the necessities of governing, and he set a high value upon Carnot's willingness to recognize the rights of the parliamentary majority that had been responsible for his—Barthélemy's—election to the Directory. After he had been in the Directory for only a short time, however, he believed he had judged the personalities of his colleagues and the general situation more acutely than Carnot. The outlook seemed blacker to him than to Carnot, and after the coup d'état of Fructidor he blamed Carnot for failing to look facts squarely in the face all through the summer of 1797. He blamed Carnot especially for not estimating correctly the qualities of Revelliere-lépeaux and the defects of those qualities.[2] To Barthélemy, Carnot was realistic in his approach to political movements but naïve in his judgment of individuals. Carnot, on the other hand, viewed Barthélemy's mysterious reserve and dogmatic pronouncements with uneasiness, and the other Directors likewise found their new colleague hard to understand.

Barthélemy's final opinion of Carnot may have been severe, but he showed insight in judging that Revelliere-lépeaux had held the balance of power from July, when the ministers were changed, onward through the coup d'état in September. During

---

[1] The first occasion dated from June 8, the morrow of his reception as member of the Directory, when he showed his colleagues the letter which Grenville had taken pains to address especially to him at the same time that he had sent a communication to the Directory as a body. The second occasion came on July 10, hardly a week before the change of ministers. Raymond Guyot, *Le Directoire et la paix de l'Europe* (Paris, 1911), Chapter XI "Les Conférences de Lille"; *Mémoires de Barthélemy*, pp. 180-181, 202-204, 221-222; AN, AF III, 6, plaquette 19 (20 Prairial An V); AN, AF III, 7, plaquette 21 (22 Messidor An V).

[2] *Mémoires de Barthélemy*, p. 242.

those six weeks Revelliere-lépeaux held the pivotal place in the Directory. Of course he did not threaten to step into Reubell's shoes as chief defender of the Directory against the councils. Reubell remained the unflinching strong man of the combination up to the very moment of the coup d'état, when for a time he lost his nerve. Also Revelliere-lépeaux and his aboveboard range of acquaintances could not win support or buy acquiescence from the four corners of France, as might Barras with his shifting but universal relationships. Yet Revelliere-lépeaux's very reputation for honesty and personal uprightness as well as his constant appeals to the principles of moderation led his political opponents to persuade themselves that he was open to conversion, and upon that possibility some of them built hopes of winning the majority of the Directory for the program of the majority in the councils. Their faith in the power of the real truth of the situation over an honest mind, such as they believed Revelliere-lépeaux's to be, was vaguely akin to his own trust in universal truth. Both he and they failed to reckon with the variations of truth; they paid the price of their mistake at Fructidor, 1797, and he in Prairial, 1799. So much for one group of legislators who respected Revelliere-lépeaux; others, who believed themselves more clever than he, may have hoped equally to convert him, without revealing to him their actual motives.

Revelliere-lépeaux, then, held the supposedly convertible vote during the month of August, but, aside from protestations of justice and moderation, there was little in his conduct to suggest that conversion was taking place. On the contrary, his success throughout the closing weeks of the summer strengthened his conviction of having acted righteously when he helped check the councils' pretensions at the moment of changing ministers. Revelliere-lépeaux as president was the member of the Directory officially most in view from the moment of his election on August 24, 1797 (7 Fructidor Year V), until the coup d'état, and Revelliere-lépeaux took official prominence seriously.

An unusually great importance was attached to this changing of presidents of the Directory in August, 1797. Carnot, who as president had not been able to guide the affair of changing ministers, was about to complete his three-month term of office as president. There had been no instance of an immediately succeeding second term in the nearly two years since the Directory had been installed, so that there was small hope and little talk of Carnot's continuing to occupy the executive chair. There was a great deal of talk, however, and apparently much hope that Barthélemy might follow Carnot.[1] Some members of the councils thought that, while technically they had been in the wrong in demanding a change of ministers that was constitutionally beyond the limits of their powers, the Directory out of courtesy to the new majority might offer the presidency to that one if its own members who most accurately represented the results of the spring elections.

In spite of this claim of the presidency for Barthélemy, supported in contemporary newspapers and memoirs, in the regular order of things it was Revelliere-lépeaux's turn to be president. Since November, 1795, the order of presidents had been: Reubell, Le Tourneur, Carnot, Revelliere-lépeaux, Barras, and again Reubell, Le Tourneur, and Carnot. Revelliere-lépeaux had once succeeded Carnot and might be expected to do so again. If Barthélemy accepted this half-established order and Le Tourneur's place in it, he would have to wait until after Revelliere-lépeaux, Barras, and Reubell had each served again, that is until 1798.

Revelliere-lépeaux took his place in the president's chair on Thursday, August 24 (7 Fructidor Year V), and three days later the following statement appeared in L'Historien:[2]

---

[1] Ibid., p. 243; Aulard, Paris...sous le directoire, vol. iv, pp. 307-308; Mémoires sur Carnot par son fils, vol. ii, pp. 162-163; Mémoires de Thibaudeau, vol. ii, pp. 326-327.

[2] L'Historien was one of the journals suppressed by the special measures modifying the liberty of the press at the time of the Fructidor coup d'état.

The time of the presidency of Carnot having expired, he has been replaced by La Revelliere. A great many of our journals have marked this time of replacement as that of the renewal of internal divisions and of the troubles that come with them.

At Lille, Malmesbury, preoccupied with his second set of negotiations which had been taking queer turns since the arrival of Talleyrand at the ministry of foreign affairs at the end of July, was informed by his Paris correspondent that " it was seen with unrest that the majority of the Directory brought La Revelliere to the presidency instead of Barthélemy." [1]

Revelliere-lépeaux was filled with the dramatic temper of the moment when he returned to the presidency. Only a week before, his nerve had been somewhat shaken by an attempt upon his life, which, more than any impersonal circumstance, had matured his belief in the reality of plots against the Directory.[2] He took the reins of office with the firm intention of dealing adequately with the sorry state of misunderstanding, of saving the republic from its enemies, of showing to one and all that a man of virtue and of principles need not be a mollycoddle. He did not have long to wait for an occasion to set the tone of his presidency. In the Directory's public session on Sunday, August 27 (10 Fructidor Year V), three days after his inauguration, he received Visconti, minister plenipotentiary of the Cisalpine republic, and then General Bernadotte, representing the Army of Italy. If his election to the presidency of the Executive Directory had brought uneasiness, Revelliere-lépeaux's addresses of the tenth of Fructidor brought the conflict into the open.[3]

Revelliere-lépeaux's discourses were provocative not only in the words he used but in the implied reproach of recent posi-

[1] Charles Ballot, *Le Coup d'état du 18 Fructidor An V, Rapports de police et documents divers* (Paris, 1906), p. 140.

[2] AN, AF III, 465, 2830; MLL, vol. ii, pp. 92-99.

[3] The text of both addresses is included in the *Pièces justificatives* of the MLL, vol. iii, pp. 49-56.

tions taken by the legislature and echoed by Carnot and Bar-thélemy in meetings of the Directory. The councils had not hesitated to criticize Bonaparte's Italian policy and his forma-tion of the Cisalpine republic on more than one occasion, and only a short time before, in a stormy session of the Directory, Carnot had come out strongly against the methods used to establish and guarantee the sister republic. In declaring: "No, the Cisalpine republic is not insecure; it will live with glory and will be the ally of France!" Revelliere-lépeaux not only gave assurance of friendship to Visconti but displayed openly the wideness of the breach between himself and two of his colleagues. When he bade General Bernadotte have confidence in the Directory in spite of the same ill-timed criticism of the heroic actions of the Army of Italy, he recalled only too clearly legislative tactlessness toward the Army of Italy and gave color to the belief that there was underground collusion be-tween the Directory and the nation's military forces, an alli-ance which threatened the existence of the two councils. Neither address was calculated to soothe the feelings of anti-Directorial forces, but one paragraph of the harangue addressed to Bernadotte left no doubt as to the course for which the majority of the Directory were prepared:

As to the Executive Directory, it will brave all in order to assure the French their liberty, their constitution, their property, their peace, and their glory, fruits truly deserved after seven years of labors and misfortunes and an unheard of train of the most astonishing victories; it will not compromise with the enemies of the republic to make a shameful bargain with them. . . The num-ber or the character of its enemies will not deter it, and if it must perish in an undertaking so sacred and with intentions so pure, well, it will share the glory of the heroes who have died for the defense of the fatherland, since it will have perished to save it, while its enemies, even victors, share the opprobrium which for posterity always accompanies the name of voluntary slaves and traitors.

No language could have been plainer. The fatherland was in danger; the Directors would not flinch before using force to save it; if they themselves perished, it would be as martyrs. Thibaudeau's estimate, " His speeches were the signal of the combat; they inflamed all heads and wrecked all hope of reconciliation," is hardly surprising,[1] or Barthélemy's conclusions:

That day should have made the people understand. It was justifiable to believe that the president of the Directory could not express himself with that lack of decorum in a solemn ceremony unless the triumvirs had adopted a desperate course.[2]

Revelliere-lépeaux said in his memoirs:

The discourses which I had pronounced on the tenth Fructidor at the reception of Bernadotte and that of Visconti had broken the ice and allowed for no more vain delays. It was imperative to be attacked or to attack, and it was clear that with unity and firmness the victory would belong to the one soonest ready.[3]

It might easily be argued that all these testimonies came after much later reflection, but police reports of the week immediately following the tenth of Fructidor, especially those of the Central Bureau of Paris, made references to the " suspicions which the reading of the discourses of Citizen La Revelliere in the last meeting of the Directory has raised in many minds," [4] and by Thursday of that week reported a positive wave of antagonism:

The discourse of the Citizen La Revelliere to the Citizen Visconti has stirred up all the ill will of those who are the most bitter against the Directory, it has spread much sorrow as well among the friends of peace who concluded that the powers are yet estranged from co-operative effort; . . . [5]

[1] *Mémoires de Thibaudeau*, vol. ii, p. 256.

[2] *Mémoires de Barthélemy*, p. 246.

[3] MLL, vol. ii, pp. 126-127.

[4] Ballot, *op. cit.*, pp. 138-139.

[5] *Ibid.*, p. 143.

One of the most interesting contentions of the days immediately following the famous addresses centers in the development of Revelliere-lépeaux's political mentality. It is the same
point which Barthélemy reproached Carnot for misunderstanding, but Carnot was not alone in believing that Revelliere-
lépeaux executed a right-about-face toward the end of the
summer. A protest, signed " A Legislator " in *L'Historien* of
Thursday, August 31 (14 Fructidor), expressed the same
feeling, that Revelliere-lépeaux had changed. Malmesbury
wrote from Lille to Grenville:

. . . if we want a more recent instance of the views and intentions
of the Directory, it is to be found in M. La Réveillière superseding
M. Barthelemi in the presidence of the Directory, and in beginning
his office by a speech which, though not in opposition, perhaps, to
his general political sentiments, was certainly very unlike the
natural phlegm and tranquillity of his character.[1]

Whether he actually changed or rather felt called upon to
reinforce his attitudes when he was named president, Revelliere-lépeaux, in his addresses to Minister Visconti and to General Bernadotte, did emphasize the increasing ill will between
the councils and the Directory. Perhaps he himself is right in
saying that after those words conflict was inevitable. At least,
the speeches convinced many people that resort to force could
not be avoided, and for practical purposes belief and reality
may well have been the same.

The last normal session of the Directory before the coup
d'état was held on Sunday, September 3 (17 Fructidor). Carnot, in his *Réponse à Bailleul*, can hardly restrain himself when
he tells of the meeting. In one paragraph Revelliere-lépeaux is
a viper, in another he is Charles IX with the tocsin of Saint

---

[1] James Harris, *Diaries and Correspondence of . . . First Earl of Malmesbury* (London, 4 vols., 1844), vol. iii, p. 519. The source for this opinion
may be in the letter written to Malmesbury from Paris on 13 Fructidor
(Ballot, *op. cit.*, pp. 144-145). For Malmesbury's reports on the Directory
and the individual Directors through the summer of 1797, see Public Record
Office F. O. 27/49 and 27/50.

Bartholomew about to ring. Revelliere-lépeaux's memoirs are scarcely more complimentary to Carnot, though they are slightly less vituperative. He explains that he could not have acted as Carnot related because he did not know the coup d'état was to be that night, nor had he proposed to kill Carnot in any case. It was the majority's plan to act only in defense, when they should know the councils were about to strike. Only after this meeting did Barras tell him that the councils were planning to act without further delay; only then did he, Barras, and Reubell decide to act. How could he have had a Saint Bartholomew attitude toward Carnot? Such is Revelliere-lépeaux's explanation of his position.[1]

---

[1] *Réponse de L. N. M. Carnot, citoyen français, l'un des fondateurs de la république et membre constitutionnel du directoire exécutif: au rapport fait sur la conjuration du 18 fructidor an 5, au conseil des Cinq-Cents, par J. Ch. Bailleul au nom d'une commission spéciale* (London, 1799), p. 154 *et seq.*; MLL, vol. ii, pp. 131-133.

Illustration on opposite page

THE FRENCH MAHOMET, English colored engraving, published in April, 1798, with the following legend: " Revolution of the 4th of September the 18th Fructidor of the 5th Year. La Revelliere Le Paux favoured by nature with a crooked back, President of the Directory at the above epoch, Protector and High Priest of the new invented Theophilanthropie Religion, appears like a true Punchinello. He is placed on his beloved point of the Republican Calendar with one hand supporting France and with the other fixing her with an iron Scepter, to prevent her leaning towards Royalism or Jacobinism. He actually Kicks the Constitution of the 3rd Year from which flyes off the Article ' Sovereignty of the People.' A bundle of kindled Straw, composed of five hundred rushes, alludes to the Council of 500. A heap of 250 Buches or billets denotes the Council of Elders, and the Director Carnot overthrown by his friends and Colleagues." The engraving, reproduced here through the courtesy of the Bibliothèque Nationale, at Paris, appeared as No. 672 of that library's exhibition on the French Revolution, from January to March, 1928.

The coup d'état was accomplished according to orders issued from the permanent session of the three Directors, lasting from five o'clock Sunday afternoon, September 3 (17 Fructidor), to eleven o'clock Tuesday night, September 5 (19 Fructidor). All the ministers and General Augereau were with the three Directors. No one was allowed to come in or go out except by special order.[1]

The measures decided upon by the three dominating Directors began to take effect not long after midnight of September 3-4. Under orders of Augereau, troops silently occupied critical points in the city, while printed proclamations were posted to explain to Parisians what was happening. Shortly after daybreak soldiers surrounded the Tuileries, where the councils were sitting in permanent session. A number of deputies were put under arrest, and the others left to find safer quarters. In the meantime Barthélemy had been arrested at the Luxembourg, while Carnot and his brother escaped from a side gate of the gardens only a few minutes before their apartments were entered by soldiers.

The remnants of the two councils met the same day at the Odéon and the Ecole de Médicine, but they accomplished little that day beside declaring themselves the legal councils. On September 5 the famous laws of the nineteenth of Fructidor

[1] Victor Pierre, *18 Fructidor; documents pour la plupart inédits recueillis et publiés pour la société d'histoire contemporaine* (Paris, 1893), pp. 47-58; Thibaudeau (*Mémoires*, vol. ii, p. 272) must have been mistaken when he described Revelliere-lépeaux as shut up with Barras in Barras' apartments as if in impenetrable sanctuary while Reubell stayed at home alone. Revelliere-lépeaux (*Mémoires*, vol. ii, p. 129) names Reubell's apartments as the place of meeting. Barthélemy (*Mémoires*, p. 252) speaks of Reubell's apartments as being lighted late in the evening and adds that a number of people seemed to be gathered there. The brother of Carnot, who was with Carnot that night, says very definitely that Revelliere-lépeaux was at Reubell's, in conference with Barras, Merlin, Sotin, Augereau, and others (C. M. Carnot-Feulins, *Histoire du directoire constitutionnel, comparée à celle du gouvernement qui lui a succédé jusqu'au 30 Prairial An 7; contenant en abrégé celle de la République française, pendant cette memorable époque; enrichie de notes curieuses et secrètes, par un ex-Représentant du peuple* (Paris, 1800), p. 205 note).

passed the two councils precisely as they had been outlined by the three Directors. The purging of the councils was legalized by retroactive declaration regarding willful errors in the elections of the spring of 1797. The penalty of deportation was voted for a number of the state's enemies, including the two minority Directors Carnot and Barthélemy, a group of former deputies, and certain journalists. Some newspapers were suppressed and the independence of others very much curtailed. Laws recently in abeyance against émigrés, and especially those émigrés who were non-juring priests, were re-enacted.

The laws of the nineteenth of Fructidor were the beginning of further repressive legislation that was to make the three victorious Directors practically dictators for some months. A number of persons were killed or died eventually as a result of the Fructidor coup d'état, but there was nothing approaching a massacre either on September 4 or in the following months. The Directory prided itself on having manipulated a bloodless revolution.

It is difficult to say whether Barras or Revelliere-lépeaux took the main initiative during this period. Thibaudeau would give the honors of a dictatorship on the seventeenth-eighteenth of Fructidor to Barras, and Barras pictures himself as head of the whole movement, deciding what was to be done and giving orders.[1] Revelliere-lépeaux, while insisting proudly that people were heard shouting his name in all quarters of Paris, uses the pronoun *we*, not *I*, in describing what went on:

We passed all the regulations which were then issued; we made out the proclamations which were then posted; we gave the general the order to act in such a manner that public tranquillity was completely maintained, and we had the satisfaction of seeing that the next day, from early morning, the crowd, seeing the order that

[1] *Mémoires de Barras*, vol. iii, pp. 15-19. These pages, however, belong to that part of the memoirs subject to the suspicion of being arranged or supplemented.

reigned everywhere, expressed its joy and ran about the quais and the promenades as on a holiday.[1]

Both Revelliere-lépeaux and Barras agree that Reubell was too timid to be of much help. Revelliere-lépeaux says that a day or two before the coup d'état Reubell was so frightened at the general situation and the threats of the councils that he was ready to resort to flight; only Revelliere-lépeaux's insistence kept him at his post. Barras goes so far as to suggest that Reubell was temporarily insane, while the coup d'état progressed.

On the whole, it seems most probable that Barras chose the moment for the coup d'état and decided what measures were most advisable. Without Revelliere-lépeaux, on the other hand, the coup d'état would certainly never have taken place. In the crescendo of irritations of that summer of 1797, Revelliere-lépeaux can hardly have been the inveterate hypocrite Barthélemy pictures, or yet have so definitely undergone a conscious and conscienceless turn for the worse at the end of August as Carnot would believe. Carnot-Feulins, the brother of Carnot, is somewhat nearer the truth when he describes Revelliere-lépeaux as a man of plain virtues swept off his feet by the rush of affairs.[2] Yet, if affairs were stronger than Revelliere-lépeaux, he never thought so; he never lost confidence in the ability of his own intelligence to work out the best solution for a given difficulty.

[1] MLL, vol. ii, p. 129.
[2] Carnot-Feulins, *op. cit.*, pp. 238-245.

CHAPTER V

NEW MORALITY

WITHOUT taking into consideration Revelliere-lépeaux's deep fervor for the coming of the millennium, and his longing for France to become the leader of Europe in bringing in the new era, all his activity over this project and that, Theophilanthropy, statues, celebrations, theatres, opera, museums, indigent men of letters—and elephants—all this appears trivial and incidental as compared with the serious problems besetting the government. Yet without surveying these scattered efforts to realize his visions of the new society, without studying through his eyes the panorama of a promised land, it would be difficult to understand Revelliere-lépeaux's enmity toward the formerly dominant church, or his intolerance of émigrés who forced him to think of the old régime. It would be impossible to explain the last years of his public achievements and the abrupt ending of his political career without remembering always his belief in society's control over the future, and society's consequent obligations which were for him the basic tenets of a new morality.

I

Revelliere-lépeaux's relation to a new cult, Theophilanthropy, has been the subject of a great deal of discussion. In a drawing that appeared early in the summer of 1797, Fragonard indicated his own ideas of the part played by Revelliere-lépeaux. Fragonard drew a picture of incense burning before a flower-

---

Illustration on opposite page

UN THEOPHILANTHROPE, caricature by Fragonard, published in color, 1797, and reproduced in black and white in the *Réimpression de l'Ancien Moniteur*, vol. xxviii, p. 722. The reproduction here is from a copy of the colored engraving in the author's collection (photograph by A. Tennyson Beals, New York).

entwined bride and groom as they approached a flower-draped altar supporting a large open book, *Manuel des Théophilan-tropes*. At one side of the altar, hung from a standard as if ready for procession, was a banner bearing the injunction: "Husbands, love your wives; make each other happy." In the center, directly before the altar, stood a man with flat dark hair falling straight over his shoulders and a red-girdled blue coat reaching a little below his knees; his left hand was half raised, palm forward in admonition, and his right arm thrust back as if to protect the grossly deformed shoulders from the weight of a long white cloak. The meaning of the sketch was painfully clear. Revelliere-lépeaux, hunch-backed member of the Executive Directory, was sponsor for the latest version of organized deism, Theophilanthropy. In jest, or in earnest, he was called Pope of Theophilanthropists, and the name stuck despite all his protests.[1]

An inconspicuous little book, the *Manuel des Théoanthropo-philes*, composed by J. B. Chemin-Dupontès, had been published in September, 1796,[2] at Paris, where the cult was already practised privately in the homes of a number of families. Valentin Haüy, director of a school for the blind, enthusiastic convert to the new deism, became one of Theophilanthropy's most ardent promoters. The first public meeting was held on January 15, 1797, at the chapel of Saint Catherine which formed a part of Haüy's institution on the rue Saint-Denis, number 34, at the corner of Lombard street.[3] Haüy, more

---

[1] The epithet *pope* was adopted abroad as well as in France. Revelliere-lépeaux himself says that the "most ministerial journal of England" considered his discourse at the Fête of the Republic "more worthy of the pope of theophilanthropists than of the president of the executive power of a great nation." MLL, vol. ii, pp. 165-166.

[2] *Précis historique sur le culte des Adorateurs de Dieu et amis des hommes*, serving as preface to the *Code* of the Theophilanthropists, appearing in the Year VII, p. xii; *Qu'est-ce que la théophilanthropie*, p. 28.

[3] M. D. Conway, *The Writings of Thomas Paine* (New York, 4 vols., 1908), vol. iv, p. 233; Abbé Henri Grégoire, *Histoire des sectes religieuses* (Paris, 2 vols., 1814), vol. ii, p. 94. Grégoire seems to have calculated the

business administrator than priest, served with Chemin and three other heads of families, Moreau, Janes, and Mandar, as the executive committee of this first society.[1] These early leaders, defending Theophilanthropy against the accusation of being just another sect, declared that their worship might serve as a moral exercise for believers of all religious cults as well as for its own followers. The tenets of Theophilanthropy were universal, they claimed, rather than exclusive, for they were based upon principles of conduct chosen from wise sayings of men of all times without reference to nationality or creed.[2] Did not Thomas Paine, for example, praise the broadminded selection in his discourse to Theophilanthropists on *The Existence of God?* [3]

Worship among Theophilanthropists was marked by the absence of elaborate rites. Moreover there was no ordained clergy. The executive committee in its weekly meetings chose readings, hymns, and subjects for simple discourses to make up the order of service. As new societies were formed, some

date incorrectly. His statement is: ". . . the first reunion is held at Paris 26 Nivôse Year V (16 December 1796)." His revolutionary date, 26 Nivôse, properly transferred, becomes January 15, 1797. *Précis historique* . . . , pp. 6-7.

[1] Grégoire, *Histoire des sectes* (Paris, 6 vols., 1828-1845), vol. i, pp. 378-379.

[2] Chemin-Dupontès, *Manuel des théophilantropes, ou adorateurs de Dieu et amis des hommes; contenant l'exposition de leurs dogmes, de leur morale et de leurs pratiques religieuses, avec une instruction sur l'organisation et la célébration du culte* (Paris, 1798) ; *Précis historique*, pp. 8-9.

[3] Conway, *Writings of Paine*, vol. iv, pp. 236-245. The discourse was delivered at one of the early meetings of Theophilanthropists, possibly in January, 1797. It is difficult to say what part Paine played in the beginnings of the cult. Conway, *The Life of Thomas Paine, with a History of his literary, political and religious Career in America, France and England* (New York, 2 vols., 1893), vol. ii, p. 256, thinks he was one of the founders of the society in Paris as well as the promoter of such a group in New York several years later. The *Précis historique* does not mention the names of any of the founders. Grégoire does not include Paine as one of the first committee of five or on the list of the later central committee (*Histoire des sectes* (1814), vol. ii, pp. 94, 102). Paine was in Paris, however, at the time of the first meetings, and his discourse and his *Letter to Mr. Erskine* show that he kept informed as to the state of the cult.

meeting on the *décadi* and others on Sunday,[1] general plans for the city of Paris were made by a central committee.[2] Before the end of 1797 a yearbook was published, including materials for worship and directions for organizing new groups.[3]

At first Theophilanthropy did not make a great public stir. Not until April 28, 1797, did the *Moniteur* print under the heading *Variétés* a brief notice: "Formation of a sect of *Theophilanthropists, or Adorers of God and friends of men.*" Ten days later, May 8, 1797 (19 Floréal Year V), a longer statement appeared under *Variétés* in the *Ami des Lois:*

> A new religious establishment has just been formed: certain fathers of families are its founders; they have collected the religious and moral principles which have appeared to them the most proper to bring men to the practice of all the social virtues, and they have published them under the name of *Manual of the Theophilanthropists or Adorers of God and men*. This religion also has its fêtes; every Sunday (old style) and every décadi at eleven o'clock in the morning, they publicly sing hymns to the God of the universe, and discourses on morality are delivered to the people. Men of every cult may take part in these solemnities, they will see and hear nothing which can contradict their belief . . . [4]

As the number of adherents grew, the need increased for public meeting places. Since the days of the National Assembly church property had belonged to the nation, and according to the Constitution of 1795 all cults were to be tolerated equally

---

[1] *Précis historique*, p. 7.

[2] Grégoire, *Histoire des sectes* (1814), vol. ii, pp. 102-103.

[3] Chemin-Dupontès, *Année religieuse des théophilanthropes, ou adorateurs de Dieu et amis des hommes; recueil de discours et extraits sur la religion et la morale universelles, pour être lus pendant le cours de l'année, soit dans les temples publics, soit dans les familles* (Paris, 2 vols., 1797-1798).

[4] Alphonse Aulard, *Paris pendant la réaction thermidorienne et sous le directoire. Recueil de documents pour l'histoire de l'esprit publique à Paris* (Paris, 5 vols., 1898-1902), vol. iv, p. 103.

before the law.[1] Theophilanthropy therefore turned to the government for permission to worship in church buildings. On June 1, 1797, application was filed for the use of Notre-Dame, but the municipal and departmental administrations did not grant the request.[2] A few weeks later a petition was addressed to the Ministry of Interior, asking that the Chapel of the Four Nations be set aside for the services of Theophilanthropy.[3] Champagneux, chief of the first division of the department of the interior, referred the matter to Ginguené, director general of public instruction in the fifth division. Ginguené, learning that the chapel was vacant, wrote his colleagues to urge upon the minister of interior the advisability of opening the building to the new society. Although the minister in turn ordered the desired arrangements to be made, for some reason, now unknown, the cult was not established at the Four Nations.

By midsummer 1797, however, Theophilanthropists were holding services in four Paris churches [4] and by the end of the year were occupying several others. The *Patriote français,* in its issue of December 3, added to a notice of installations at Saint-Roch and Saint-Sulpice the comment:

Thus their cult is actually practised in all quarters and in the largest religious buildings in Paris. They are also established in the commune of Franciade, and it is estimated that there are not a dozen cantons in the department of the Seine which do not have

[1] *Constitution de l'An III,* Article 354: "Nul ne peut être empêché d'exercer, en se conformant aux lois, le culte qu'i! a choisi. Nul ne peut être forcé de contribuer aux dépenses d'un culte. La République n'en salarie aucun."

[2] *Catalogue d'une importante collection de documents autographes et historiques sur la révolution française depuis le 13 juillet jusqu'au 18 brumaire an VIII* (Charavay, Paris, 1862), p. 133, no. 191, Théophilanthropes, Temple de l'Etre-Suprême (Notre-Dame).

[3] Albert Mathiez, *La Théophilanthropie et le culte décadaire 1796-1801, Essai sur l'histoire religieuse de la révolution* (Paris, 1903), p. 180. The reference for this incident is drawn from AN, AF *III, 75-76.

[4] *Ami des Lois,* July 21, 1797 (Aulard, *Paris sous le directoire,* vol. iv, p. 230).

Theophilanthropist societies; so weary are people of priests selling absolutions; which proves that morality without charge is better than dogmas for silver.[1]

Outside the department of the Seine several societies were organized during the summer of 1797, notably at Dijon and Mâcon.[2] In the north, where Catholicism was particularly strong, the rational cult did not take firm root; yet in the department of the Aisne there were efforts to practise a cult built on principles closely related to Theophilanthropy. There is almost no trace of the cult in western France, but farther south it took strong hold at Bordeaux. Organizations in the central region, at Bourges and in the departments of Loir-et-Cher and Vienne, were fairly successful, but the new deism proved especially vigorous in the east where, in addition to Dijon and Mâcon, there were groups at Châlons-sur-Marne, Troyes, Autun, Epinal, and Coligni. The cult was to live longest of all in the department of the Yonne, southeast of Paris.[3]

In April, 1798, after a second request for the use of Notre-Dame was granted, schismatic Catholicism with its constitution-supporting clergy was obliged to share even this sacred place with deism.[4] In June, 1798, the commissioner of the depart-

---

[1] Aulard, op. cit., vol. iv, pp. 471, 476.

[2] Lachapelle, " Réflexions sur le culte des Théophilanthropes," Moniteur, August 11, 1797.

[3] Grégoire, " Culte Théophilanthropique dans les départemens," Histoire des sectes (1814), vol. ii, pp. 130-157; Mathiez, "Le Lendemain de Fructidor dans les départements et à l'étranger," La Théophilanthropie et le culte décadaire, p. 8, note 2; pp. 307-379.

[4] The inaugural service of Theophilanthropy at Notre-Dame was held on April 29, 1798 (10 Floréal Year VI). L'Ami des théophilanthropes, no. xii; Mathiez, La Théophilanthropie et le culte décadaire, p. 410, note 1; Augustin Gazier, Etudes sur l'histoire religieuse de la révolution française, d'après des documents originaux et inédits (Paris, 1887), pp. 333-334, asserts that the celebration of Theophilanthropy in Notre-Dame was short-lived, being conducted for the last time on May 28, 1798. Official records show, however, that interferences with the cult's use of the cathedral caused difficulties in September of that year. A. Schmidt, Tableaux de la révolution française (Leipzig, 3 vols., 1867-1870), vol. iii, p. 327; Mathiez, op. cit., p. 545, note 2.

ment of the Seine reported to the minister of general police that Theophilanthropy was using all the churches in Paris except two.[1]

Theophilanthropy reached the peak of its influence in the late autumn of 1798, when it was holding services in all the churches of Paris;[2] but this surprising achievement was not long maintained. Toward the end of December, 1798, Dupin, commissioner of the department of the Seine, wrote to the minister of interior:

> The Theophilanthropists seem to disappear. Those who joined their assembly because of patriotism prefer the Fêtes Décadaires. Those who went through curiosity no longer find there anything attractive. And those who attended for the sake of religious principles have conceived prejudices justified by several unfortunate choices of Theophilanthropist orators.[3]

From the beginning of 1799, Theophilanthropy is less frequently mentioned in municipal and departmental reports. Late in January, Dupin wrote briefly: " The Theophilanthropists still live, but their number does not grow and their existence is not remarked." [4] It must be noted that Grégoire

[1] Aulard, *Paris sous le directoire*, vol. iv, p. 732: " Compte rendu au ministre de la police par le commissaire du directoire exécutif près le département de la Seine, de la situation politique de ce département pendant l'an VI." The material in this report dates from September, 1797, to June, 1798.

[2] The date should be placed in November or December, 1798, with the occupation of Saint-Roch and Médard rather than in September as an earlier report might seem to indicate. Aulard, *op. cit.*, vol. v, pp. 108 (" Compte rendu par les administrateurs du département de la Seine de leur gestion depuis le 27 Floréal an VI jusqu'au 1er Vendémiaire an VII, en exécution de l'article 200 de la Constitution "), 215.

[3] *Ibid.*, vol. v, p. 273: " Tableau analytique de la situation de la Seine, pendant le mois de frimaire an VII, adressé au ministre de l'intérieur par le commissaire du pouvoir exécutif près l'administration centrale dudit département."

[4] *Ibid.*, vol. v, pp. 326-327: " Tableau analytique de la situation du département de la Seine, pendant le mois de nivôse an VII, présenté au ministre de l'intérieur par le commissaire du pouvoir exécutif près l'administration centrale dudit département."

credits Theophilanthropists with holding services in eighteen Paris churches as late as June, 1799,[1] although the *Ami des Lois* of July 9 describes the religion as losing its adherents.[2] In any case, the cult was declining before the end of the Directory, while at no period during the Consulate was it able to regain its former prosperity.[3] The public career of Theophilanthropy was ended by the order of Bonaparte on October 4, 1801, denying the cult the use of public buildings not only in Paris but also in the departments.[4] Bonaparte was smoothing the way for his Concordat.

When appeals to the police and to the Consuls proved of no avail,[5] all hope of public meetings was finally abandoned. Theophilanthropy, having at one time held its services in every church in Paris, survived only among small groups such as the one described in a police report of December 1803 :

There meets with a man named Drouet, living in the blind alley Férou, a group of respected patriots which is called *Society of Morality*; it is for the most part composed of former Theophilanthropists ; one is admitted into that society only when he is presented by a member and vouched for by another. He is then inscribed on a register as is also his sponsor and receives a card of admission to the assembly. The number of members is nearly one hundred, but the meetings are never attended by more than fifty.[6]

---

[1] Grégoire, *Histoire des sectes* (1814), vol. ii, p. 98.

[2] Aulard, *op. cit.*, vol. v, p. 610.

[3] Alphonse Aulard, *Paris sous le consulat, Recueil de documents pour l'histoire de l'esprit public à Paris* (Paris, 3 vols., 1903-1906), vol. i, pp. 187, 265-266, 280, 288, 300, 340, 345, 377-378, 479, 642, 801 ; vol. ii, pp. 124, 128, 155, 257, 439, 506.

[4] *Ibid.*, vol. ii, p. 418 : "Rapport de la préfecture de police du 3 thermidor"; p. 539 : "Ministère de la Police, Tableau de la situation de Paris du 4e jour complémentaire"; p. 583 : Journal des débats du 28 vendémiaire. *Correspondance de Napoléon Ier*, vol. vii, p. 345.

[5] Aulard, *Paris sous le consulat*, vol. ii, p. 581 : "Rapport de la préfecture de police du 28 vendémaire"; p. 589 : "Rapport de la préfecture de police du 4 brumaire."

[6] "Rapport de la préfecture de police du 14 frimaire an XII" (AN, F7, 3832). This report is quoted in Mathiez, "La Théophilanthropie sous le consulat," *La Révolution française, revue*, vol. liii, p. 278.

Theophilanthropy had lived as a public cult only four years, from 1797 to 1801. The summit of its power had been reached at the end of 1798, not quite two years after the initial meeting at the chapel of Saint Catherine.

To what extent was its growth and decline due to governmental protection and disfavor, and to what extent was Revelliere-lépeaux responsible for the governmental policy? How far was Revelliere-lépeaux personally concerned with the fortunes of Theophilanthropy? Enough conclusive evidence for a definitive solution of these problems has never been uncovered, but this much is certain: Revelliere-lépeaux was deeply interested in Theophilanthropy, and the government did at times favor the cult. On the other hand Revelliere-lépeaux renounced unqualifiedly the title of founder of Theophilanthropy, and his assertion has not yet been disproved. Yet, in writing his memoirs, he insisted that Theophilanthropy was based upon principles set forth in his published writings, his ideas being incorporated into the new cult without his knowledge.[1] To enforce this claim of intellectual parenthood, he mentions the *Réflexions sur le culte, sur les cérémonies civiles et sur les fêtes nationales* which he read at the Institut on May 1, 1797. And, in truth, it must be admitted that the language of the *Réflexions* has a great deal in common with the language of Theophilanthropy. The new cult takes its place in Revelliere-lépeaux's three-fold scheme of religious cult, civil ceremonies, and national fêtes as if it were made to order. Revelliere-lépeaux's account of the founding of a religion upon basic ideas such as he had set free to filter as they might into the thought of the day makes a beautiful story: ideas gathered together for their own sake by men virtually strangers to him, then a visit from these founders to acknowledge their debt to the true author of their religion, then a request that the wise author present the cause of the new cult to his colleagues of the Directory.[2] Unfortunately for Revelliere-lépeaux's story,

[1] MLL, vol. ii, pp. 166-167.
[2] MLL, vol. ii, p. 166.

the dates in the case contradict him. The *Manuel des Théo-anthropophiles* appeared in September, 1796, and Theophilan-thropy's first public meeting occurred in January, 1797, whereas Revelliere-lépeaux did not read his *Réflexions* at the Institut until the first of May, 1797.

Finding the source of the basic tenets of Theophilanthropy is not, however, so important as it might seem; the critical point is rather the question of time. Such ideas were in every-one's mind; even the phraseology was to be found currently in the writing of more than one eighteenth-century deist. Revelliere-lépeaux's arrangement of cult, ceremony, and fête in the *Réflexions* may have been his own, but he had no patent on the concepts. As for the question of time, when did Revelliere-lépeaux first hear of Theophilanthropy, and when did he establish relations with the leaders of the cult? Did he first speak of Theophilanthropy to his colleagues in March or April, 1797, as Barras reports,[1] or did Barras perhaps describe Revelliere-lépeaux's habitual enthusiasm for religious reform in terms of his later reputation as protector of Theophilanthropy? Revelliere-lépeaux says frankly that he became the cult's advo-cate in the Executive Directory and that Sotin was ordered to draw upon secret funds put at the disposal of the minister of police.[2] Since Sotin became minister of police only in July, 1797, it would seem to follow that the era of active govern-mental protection began about midsummer, 1797.

Of what did the protection consist? Money subsidies, cer-tainly, but such money subsidies scarcely reached the fabulous sums that opponents of Theophilanthropy were wont to sup-pose. The amounts indicated in the scattered records of these transactions do not run into thousands and thousands of francs. For example, one list of secret expenditures shows that on three successive occasions twelve hundred francs were paid to Valentin Haüy; only one of these payments, however, was

[1] Paul François Jean Nicolas, Vicomte de Barras, *Mémoires* (Paris, 4 vols., 1895), vol. ii, pp. 304, 337-338, 383.

[2] MLL, vol. ii, pp. 166-167.

clearly marked for Theophilanthropy.[1] At another time, a certain Guffroy, who happened to be editor of the *Ami des Théophilanthropes*, received fifteen hundred francs. Such sums of money, given to meet specific requests, seem to have been spent to pay expenses of installation necessary for the relatively simple rites of the cult's worship and perhaps also to help publish the two newspapers *Ami des Théophilanthropes* and *Feuille citadine et villageoise*.[2] Such grants had to be paid from secret funds, or they would have violated too flagrantly the constitutional provision against governmental support of religion. They would have violated equally Revelliere-lépeaux's conception of the proper relation of state to cult. In the *Réflexions* he had stated positively:

. . . it is the duty of the heads of the State to favor, without appearing to, the establishment of our maxims and their propagation by all the possible means of governmental administration; but however pure and wise a religious cult may be, whenever the law recognizes it, it is impossible that it be not altered from its foundation, by the ambition of ministers and that of the followers themselves, who will soon have forgotten all the maxims of universal tolerance and general fraternity in order to render themselves dominant and exclusive, by means of the supremacy which will have been given them. You will then see promptly resurrected the riches and tyranny of a clergy not less ambitious . . . than the Roman clergy, . . . [3]

[1] Mathiez, " Subventions du directoire aux théophilanthropes," *La Révolution française, revue*, vol. xlvii (1904), p. 66.

[2] Theophilanthropy's first newspaper, the *Echo,* changed titles several times. According to Tourneux, *Bibliographie de l'histoire de Paris pendant la révolution française* (Paris, 5 vols., 1890-1913), vol. iii, p. 437, the *Echo des cercles patriotiques*, managed by " Barbet et Darcet neveu," beginning with the fourteenth number added the words " et des réunions de théophilanthropes " to its title and came to be edited by Etienne-Marie Siauve. In 1798, the *Echo* was replaced by the *Journal des théophilanthropes ou Recueil de morale universelle* . . . which was almost immediately afterward called the *Ami des théophilanthropes*. Guffroy was editor of the *Ami*. Beginning with the nineteenth number, the *Echo* carried the sub-title *Feuille citadine et villageoise*.

[3] MLL, vol. iii, p. 12.

Yet Revelliere-lépeaux was annoyed when, having published his views about secret aid to cults, he found that secrecy was no longer possible.

In certain cases the Directory could grant money openly in such a way that Theophilanthropy profited indirectly. From funds voted by the Directory on November 12, 1797 (22 Brumaire Year VI), the minister of the interior paid to Chemin one hundred and fifty francs for one hundred and fifty copies of the *Instructions sur la morale* of the Theophilanthropists.[1] These copies were to be used at the discretion of the committee that supervised orphanages and other charitable institutions. Only a few days earlier the Directory had ordered the minister of interior to pay two hundred francs to Chapuis, a leading Theophilanthropist who had labored throughout the summer to establish a school where good morals and republican principles should be inculcated. Revelliere-lépeaux had favorably annotated the petition of Chapuis who, after the failure of his strenuous endeavors to promote character and patriotism, was entirely without resources.[2] The same autumn of 1797, the minister of interior gave fifteen hundred francs to Parent, a former priest who had become one of the most active Theophilanthropists, to pay for printing a collection of nearly one hundred hymns which he had put in plain-song to make them more adaptable to the use of people in the country who were accustomed to that sort of music.[3] Such expenditure was justified on the ground that hymns would serve to encourage patriotism.

Grants of money, avowed or secret, were not the government's only means of showing favor. State control of church buildings opened another channel for patronage. For more

---

[1] AN, AF III, 112, 528: Etat de Répartition de la somme de 404, 901.26 faisant partie du fonds disponible de 500,000 par décision du Directoire exécutif, du 22 Brumaire an 6, 5e division.

[2] AN, F17, 1021A, 7.

[3] AN, F17, 1021A, 7, 110; Grégoire, *Histoire des sectes* (1814), vol. ii, pp. 124-125.

than a year, from the summer of 1797 until late in 1798, Theophilanthropy was allowed to occupy, one after another, the churches of Paris jointly with schismatic Catholicism, arrangements being for each cult to worship as it chose at an allotted hour that did not disturb the other. The régime of joint occupation gave rise to disputes over the choice of hours and the furnishing of the interior of the building,[1] but the discomforts of sharing churches were as nothing compared with the real difficulties of agreeing upon an hour for worship after the order of September 18, 1798, issued by the central administration of the department of the Seine.[2] This new order, although not actually depriving Theophilanthropists of the use of churches, practically excluded them by assigning the best hours to the new *Culte Décadaire* which was growing by leaps and bounds.

Did the launching of the *Culte Décadaire* prove that the Directory had ceased to protect Theophilanthropy? If the national government meant to continue favoring the deistic cult, why did it not force the central administration of the Seine to refrain from showing preference to the *Culte Décadaire* in respect to hours of worship? Had Revelliere-lépeaux, for some reason or other, ceased to be the friend of Theophilanthropy? Or was he obliged to give up protecting it because of opposition among his colleagues?

One of the more credible theories advanced to explain the change in the relations of the Directory, and especially of Revelliere-lépeaux, to Theophilanthropy is founded upon a supposed rapid development toward Jacobinism among Theophilanthropists.[3] Certainly accusations were not lacking that deists were using their religious committee meetings as cloaks for radical activities; they were supposed to be working to swing

---

[1] Mathiez, *La Théophilanthropie et le culte décadaire*, pp. 223-233.

[2] Schmidt, *Tableaux*, vol. iii, pp. 326-327.

[3] Mathiez, *La Théophilanthropie et le culte décadaire*, p. 400 *et seq.*; Aulard, *Paris sous le directoire*, vol. iv, pp. 170-171: *Miroir*, 25 Prairial An V (June 13, 1797).

elections toward the left. The cry of radicalism was quickly taken up by the newspapers. As early as June 23, 1797, the *Rédacteur* objected to the characterization of Theophilanthropy as a political association with Jacobin principles:

It has been said in one journal, and repeated in perhaps ten others (for foolishness and lies spread quickly in Paris) that the assembly of the Theophilanthropists is a reunion of Jacobins. But they do nothing in that assembly except sing pious hymns, listen to moral readings, address prayers to the Supreme Being. It is a cult freed from mysticism, and one which admits only the two fundamental dogmas of all religions: the existence of God and the immortality of the soul. The divine service is conducted with decorum and order. Thus, not only is it lying very insolently to represent the Theophilanthropists as factionists, but it is violating in their regard the law of the liberty of cults.[1]

Journalistic attack and counter attack aroused the Theophilanthropists and brought out in the *Moniteur* of August 11, 1797, a long article signed by J. Lachapelle, asserting that the religion was not a center of political scheming. He represented Theophilanthropy, on the contrary, as a logical and natural attempt to cope with irreligion and immorality. After describing the purposes and procedure of the cult, Lachapelle protested against the stories of its treasonable activities. He denied the charge of the *Censeur des Journaux* that Theophilanthropist meetings

are nothing but clubs where, under pretext of adoring God in spirit and in truth, they deliberate very seditiously on affairs of the time. They meet at night, . . .

and finally concluded his discussion:

I shall end these reflections by saying that an institution whose sole object is to reclaim for religion little by little those who, for whatever cause, have not for a long time belonged to any cult, to encourage effectually, by regular and fitting instruction, adults as

[1] Aulard, *Paris sous le directoire*, vol. iv, pp. 187-188.

well as children to fulfill all the duties of civil and domestic life; a religious association . . . ; which, perfectly strange to political affairs, only mentions the fatherland in order to make known to the citizens the sacred obligations which it imposes upon them . . . ; such an institution, I say, far from meriting unjust attacks, appears to me on the contrary to have, as every one which is useful to society, some right to the esteem, to the respect, and to the moral protection of all good people.

Lachapelle's published statement and the protests of other Theophilanthropists did not stop the talk about the cult's political activities, and gossip had it that the cult was in league with the government, not against it.[1] A report of the central bureau of Paris on November 20, 1797, noted the rumor

that the Theophilanthropists are paid by the government, supported by a member of the Directory, that by preference they will be chosen for public offices.[2]

In this belief is to be found the source for the story that Revelliere-lépeaux, by protecting the Theophilanthropists and becoming their pope, was aspiring to dictatorial power in the Directory, and the increasing success of Theophilanthropy after Fructidor seemed to support the story.

The published doctrines of Theophilanthropy expressed patriotism only in general terms;[3] the exhortations to be useful to the fatherland mentioned only non-partisan virtues such as industriousness, promptness in paying taxes, and willingness to defend the country in time of war. Nevertheless, the Directory was a republican government, and sermons on patriotism were in terms of republicanism.

[1] Mallet du Pan, *Correspondance inédite . . . avec le cour de Vienne 1794-1798 publiée d'après les manuscrits conservés aux Archives de Vienne* (Paris, 2 vols., 1884), vol. ii, pp. 368-369.

[2] Aulard, *Paris sous le directoire*, vol. iv, p. 461: Rapport du Bureau Central du 30 Brumaire An VI.

[3] Chemin-Dupontès, *Manuel des théophilantropes*, Section III of the *Morale des Théophilantropes*, " Rendez-vous utiles à la Patrie," pp. 24-27.

Did the republicanism of Theophilanthropy in actual practice go further than the government wished? Mathiez, with
his hypothesis of a probable last stormy interview between
Revelliere-lépeaux and a group of Theophilanthropist leaders
in March or April, 1798, holds that it did.[1] After detailed
studies, Mathiez has concluded that Revelliere-lépeaux withdrew his support from the cult, because he was incensed at its
radical activities. Although Revelliere-lépeaux nowhere in his
writings acknowledges this sharp break, Mathiez minimizes the
omission with the explanation that " that hour was painful to
his sensitive mind, so painful that he did not have the courage
to record the reminiscence in his *Mémoires*." Mathiez very
logically sets forth the theory that the Directory, through its
ministers and commissioners, had controlled the attitude of the
police toward religion and that the lower police, although never
friendly toward Theophilanthropy, " kept their hostility secret
and postponed their revenge as long as the Directory protected
the new republican deist church." [2] When the national government became unfriendly, municipal authorities were free openly
to favor Catholicism and to oppose Theophilanthropy. To
complete his hypothesis of a stormy interview between Revelliere-lépeaux and Theophilanthropist leaders, Mathiez supposes
a subsequent right-about-face among the members of the cult,
with a sincere attempt to modify too radical activities in the
hope of rewinning governmental confidence.[3]

Either this hypothesis is correct, and Theophilanthropy
began retrieving the Directory's good will, or the break in the
early spring of 1798 was not as sharp as Mathiez believes, for
in June the Directory's commissioners in the department of the
Seine appear far from hostile to Theophilanthropy; Dupin

[1] *Qu'est-ce que la théophilanthropie*, p. 13; Mathiez, *La Théophilanthropie
et le culte décadaire*, p. 405.

[2] Mathiez, "Les Théophilanthropes et les autorités à Paris sous le directoire," *La Révolution et l'église* (Paris, 1910), pp. 208-209. This article was
reprinted from *Annales révolutionnaires* of April, 1909.

[3] Mathiez, *La Théophilanthropie et le culte décadaire*, pp. 405-406.

even advised the minister of general police to give the cult three hundred francs so that its worship could be extended into the few churches of Paris which it had been unable to occupy.[1] In making this recommendation, Dupin was carrying out the wishes of Chapuis, then serving as commissioner of the Directory in the twelfth arrondissement of Paris.[2] As a result, not only three hundred but four hundred francs were granted, so that on September 6, 1798 (20 Fructidor Year VI), Theophilanthropy could be installed in the church Saint-Jacques-du-Haut-Pas, and very shortly afterward in the church Médard.

The relations between the Directory and Theophilanthropy from the autumn of 1798 until the summer of 1799 are difficult to trace. It cannot be proved that Revelliere-lépeaux gave the cult his unqualified approval, as in the preceding year; nor can he be said to have abandoned it completely. More than one petition was addressed to him, and in several instances he seems to have done his best to help the deists. On the other hand, he was either unwilling or unable to protect Theophilanthropy against the encroachments of the *Culte Décadaire*.

Throughout the first two years of its existence, Theophilanthropy had met only two rivals: Catholicism and the natural inertia or hostility of society toward a new and unknown religious movement. Revelliere-lépeaux's attitude against these two enemies was predictable and sure. He was constantly anticlerical, and in his case anti-clericalism was directed exclusively against the Catholic Church. He saw in public indifference to the new deistic cult only an invitation for zealous labor and proselytism. In 1798, however, Theophilanthropy was in danger of being outstripped by another faith, born of the need of the state to concentrate the loyalty of its people and clothed in a pageantry more appealing than the simple ceremonies of Theophilanthropy. Did Revelliere-lépeaux fail to see that even his own idea of national fêtes, once entrenched, might develop

[1] Aulard, *Paris sous le directoire*, vol. iv, p. 732.

[2] AN, F⁷, 7419; Mathiez, *La Théophilanthropie et le culte décadaire*, pp. 411-413.

into a civil religion which would supplant rather than supplement his favorite religious cult? Or did the situation pass beyond his control?

Constitutional provisions for a series of celebrations throughout the year to be organized under the auspices of the state had remained practically a dead letter during the first two years of the Directory, and in all that time the *Culte Décadaire,* namely a system of regular meetings every tenth day according to programs sent out by the minister of interior, was not being considered. Although Revelliere-lépeaux never relaxed his interest in developing patriotism by education and ceremonies, two other men, Merlin de Douai and François de Neufchâteau, were principally responsible for putting life into the system of fêtes and for creating the *Culte Décadaire.*[1] These two entered the Directory immediately after Fructidor, 1797, taking the places of Carnot and Barthélemy. Merlin de Douai first, and then François de Neufchâteau, championed the cause of patriotic fêtes so that during the spring and summer of 1798 the celebrations assumed for the first time something of the pomp and ceremony that had been intended. François de Neufchâteau was removed from the Directory in the spring of 1798 by the drawing of lots, but shortly afterward he was reappointed minister of interior, and from the summer of 1798 his indefatigable labors began building the *Culte Décadaire,* encouraging and requiring tenth-day services for instruction in the affairs of state and the inculcation of personal and social virtues without the aid of supernatural religion.

The two councils passed laws authorizing the *Culte Décadaire* in August and September, 1798.[2] In spite of circulars and exhortations issued faithfully from the ministry of interior, the new cult was not welcomed in all of France. The country districts were particularly slow in accepting it. The

[1] Mathiez, *La Théophilanthropie et le culte décadaire,* Chapter VI, pp. 400-459.
[2] *Ibid.,* pp. 414-429.

energy of François de Neufchâteau, however, knew no bounds, and gradually his enthusiasm, re-enforced by laws of the councils and orders of the Directory, appeared to be winning the populace. For six months, from the late autumn of 1798 until the late spring of 1799, it became progressively stronger. Although the *Culte Décadaire* pretended not to replace religious cults, the orders that gave it precedence in church buildings— which were, of course, state buildings—made it the enemy of both Catholicism and Theophilanthropy.

Revelliere-lépeaux lent his influence to the state cult. When his friend the poet Ducis came to visit him at Andilly, the two men poured over verses of hymns which Ducis was writing to be used for marriage ceremonies. These hymns were later presented to François de Neufchâteau [1] and accepted as part of the ritual he was constantly engaged in adapting for his *Culte Décadaire.* On the other hand, Revelliere-lépeaux did not disregard petitions of Theophilanthropists who continued to seek his aid in their struggle to hold their own in the occupation of churches.[2] Yet, whether he was unable to command the assent of the other Directors, or whether François de Neufchâteau in spite of the Directory contrived to favor the *Culte Décadaire,* Revelliere-lépeaux's good will toward Theophilanthropy seems to have spent itself in favorable recommendations to the minister of interior or to the minister of police. It is to be doubted that Revelliere-lépeaux ever fully approved usurpation of the place of religion by any ceremony which ignored the concept of God, but even in his memoirs he left no explanation of his attitude toward the *Culte Décadaire.*

Any hypothesis that undertakes to explain the complicated relations of church and state during the four years of the Directory may be subject to question, but certain assertions regarding the rôle of Revelliere-lépeaux in the government's policy seem tenable. In the first place, he was anti-Catholic.

---

[1] AN, AE II, 1475; Musée des Archives Nationales, Vitrine 152.

[2] Mathiez, *La Théophilanthropie et le culte décadaire,* pp. 544-551.

His earlier desires had been to reform the Catholic Church, giving congregations the right to choose their religious leaders and making marriage optional with the clergy. By the time of the Directory he was fixed in a determination to destroy Catholicism root and branch. In the language of the time, he attacked the church as the teacher of superstition and branded the confessional as immoral. The key to his hostility lay, however, in his conviction that the Catholic Church was the enemy of the republic, for he had come to believe that the old religion was corrupting society as well as the individual. Therefore, while he never ceased to maintain friendly relations with some members of the Catholic clergy, he opposed the church itself with all his might. In the second place, although he heartily approved of attempts to encourage patriotism and virtue by fêtes and was far from disliking the *Culte Décadaire,* the deistic cult of Theophilanthropy won his particular enthusiasm and support. Beginning in the summer of 1797, and continuing for nine months or a year, he was Theophilanthropy's chief advocate in the Executive Directory. The protection he was able to obtain for the cult consisted, for the most part, of relatively small amounts of money paid from secret funds of the police, and of certain privileges such as the use of churches and the assurance of police protection against disturbance to the worshippers. This protection was supplemented by minor encouragements such as approval of books of moral instruction composed by Theophilanthropists, or the payment of small sums of money to individual Theophilanthropists, as in the case of Chapuis the educator. During the last year of the Directory, Revelliere-lépeaux's attitude cannot be demonstrated so pre-

---

Illustration on opposite page

THE NEW MORALITY, caricature by Gillray, published as a colored engraving in the *Anti-Jacobin Review and Magazine* (London, July 1798, p. 114) and shortly afterward reprinted in color and in black and white. The caricature is reproduced here from an authorized photostat of a copy in the British Museum.

cisely. He may have broken with the leaders of Theophilanthropy temporarily in the spring of 1798, but at least he remained in sympathy with the movement even during the
months when the *Culte Décadaire* was threatening to sweep the
entire country. When he left the Directory in June, 1799,
Revelliere-lépeaux had not for some time been of great assistance to Theophilanthropy; accusations that he had favored
the cult were then slightly out of date. The charge that he had
treasonably used the cult for political ends and was aspiring
through control over Theophilanthropists to gain still more
power in government has been impossible to prove and now
appears a little ridiculous. From the incongruity of Revelliere-
lépeaux's too serious and often intolerant good intentions,
from the mistaken hopes of deists and the hostility of Catho-
lics, came the irrepressible mixture of humor and bitterness
which has left the caricature of a Citizen Director as Pope.

II

While he encouraged deism in the belief that it would help
reconstruct society, Revelliere-lépeaux continued to occupy
himself with utilizing art and learning as bulwarks of the new
republic. Progress had been made in importing treasures from
conquered regions. When Labillardière left Coni on September 30, 1796, on his way to Paris with the first shipment of
artistic booty from Italy, he had been obliged to leave behind
twenty-three cases of paintings.[1] Toward the end of October,
Citizen Escudier, a resident of Paris but a native of Toulon,
was appointed to bring the rest of the paintings to Paris, and
with them eighteen cases of objects chosen in the meantime at
Modena.[2] Charging an assistant, Bertrand, to look after the
treasures from Modena, Escudier went directly to Coni. Arriv-

[1] Collection Pasquier, Letter a. s. Labillardiere to Citizen Lareveilliere
Lepeaux, Paris, 10 Frimaire An V, Pièce justificative no. 10.

[2] Blumer, "La Commission pour la recherche des objets de sciences et
arts en Italie," *La Révolution française, revue*, vol. lxxxvii (1934), p. 225
et seq.

ing there on November 13, he was able to arrange a safe escort soon enough to join Bertrand at Genoa by December 3 (13 Frimaire Year V).[1] Embarking from Genoa on December 11, Escudier arrived four days later at Toulon. After a delay of nearly seven months at the French port, the precious cases from Coni and Modena were loaded on a caravan of seventeen wagons for their journey northward. In twenty-five days they reached Paris, July 30, 1797.

Neither Labillardière's expedition nor Escudier's caused a great public stir. Publicity and acclaim were reserved for the third installment, which did not find its way to Paris until the summer of 1798. Conquests from Rome formed the nucleus of this third shipment; in pursuance of the terms of the armistice of June 1796 with the Pope and the subsequent treaty of Tolentino concluded in February 1797, four shipments left Rome for Leghorn in the course of the summer of 1797. While the other members of the commission went to Venice to carry out the provisions of a secret treaty concluded in May 1797, providing for the surrender of twenty paintings and five hundred manuscripts of the victor's choice, Thouin and Moitte had the Roman consignment placed on boats that sailed from Leghorn on August 9, 1797, arrived at Marseilles on August 15, and after waiting in quarantine were unloaded on August 27.

At this point, Thouin wrote at length to Revelliere-lépeaux, sparing no detail of the difficulties of the journey. Funds were exhausted. It was necessary that the Directory and the various ministers at Paris take immediate steps to meet the situation. Yet the commissioners continued to dream of immeasurable glory for France, and to that end all their labors were being consecrated.[2]

---

[1] AN, AF III, 71, 2: "Extrait d'une dépêche des Commissaires à la recherche des objets des sciences et arts, Milan 15 frimaire an 5." For record of payment, see AN, AF III, 112, 528.

[2] AN, F17, 1275, 2. Two days later Thouin wrote a second letter to Revelliere-lépeaux (AN, F17, 1275, 2, 323).

This letter, my respectable friend, is not official. It is not at all to the president of the Directory that I write; it is to my zealous friend of the arts and the sciences and the glory of his fatherland that I address it. To whom could we better appeal than to you the promoter of the expedition of the commission in Italy? We have written to the ministers; their pressing occupations have kept them from answering us. Yours without doubt are infinitely more considerable and more important, but I hope that overlooking customary procedure you will be so good as to bring our work to its fulfillment . . .

We ask you with confidence, my worthy friend, 1° to hasten the decision of the Executive Directory as to the kind of entrance into Paris for the monuments from Rome, and to notify General Bonaparte and us of the decision so that we may execute it punctually; 2° to have the minister of interior send us the orders essential to prevent the convoy from being delayed en route and to make indispensable repairs on the canals; 3° and finally to have the minister of war arrange to have the convoy guarded as it crosses France.

Delicately reminding Revelliere-lépeaux of his success in Fructidor, Thouin ended his letter with a flourish: " You have saved the Republic by your courage; she will owe you as well the monuments which are to make her learned, illustrious, and forever happy." In spite of the unofficial character of Thouin's message, it proved the turning point in the work of the committee for Italian treasures and outlined the program actually followed in completing the transportation of artistic, scientific, and literary objects from Italy to Paris and in receiving the precious cargoes on their arrival.

Revelliere-lépeaux set to work straightway. The Directory communicated with the minister of interior,[1] the minister of foreign affairs, the minister of war, and the board of administration of the Musée Central des Arts. Notwithstanding Thouin's complaints, these ministries had not been entirely ne-

[1] AN, F17, 1055, 9: Letter a.s. Revelliere-lépeaux to the minister of interior, Paris, 16 Vendémiaire An VI; AN, F17, 1275, 2.

glecting the matter in hand,[1] but direct word from the heads of the government made the wheels turn faster. The minister of interior wrote to Thouin and Moitte, sending a copy of the letter to Revelliere-lépeaux; the minister was proposing a new apportionment of money to pay for transportation charges, but he hoped that Bonaparte would carry out his promise of financial aid;[2] he was asking companies for bids on contracts to bring the treasures from Marseilles to Paris; he was turning over in his mind projects of receiving the convoy with due honors.[3] The minister of war, for his part, exchanged letters with the minister of interior; he had ordered a substantial guard to protect the convoy and was issuing commands to military officers along the proposed route to facilitate the passage of the consignment.[4] Accordingly, after a delay of six weeks at Marseilles, the cargo, re-embarked on river boats, set sail up the Rhône toward Arles on November 7. At Arles there was another long wait until collections from Venice and Verona[5] caught up with the procession. These forty-five cases,

---

[1] Archives du Musée du Louvre (AL), *Correspondance de l'Administration du Musée Central des Arts*, vol. i, p. 81 : Letter of 27 Fructidor Year V to La Réveillère Lépaux member of the Directory; Letter of 27 Fructidor Year V to the director general of public instruction. *Ibid.*, vol. i, p. 82 : Letter of 28 Fructidor Year V to commissioners of the French government for the collection of objects of sciences and arts in Italy; Letter of 29 Fructidor Year V to the minister of foreign affairs. AAE, Mémoires et Documents, 1414 (Affaires intérieures, 674) 1796-1802 : Letter of 5 Vendémiaire Year VI, minister of foreign affairs to the administrators of the Musée Central des Arts.

[2] The Directory had not ceased exhorting Bonaparte to do everything he could toward promoting and supervising the work of the commissioners in Italy. *Cf.* letter from the Executive Directory to Bonaparte, May 12, 1797 (23 Floréal An V), AHG, B *3, *119, fol. 164 r.

[3] AN, F17, 1275, 2, 379-381.

[4] AN, F17, 1275, 2, 375.

[5] Collections from Verona had arrived in Venice by September 10, 1797 (24 Fructidor Year V) ; *cf.* letter from Monge to Dessole, *chef de l'état major* of the Army of Italy (AHG, B *3 *119). A week later, September 17, 1797, the commissioners at Venice notified the Directory that their mission in Italy was completed (AN, F17, 1275). The entire collection from Venice

having arrived by sea at Toulon on January 22, 1798, joined the lot at Arles on March 7. One last part of the shipment from Venice, including the famous four horses and the lion of St. Mark, did not come for so long that Thouin finally gave up waiting and ordered the boats to turn north from Arles. The bronze horses and the lion left Toulon only on April 18, to join the principal shipment at Digoin on June 19. In the meantime, the water route had been followed according to plans worked out between Thouin and the Paris ministers: up the Rhône to Lyons, then following the Saône river to Châlons, where it was necessary to take the Canal du Centre to reach the Loire at Digoin; then along the Canal Briaire to Montargis, the Canal du Loing to the Seine, and by that river to the outskirts of Paris.[1]

Since this third shipment of precious objects reached Paris on July 15 just too late for Bastille Day, the next public fête of the calendar, July 27-28, 1798 (9-10 Thermidor Year VI), was set aside for celebrating the arrival of the monuments of science and the arts from Italy.[2] No effort was spared in the intervening two weeks to organize a fête worthy of the treasures and of the republic. The outstanding feature of the first day's program was a parade of gigantic proportions, beginning near the Jardin des Plantes, where the sculptures and paintings and even wild animals — a consignment of living specimens from Africa had been joined to the Italian shipments at Marseilles so that both arrived at Paris at the same time—[3] were removed from barges to wagons and cages. Each statue bore its name and an appropriate inscription; paintings and manuscripts and other objects which might have been damaged through undue exposure were left in their cases but marked clearly so that people along the streets and crowds

and Verona was ready to turn over to the commanding officer of the marine to be shipped to Marseilles or to Toulon, as seemed wisest.

[1] Blumer, *op. cit.*, pp. 229-236.

[2] *Ibid.*, pp. 237-241; Saunier, *op. cit.*, p. 39 *et seq.*

[3] AN, F17, 1055, 4.

gathered at the Champ-de-Mars could not mistake their identity. Certain accounts tell of enthusiasm checked by rain, while
others suggest that there was more excitement over the new
animals than appreciation of the objects of art. The procession finally resolved itself into a great circle at the Champ-de-
Mars, and a complete list of trophies was formally presented
to the minister of interior, François de Neufchâteau, by four
members of the commission who had chosen the works of art
in Italy. All these details, reminiscent of ancient Roman tri-
umphs, touched popular imagination and pride.

At a public session of the Executive Directory the next day,
Reubell, at that time president, congratulated the commissioners
on behalf of the government and pinned upon each one a medal
engraved with the words " Les sciences et les arts reconnais-
sants." Thouin thanked the Directory and praised the spirit
of liberty, which had freed the work of so many great masters
from oblivion and decay.

The next problem was to arrange the paintings and marbles
against a background suitable for public exhibition. The matter
of location and appropriate means of display had been discussed for nearly a year. In his notable letter of September 29,
1797, written from Marseilles to Revelliere-lépeaux, Thouin
had pleaded for prompt display of the treasures from Italy:

I shall close this letter—too long already—with a matter which
seems important to us. We would not have these works of ancient
genius abandoned for years on end in gloomy storehouses, but
rather put on exhibition as soon as possible for art lovers of all
nations, thus serving at once to instruct and develop the genius
of our artists. If this course is not followed, it is to be feared that
evil-minded and even well-intentioned tourists who come to see
these rare objects may have a justifiable pretext for regretting
their removal from the sumptuous galleries of the Vatican and
of the Capitoline, where they could be seen by everybody, to be
hidden away from all eyes in obscure storage. Certainly it will be
impossible to arrange them in Paris immediately upon their arrival
as advantageously as they were displayed at Rome and as they

deserve to be shown. I do not believe that a museum worthy of them even exists, and if we wait until one is arranged years will pass before they can be seen by the public. Would it not be possible to consecrate an unused church to these treasures? One could easily be found suitable for the purpose, such as that of the Feuillants, of the Capucines, the church of the Assumption, or others near the museum. These gods of antiquity were displaced from their temples to make way for divinities who are no more useful for being less ancient. They will re-enter their sanctuaries with a more worthy consecration, since they will contribute to developing the arts. They could be placed on simple stucco-covered pedestals until the place destined to receive them in the museum is properly and entirely prepared to receive them.[1]

The minister of interior, to whom Revelliere-lépeaux communicated Thouin's letter, replied briefly, " I understand how much you must desire that these monuments be made ready for public exhibition promptly, and I will leave no stone unturned in order that your wish may be gratified," and inclosed with the note a copy of his longer answer to Thouin and Moitte, setting forth his own opinions and explaining his plans for housing the Italian art conquests.[2]

Your reflections on the necessity of placing them temporarily in a church seemed to me very well taken. The plan at first was to turn over to them certain halls of the rez-de-chaussée underneath the Gallery of Apollo. I had these halls inspected, and they seem to lack majesty. Their gilt, their ornamentation of a bizarre taste, would seem to contrast disagreeably with the beautiful and noble simplicity of the Ancients. Therefore I believe we shall have to give up the plan. Perhaps a handsome museum of sculpture could be arranged in long lines with an aisle in between where the public might walk and admire. This plan, however, would necessitate rather large expenditures, aside from the fact that modern sculpture would adapt itself better to the location than ancient marbles.

[1] AN, F¹⁷, 1275, 2.
[2] AN, F¹⁷, 1275, 2, 379-381.

Therefore I adopt your idea of setting up our antiquities temporarily in a church, and consequently I am looking to see which one would best suit the purpose. The chapel of the Collège des Quatre Nations has been suggested to me. As a matter of fact it would seem very well suited, if it is large enough.

As soon as I have definitely chosen a place, I shall have pedestals prepared there, and, since the dimensions of the principal statues which are coming are perfectly known, the places for them will be designated in advance, and we shall have only to put them there when they arrive.

The administrators of the Musée Central des Arts took offense, however, at the idea that the new treasures were not to be entrusted exclusively to their care. Having heard from Revelliere-lépeaux of Thouin's proposals, they immediately questioned the policy of establishing any important collection at Paris separate from their own museum. They wrote to Thouin to that effect on October 16 (25 Vendémiaire Year VI). The commissioners replied that they never would have suggested to Revelliere-lépeaux the advisability of placing the objects from Italy in an unused church, if they had believed for an instant that the museum had enough room or indeed any place ready to receive the treasures on their arrival in Paris.[1] The museum's administrative committee gained its point. The Italian treasures were first displayed in what is today the Louvre and, except for paintings and statues confided to provincial museums, remained there until 1815. On February 6, 1798, while Thouin and Moitte were still worried about sending their convoy north from Arles, an exhibition was opened at the Musée Central,[2] composed chiefly of the paintings brought from Parma, Piacenza, Milan, Cremona,

[1] AL, *Registre des Procès-Verbaux de l'Administration du Musée Central des Arts*, vol. i, p. 153, 82nd session, November 18, 1797 (28 Brumaire Year VI). The administrators had written to Revelliere-lépeaux on September 13, 1797 (27 Fructidor Year V), asking help to improve the museum's facilities for displaying the collections; cf. *Correspondance de l'Administration du Musée Central des Arts*, vol. i, p. 81.

[2] Saunier, *op. cit.*, p. 39.

Modena, and Bologna, which had arrived in November 1796 under the care of Labillardière and in July 1797 under the care of Escudier.

The considerably enlarged collections at the museum demanded additional care and oversight. On April 11, 1798 (22 Germinal Year VI), the administrators wrote to Revelliere-lépeaux begging him to urge upon his colleagues the wisdom of enlarging their number by appointment of Barthélemy and Moitte, both commissioners of the Italian art expedition. They also wrote to Bonaparte in Italy, asking him to use his influence with the Directory toward the same end.[1] As a result, Barthélemy and Moitte received the desired appointments. The board of administrators worked steadily at the problem of opening the main part of the Italian collection to the public; but various delays postponed the second exhibition until November 9, 1799 (18 Brumaire Year VIII), curiously enough, the very last day of the Directory. This time the treasures of Venice, Verona, Mantua, Pesaro, Fano, Loretta, and Rome were displayed. The following March, 1800, pictures and marbles from Florence and Turin were added to the collection.[2] Bonaparte, the First Consul, was continuing the work of Bonaparte, General of the First Italian Campaign.

While paintings and marbles were arriving in Paris by divers routes, Hans and Marguerite, the elephants, presented a very live and resisting problem in the Netherlands, where they appeared only too content to remain and only too happy

[1] AL, *Correspondance*, vol. i, pp. 125-126.

[2] Saunier, *op. cit.*, p. 39. Removals from Florence had not begun until 1798 (Müntz, *op. cit.*, 1896, p. 502 *et seq.*). On December 19, 1798, Revelliere-lépeaux was writing the first draft of a letter sent by the Executive Directory to General Championnet, exhorting him, if the chance of war took him to Naples, to take every precaution to prevent the looting of art collections which must be perfectly preserved for France (AN, AF III, 563, 3815). At this point, events moved faster than intentions; the collections of Naples were pillaged; choice objects from that city came into the personal possession of Bonaparte during the Consulate, but neither then nor during the Directory did Neapolitan treasures enrich public collections in France (Müntz, *op. cit.*, 1896, p. 506).

to thwart every well-laid plan for taking them south. The lively three-cornered correspondence continued—Directory, museum of natural history, menagerie headquarters at Loo—with occasional interpolations by one minister or another. When especially constructed wagons repeatedly broke down, the project of bringing the animals to Paris on foot was discussed and given up as impractical. The final conclusion was a mixed plan of beginning the journey by river boat and completing the last laps with bigger and stronger wagons than had yet been constructed.

In October, 1797, Revelliere-lépeaux forwarded to the museum's administrative council a letter from Noël, still minister at The Hague, with his account of the elephants' final departure. After a slow first journey, the animals wintered at Cambrai under military protection, achieved the final part of the route by land, passed through Reims so as to arrive in Paris at the end of March, 1798. Hans and Marguerite were greeted with enthusiasm, and their appearance at the Jardin des Plantes was heralded near and far, as far as the London *Times*. One of their specially constructed wagons was sent as a gift to the Conservatoire des Arts et Métiers, while the administrators of the department of the Aisne were granted two thousand francs to repair roads damaged by the wagon in passing from Cambrai to Reims. Quarters for the elephants had been scrupulously prepared, with attention paid to heating and ventilation. After Hans and Marguerite had become somewhat accustomed to their new surroundings, the public was admitted to see them at certain hours each day. Artists were given permission to make drawings and paintings of the strange beasts, and scientists to examine them at leisure. Twice, so the minutes of the natural history museum's administrative committee solemnly relate, the orchestra from the Conservatoire de Musique came to give concerts for Hans and Marguerite so that their emotional reactions might be carefully observed and recorded.[1]

[1] BMHN, *Procès-Verbaux des séances*, vol. iii, pp. 44, 52, 78, 97, 108, 120, 122-123, 133, 146, 153, 155, 158, 159, 160, 164, 165, 170, 175, 177; vol. iv,

III

Revelliere-lépeaux's eagerness to promote learning and the arts was as constant during the last two years of his Directorial career as in the first eighteen months. At the Institut, however, his interest could not express itself through attendance at meetings, for politics was too preoccupying. He went only twice in 1797, the first time on the first of May to read his *Réflexions sur le culte,* and again on October 13 (22 Vendémiaire Year VI), to read his short *Essai sur les moyens de faire participer l'universalité des spectateurs à tout ce qui se passe dans les fêtes nationales.* In 1798 he appeared not at all, nor up to his resignation from the Directory in 1799. That his interest did not flag is demonstrated, none the less, by the assiduity of his attendance as soon as the storms that closed the Directory had died down.[1] Revelliere-lépeaux's relations with the museum of natural history continued to be close and personal. His interests did not confine themselves to bringing two elephants down from the Netherlands. In December, 1797, he sent tickets to the members of the museum for the fête celebrating the recent signing of peace with Austria.[2] In January, 1798, he made the museum a present of two rare nuts recently brought back from Java.[3] That October, he wrote directly to Thouin, asking that a collection of seeds of both grains and vegetables be sent to a group of landed proprietors in Maine-et-Loire in order to make experiments to improve crops there. The request was taken up by the council of administrators and an order sent to the professor of plant culture to be filled.[4] When questions of the museum's housing came up from time to time, Revelliere-lépeaux took the trouble to inform himself

pp. 3, 8-9, 19, 20, 24, 117; AN, AF III, 112, 528: Ministère de l'Intérieur, Etat de Répartition, Distribution du 18 Ventôse an 6, No. 49; AN, AF III, 112, 529: Ministère de l'Intérieur, Etat de Répartition, Distribution du 23 Germinal an 6, No. 25.

[1] Communication of M. Lyon-Caen: *La Revelliere-lépeaux Membre de la Classe des Sciences morales et politiques 1795-1803.*

[2] BMHN, *Procès-Verbaux,* vol. iii, p. 132.

[3] *Ibid.,* vol. iii, p. 134.   [4] *Ibid.,* vol. iv, p. 30.

about the improvements and exchanges of property under consideration.[1]

Moreover Revelliere-lépeaux's contacts with the Muséum Central des Arts, the forerunner of the present-day Louvre, were not limited to consultations about the disposition of artistic treasures brought back from Italy, although that subject figured largely in his relations with the museum's administrators. Most of the museum's correspondence was carried on with the minister of interior rather than with individual Directors, but, when it was necessary to appeal immediately to the highest governmental executives, Revelliere-lépeaux seems to have been consulted in preference to the others, in fact almost exclusively.[2] When the moment came to consider disposing of paintings and statues not vitally essential to the Muséum Central at Paris, Revelliere-lépeaux urged the claims of provincial museums and warmly seconded the requests of the recently founded central school and museum at Angers for a share in the national treasure.[3] In matters of general administration, he did not hesitate to call the managers of the Muséum Central sharply to account whenever he thought they had overstepped the bounds of their powers.[4]

At the Opéra, too, Revelliere-lépeaux was the favorite Director, when money was lacking or petitions were to be presented for other needs. During the spring of 1798 he was particularly active in receiving delegations and championing the cause of opera before his colleagues, whether it was the question of granting a general subsidy or of contriving to allot a pension for some aging musician, or of intervening at the

---

[1] BMHN, *Procès-Verbaux*, vol. iv, p. 60.

[2] AL, *Registre des Procès-Verbaux*, vols. i and ii (8 Pluviôse An 5-28 Fructidor An 8); *Registre de Correspondance* (11 Pluviôse An 5-27 Fructidor An 8).

[3] AL, *Registre des Procès-Verbaux*, vol. i, pp. 208, 231-235; vol. ii, p. 107; AML, L 918, dossier Musée de peinture; Port, *op. cit.*, vol. i, p. 86; Louis Tavernier, *Le Musée d'Angers* (Angers, 1855), p. 21.

[4] AL, *Registre des Procès-Verbaux*, vol. i, p. 208; AN, AF III, 489, 3056.

ministry of war to exempt from military service young artists needed for operatic presentations.[1]

In August, 1797, Revelliere-lépeaux wrote directions for investigating the state of the Observatoire and taking steps to stimulate its activities, but although the newly founded Bureau des Longitudes kept in close touch with the Directory, there is nothing in its records to suggest that Revelliere-lépeaux played any greater rôle than his colleagues in working out its problems from 1795 to 1799.[2]

Beside the hundred and one organizations demanding attention, there were always favorite friends and protégés. Revelliere-lépeaux saw that the naturalist Adanson's pension was continued [3] and that Bernardin de Saint-Pierre was granted an additional and much-needed subsidy.[4] When foreign residents were a second time menaced with expulsion from Paris, Revelliere-lépeaux's intervention saved Tortoni, Roman brother-in-law of the painter Gérard, from being obliged to leave the country.[5] At another time his word helped the brother of the poet Ducis, when he needed a position.[6]

In June, 1798, according to Revelliere-lépeaux's request, a special messenger brought from Rome molds for making a particular type of character, which it was hoped would encourage the development of fine printing in France.[7] The next

[1] Archives de l'Opéra: General funds for Opéra, Cartons A 44 (Liasse 10), A 49 (Ventôse An 6); Exemption from military service, Registre 121 (Floréal An 7); Larrivée petition, Cartons A 49 (Floréal), A 50 (Vendémiaire), Registres 116, pp. 26, 35, and 117, fols. 8 r., 48 v.

[2] AN, AF III, 460, 2768, plaquette 28 Thermidor An V; Archives du Bureau des Longitudes, Procès-Verbaux des Séances 1e à 160e (6 Juillet 1795–10 Septembre 1797); Séances 161e à 609e (1797-1804). The Archives of the present-day Observatoire shed no light on Revelliere-lépeaux's rôle during these years.

[3] AN, F17, 1021A, 8.

[4] AN, F17, 1021A, 7.

[5] AN, AF III, 452, 2684.

[6] AN, AA 64, 2, 291-333, fols. 43-45.

[7] Collection Pasquier, Letter a. s. "Saint Martin au Citoyen Lareveillère Lépeaux Membre du Directoire Exécutif, 1er Messidor An 6."

month, Revelliere-lépeaux received word from Ginguené, who had passed from his position in public instruction to the post of minister to Turin and from there to a place as publicist and propaganda secretary in Italy, that a remarkably talented Italian violinist was coming to Paris with her family. Ginguené hoped that the Director and his wife and daughter would invite the young virtuoso to some of their receptions and act as sponsor for her and her playing whenever it might be possible.[1] These experiences in advancing the work of scholars and artists served to widen Revelliere-lépeaux's horizon and encouraged him to include more than armies and boundaries in his conception of foreign affairs.

IV

In January, 1798, there appeared a slender volume of ten essays, *Opuscules moraux de L. M. Revelliere-lépeaux et de J. B. Leclerc,* with, the explanatory note " the same principles, the same views, the same sentiments united them from their earliest youth in bonds of friendship which death alone can break " upon the title page. Published at the height of Revelliere-lépeaux's political prestige and while Leclerc was still continuing his legislative career in the Council of Five Hundred, the book served as an abridged anthology of the two men's occasional writings. Of the five items written by Revelliere-lépeaux, two were the essays read at his class of moral and political sciences at the Institut in 1797, two were short addresses pronounced in his official capacity as president of the Directory in the autumn of 1797 at the celebration of the Fête of the Founding of the Republic and at the funeral ceremonies for General Hoche, while the fifth, setting forth projects for a Panthéon and for a national theatre, had already appeared in pamphlet form but had not been presented as a public oration. The five contributions of Leclerc had been delivered in

[1] BN, MSS fr., Nouvelles Acquisitions, 21566, 29. For Ginguené's appointment, see AN, AF III, 478, 2955, no. 16: Letter from Executive Directory to Bonaparte, 23 Brumaire An 6.

part or in whole during the course of his parliamentary activities as deputy from Maine-et-Loire. Leclerc's dominant idea was the importance of a well conceived framework of institutions as a factor in good government. In expanding this theme he first pointed out the utility of poetry and music in the achievement of an adequate program of instruction in state schools. Subsequently he insisted upon the worth of civil religion as a factor in developing upright, faithful citizens. Both Revelliere-lépeaux and Leclerc envisaged the republic as a transformation of society from cellar to garret; all was to be remade, everything built again from first principles. Since human nature was human nature, each person could not be expected to reason out every new situation from the clear blue sky, and, even if such a course were possible, excessive individualism would mean the loss of the impetus and enthusiasm of group co-operation. The integral parts of the social framework should be conceived, however, so in harmony with universal truth that they would represent what every man could find for himself had he the time and inclination to search for the essence of living at its source. The social pattern of a design for living should be founded upon universal instinct, reason, and emotion, so that every man, woman, and child would rejoice as one person in the resultant collective expression.

Throughout the rest of his life, Revelliere-lépeaux set down no clearer exposition of his social philosophy.

CHAPTER VI

PRAIRIAL

Je ne sais si l'on a jamais entrepris d'écrire une biographie en essayant à chaque instant d'en savoir aussi peu sur l'instant suivant que le héros de l'ouvrage en savait lui-même au moment correspondant de sa carrière. En somme, reconstituer le hasard à chaque instant, au lieu de forger une suite que l'on peut résumer, et une causalité que l'on peut mettre en formule.

Paul Valéry, " Suite "
La Nouvelle Revue Française
1er Décembre 1933

It is not quite fair to introduce an account of Revelliere-lépeaux's political rôle from 1797 to 1799 with a quick glance over the twenty-one months and twelve days between the coup d'état of Fructidor and the one of Prairial, for in September, 1797, Revelliere-lépeaux did not know that he would be in the office twenty-one months and twelve days longer, nor did the date of Thirtieth Prairial hold any portent of tragedy for him. It is hardly permissible to hint that his admiration for Bonaparte would fail, since in September, 1797, he and his colleagues were still trying to reassure their general in Italy and dissuade him from resigning by giving him greater liberty in negotiating peace with Austria. Without pre-vision, Revelliere-lépeaux entered upon what both contemporaries and later historians called the Second Directory and what it pleased Carnot-Feulins to name the Unconstitutional Directory.

Illustration on opposite page

Portrait of Revelliere-lépeaux, oil on canvas, painted by François Gérard (flowers by the naturalist Van Spaendonck) during the Directory, perhaps in 1795 or 1796. This reproduction is from a photograph (J. Evers) of the original in the Musée d'Angers.

I

Grâces te soient rendues, souverain arbitre des destinées de
l'univers; grâces te soient rendues, la France est république!

This refrain, echoing through Revelliere-lépeaux's triumphant prayer-oration on the occasion of the first day of the
sixth year of the republic, September 22, 1797 (1 Vendémiaire Year VI), was his hymn of thanksgiving, chanted as president of the Directory for the success of the coup d'état of
Fructidor that he had achieved barely two weeks earlier. He
rejoiced that the sons of Gaul were slaves no longer, that they
had discovered their dignity as men. He described the self-
seeking enemies of the reborn liberty who had been ready to
destroy the republic. In a moment more, he pointed out, the
constitution would have been overturned, the republic would
have perished, the republicans would have been massacred, and
France, covered with ruins and corpses, would have fallen prey
to civil war. Then, before it was too late, a power from on high
had confounded the traitors and caught them in their own traps.
The republican constitution was strengthened by the very
efforts bent upon its ruin.[1]

In blissful contemplation of his state of oneness with the
ruler of the universe who had snatched France from the edge
of the precipice, and in joy at having performed faithfully his
duty as vice-regent on earth, Revelliere-lépeaux was not
troubled in conscience by the course he and Barras and Reubell
had taken. Carnot and Barthélemy, and the mass of deputies
who had been excluded from the councils, were either sinister
plotters or sadly mistaken mortals. Both categories of opponents were equally unholy and dangerous to the fatherland.
The majority of the Directory had chosen the one righteous
way and the one condition of grace.

---

[1] *Discours prononcé comme président du directoire à la fête de la république,
le 1er Vendémiaire an VI*, MLL, vol. iii, pp. 40-44.

Revelliere-lépeaux would have felt uneasy, however, in resting upon his laurels. The whole of France had to be assured of guidance by true patriots. The victory had to be consolidated. Not only were laws against émigrés and disloyal priests to be revived, but the government's personnel had to be purified. The Directory saw fit to discharge commissioners and name new ones from north to south and from east to west. Revellierelépeaux forgot his lack of health and his weariness in helping to supervise long and frequent lists of new appointments.[1]

Almost before the work of administrative purification was well under way, attention was drawn again to military affairs by the death of Hoche. Only ten days after celebrating the republic's birthday with shapely phrases, Revelliere-lépeaux gave the funeral oration for this greatly mourned general. He must have thought back over the last summer to the moment when Hoche and his troops had come closer to Paris than the constitution allowed, and he must have recalled the vigorous protest of the councils and the resulting scenes. He had thought Barras responsible for the mysterious orders, which no one was willing to own or explain; and, because he had a real affection and respect for Hoche, he had tried to ease the situation at the tense meeting of the Directory, where Hoche defended himself as best he could while Barras sat in stony silence.[2] The incident was unfortunate, but given another turn of events Hoche might have proved more to the Directory's liking as a protector than the blustering Augereau. All these thoughts, and more, must have gone through Revelliere-lépeaux's mind; but they did not disturb the even tenor of the funeral oration. He used the occasion rather to extol Hoche's success in the delicate task of pacifying the west of France and to hold up his example of astonishing exploits to both civilian and soldier. " When the first tribute has been offered to nature and the last respects paid

---

[1] MLL, vol. ii, p. 364. For appointments in the various departments, *cf. infra*, Appendix B, pp. 275-277.

[2] MLL, vol. ii, pp. 122-125; Pierre, *op. cit.*, pp. 5-7.

to the ashes of great men, it is in imitating them that we honor them." [1]

Revelliere-lépeaux was ready to make sacrifices for peace with honor, but ignominious peace was not to be considered. Thus, in spite of his desire that the wars of the previous five years come to an end, and preferably so within the months of his presidency, he did not waste tears over the failure of negotiations at Lille. In his attitude toward Great Britain, he was unyielding. To his way of thinking, if Great Britain did not appreciate and respect the dignity of the French republic, if she supposed for a moment that France would give up colonial possessions won by the honest strength of arms or desert her allies by abandoning their possessions, then she deserved to lose the blessings of peace and to feel the heavy hand of France.[2] For a time in the early autumn of 1797, Revelliere-lépeaux faced the possibility of seeing his term as president marked by the resumption of war with Austria as well as with Great Britain instead of blessed with the signing of a general peace.

Napoleon Bonaparte, after his summer at Montebello, was not the same Bonaparte who had left Paris for Italy in the spring of 1796. It was disconcerting for the Directory to have the general proceed with peace plans as if he and not they or their diplomatic agents held final authority over treaties. It was disconcerting to have him offer to resign in the middle of the negotiations. The Directory, unable to reach an understanding with Bonaparte by correspondence, sent a trusted messenger to Italy to confer with him and bring back a report. Dispatching a special envoy in this way was not at all without precedent, but the Directory waited with unusual impatience to hear the account which would come back with Botto, secretary of Barras, whom they charged with the mission. Botto's long report was in the Directory's hands toward the end of Vendé-

[1] AN, AF III, 467, 2842; *Discours prononcé comme président du directoire à la cérémonie funèbre exécutée en mémoire du Général Hoche au Champ de Mars, le 10 Vendémiaire an VI*, MLL, vol. iii, pp. 45-48.

[2] MLL, vol. ii, pp. 73-74.

miaire. Revelliere-lépeaux annotated the manuscript fully and meticulously, and according to these notes the Directory's letter to Bonaparte was prepared, discussing and recommending courses of action to meet the alternate exigencies of war or peace. This letter, dated October 21, 1797 (30 Vendémiaire Year VI), four days *after* the treaty of Campo Formio was actually signed, showed Revelliere-lépeaux and his colleagues laying even chances on the success or failure of making peace with Austria.[1] Perhaps the most striking part of this annotated report and the consequent reply to Bonaparte was precisely this pessimism as to the coming of peace and the resultant anxiety to provide adequately for resuming hostilities. The Directory almost begged Bonaparte's pardon for the plan of campaign it had submitted to him a month before; the proposal had been meant only as a suggestion, and Bonaparte's criticism had been heartily welcomed; they assured him that arrangements were being made for the re-enforcements he considered necessary. Bonaparte's objections to Schérer as minister of war were given less consideration, on the other hand, but his request for men of letters to serve as publicists was greeted with enthusiasm. The general's disavowal of intention to confound the military with the law, or to allow any encroachment upon legislative authority by the army, was approved energetically by Revelliere-lépeaux and the letter of his Directory to Bonaparte.

Revelliere-lépeaux and his Directory—but how much of the Directory was really his? The truce with Great Britain was broken during his presidency, and peace made with Austria, but had he determined either step? He and Barras and Reubell had accomplished Fructidor together. Merlin and François de Neufchâteau were only newcomers, not destitute of talent or experience, but valuable at first chiefly because they were not Carnot and Barthélemy. They would not immediately take as active a part in foreign affairs as their two predecessors. In the

[1] AN, AF III, 473, 2906; MLL, vol. ii, pp. 274-275.

nature of the case, more influence on foreign relations might be expected from Revelliere-lépeaux than before Fructidor. Reubell was likely to differ from him in conceptions and methods; Reubell, Alsatian that he was, emphasized the importance of the German aspects of foreign problems. Italy was important, he granted, but chiefly as the meeting ground of France and the Emperor. Any other extension of activities beyond the regions already involved he considered both foolish and wasteful. Barras and Revelliere-lépeaux were left to insist upon the importance of a strong policy among the Italians. Moreover, Reubell's health was showing signs of strain, and that fact lessened the probability that he would violently contradict his colleagues. As for Barras, he was everywhere and nowhere. Revelliere-lépeaux never succeeded in feeling entirely at ease with him. Did Botto really tell all in his official report, or were there other confidences for the secret ear of Barras? Barras had agents placed in most unexpected places, and Revelliere-lépeaux, ready to champion openly a program of proselytizing and reorganizing Italy, was forced to acknowledge that many an inexplicable turn of events might be due to the underground influence of Barras. Yet what could one do with a colleague, especially such an able one and one who had proved his far-seeing qualities at Fructidor, except take his official word and hope for the best?

Italy, for Revelliere-lépeaux at the end of 1797, divided itself into two sorts of territories: sister republics of France, and kingdoms or duchies capable of becoming sister republics. Venice was unfortunately subtracted from Italy for the time being, but the future might change its fate.[1] In respect of missionary fervor, Revelliere-lépeaux had changed not one whit since he sponsored the decree of November, 1792, offering liberty to all nations. His vision of a strong France, surrounded by a galaxy of small buffer states infinitely grateful for

[1] MLL, vol. ii, pp. 34-35.

France's tutelage, was the logical sequel to his views of 1792.[1] In France and among her neighbors there might be opposition from misguided souls and from cliques of unenlightened or evil-intentioned men; but the republican path, he was persuaded, was the one way to salvation, and the privilege of making and following that path repaid a thousand times the effort. France was to be the Grand Nation, shedding light upon all; and the Italians, though not her first pupils, would be among the earliest to enjoy the blessings that republican constitutions would eventually bring to all mankind.

With pride in the accomplishments of his term of three months, Revelliere-lépeaux left the president's chair to his successor Merlin at the end of November, 1797, and returned to his place as simple Director. He looked forward with confidence to the year of 1798.

II

In the era of the first constitutional republic, with its republican calendar, the new year began on the first of Vendémiaire (September 22). Politically speaking, however, the year began on the first of Prairial (May 20), when the newly chosen deputies took their seats in the Council of Five Hundred and the Council of Ancients. The annual parliamentary change might have momentous consequences. Not only could an unfavorable legislature annihilate the Directory's policy after the first of Prairial, but each year Revelliere-lépeaux and his colleagues faced the hazard of lot to decide which one would leave the Directory. Revelliere-lépeaux persuaded himself that he would be glad to withdraw, but when the spring of 1798 approached he suffered from nervous premonitions.

Justifying by the fact of their own survival at Fructidor the executive right to determine the choice of deputies, the Directors set about systematically to control the course of the

[1] Revelliere-lépeaux claims to have taken from the writings of d'Argenson, minister of Louis XV, his ideas of guaranteeing the independence of Italian states as a precautionary measure against Austria (MLL, vol. ii, p. 34).

elections. Revelliere-lépeaux saw nothing wrong in pointing out to the French electorate the qualifications which their representatives should have, or in warning them of the pitfalls which lay to the right and left of the narrow but righteous path. His colleagues appointed him to frame his ideas in a proclamation to enlighten the voting public, and since he wrote exactly as he felt the task was not difficult.

On March 23, 1798 (3 Germinal Year VI), the Directory dispatched its electoral address to the minister of interior, the minister of finance, and the *Rédacteur*. In drafting the document Revelliere-lépeaux had emphasized the qualities of republicanism, honesty, intelligence, energy, and wisdom as criteria by which the electors were to measure candidates. He added a general warning to avoid selecting aristocrats but urged electors against reacting too far in the opposite direction, because the elections of 1795 and 1797, with their disastrous tendency toward monarchy, might thereby be so reversed that dangerous radicals and anarchists would come into power. He concluded with an appeal to the electors' pride, assuring them that the fate not only of France but of all humanity waited upon their careful judgments.[1]

This address was not startling, nor did Revelliere-lépeaux emphasize unduly the uneasiness he felt. Yet through the days following the release of the address, he was increasingly anxious. His colleagues, too, feared or seemed to fear a revival of the Terror, if too radical a group of deputies came into power. The Directors began to credit rumors that royalists, foreseeing their own defeat, were backing the radical groups in the hope of coming into power upon the crest of the wave of despondency sure to follow a reign of irresponsible anarchy. Revelliere-lépeaux, always susceptible to insinuations of intrigue against the Directory, became convinced that this combination of plotters was a reality, and, when the first election returns began coming in, he had no longer a doubt. Then he

[1] AN, AF III, 513, 3255.

and Merlin composed a short emergency proclamation, announcing to the whole French population the discovery of a plot to destroy the republic. The Directory, having saved the nation from one horrible conspiracy at Fructidor, begged its constituents to defeat this new strategy by watching over the results of the elections already taking place or about to take place.[1] There was no time to lose. Merlin as well as Revellierelépeaux was in despair, for Merlin realized that all his part in preparing the elections had been of little help. He had worked ingeniously, and with remarkable quietness, to advance the cause of candidates favorable to the government. He had arranged a system of special agents whose apparent duty, as they penetrated nearly every department, was to inspect the repair and building of roads and highways which were, truly enough, in a miserable condition. The instructions and reports, all in terms of roadbuilding, had generally escaped detection, and in some cases the work was not entirely in vain, but for the most part these agents were as powerless as Revelliere-lépeaux's first rhetorical statement to stem the tide against the Directory.[2] Revelliere-lépeaux thus found Merlin ready to join forces with him in another public appeal.

Rhetoric failed, secret influence failed, and the Directory faced the certainty of a hostile majority in the councils. The old legislature continued in office, however, for several weeks after the elections, and the old legislature was docile. The Directory, working through its champions in the councils, had the councils declare election returns fraudulent or incorrect where the vote had been unfavorable to the Directory. The legislature then passed upon the eligibility of new deputies with the result that the evident will of the electorate was disregarded and the decisions reversed in enough cases to assure a majority in the new legislature favorable to the Directory. This anticipatory purge, completed on the twenty-second day of Floréal

[1] AN, AF III, 514, 3276.

[2] Albert Meynier, *Les Coups d'état du Directoire*, vol. ii, *Le Vingt-deux Floréal et le Trente Prairial* (Paris, 1928), pp. 43-51.

(May 11, 1798), was equivalent to a coup d'état. Revelliere-lépeaux, with no qualms of conscience, found the Twenty-second Floréal good because the Directory, in its wisdom, had once again saved the misguided electorate from the disaster of its folly.

III

Not entirely free from suspicion that the councils might encroach upon the executive power, yet reasonably sure that the most objectionable element had been removed, Revelliere-lépeaux, beginning with the spring of 1798, had more leisure to consider other problems pressing on every hand. In March, shortly before the elections, he had been instrumental in defining the Directory's policy toward the opposition raising its head in the west of France. When the minister of war reported that organized trouble might be expected from the former Vendean chiefs, Revelliere-lépeaux ordered information gathered from what he considered reliable sources as to the identity of these rebel chiefs.[1] Within two weeks the Directory sent instructions to General Victor, in command of the Twelfth Division with a jurisdiction including the departments of Maine-et-Loire, Loire-Inférieure, Deux-Sèvres, and the Vendée. General Victor was ordered to watch the former leaders of revolt with care but neither to offend them nor to associate familiarly with them. The rank and file of former rebels were to be assured of every kindness on the part of the government as long as they behaved themselves. In concluding its orders, the Directory named certain responsible citizens in each department upon whose judgment General Victor could rely with entire confidence.[2]

At the end of May, when the new councils met, the west of France was thus under careful supervision. To the north of France, Holland, although suffering dissensions, was maintaining her status as a republic officially faithful to her alliance

[1] AN, AF III, 508, 3212.

[2] AN, AF III: 512, 3250; 566, 3837.

with France.[1] To the east, Switzerland had been the scene of the establishment of the Helvetian republic at the end of March. The government's enemies spread rumors that quarrels had been stirred up among the cantons because Bonaparte wished to gain control of mountain passes to Italy, but Revelliere-lépeaux in his memoirs presented the interpretation that the change came because back in the sixteenth century France had assumed the responsibility of protecting certain cantons from aggressions upon their liberty.[2] To the south, in Spain, where since the beginning of the French Revolution the king and his court had swung back and forth from alliance with England to anomalous friendship with the French republic, Perrochel, a former ecclesiastic from Maine-et-Loire, had been named chargé d'affaires to fill the interim between Pérignon and Truguet.[3] Revelliere-lépeaux was responsible for his appointment to Madrid and was pleased with reports of his work there, more pleased than with Truguet. In Paris, Napoleon Bonaparte on returning at the end of 1797 had praised the simple virtues and extolled the heroes of Plutarch and had proved in various ways to Revelliere-lépeaux's satisfaction that his head was not turned by successes in Italy.[4] In consequence, Revelliere-lépeaux's objection to Bonaparte's cherished Egyptian campaign was more perfunctory than serious, when the question came to be decided by the Directory.[5] The expeditions to Eng-

---

[1] MLL, vol. ii, pp. 68-74, 194-198; AN, AF III, 528, 3443; Collection Pasquier, letters: Champigny-Aubin to Revelliere-lépeaux, Desmazieres fils to Revelliere-lépeaux, and Daendels to Revelliere-lépeaux.

[2] MLL, vol. ii, pp. 199-237; AN, AF III: 483, 3000; 560, 3784; 571, 3887; Collection Pasquier, correspondence and memoirs regarding Switzerland.

[3] MLL, vol. ii, pp. 252-257; A. Dry, *Soldats ambassadeurs sous le directoire An IV- An VIII* (Paris, 2 vols., 1906), " Pérignon," " Truguet "; Collection Pasquier, letters from Champigny-Aubin, Perrochel, and Seignette to Revelliere-lépeaux.

[4] MLL, vol. ii, p. 339.

[5] Revelliere-lépeaux points out (MLL, vol. ii, pp. 340-358) that he opposed the Egyptian expedition as rash and untimely, but that when the majority favored it he insisted that Bonaparte be given the full powers necessary for

land had been failures; this new method of attack, while perhaps chimerical, if it should succeed might be the very means of wounding Great Britain.

There remained Italy, with its five leading centers, Turin, Genoa, Milan, Rome, and Naples, capitals of three republics and two monarchies. Of the five, Turin was in the least tenable position. It was a monarchy guaranteed by treaties of peace and alliance with France, but it was also a monarchy surrounded by republics who vied with each other in revolutionary zeal seasoned with the hope of spoils from the court of Turin. One of Revelliere-lépeaux's best friends, Ginguené, fresh from the concerns of public instruction but with no diplomatic experience, had been named ambassador to Turin in December, 1797, in the general turnover of diplomats following the coup d'état of Fructidor; but he had not arrived at his post until toward the end of March, 1798. The French diplomatic corps throughout Europe had been rearranged with the idea of purifying and republicizing the various ministries and embassies. Ginguené suffered the contradictory plight of being an ardent republican sent to his post with definite instructions to maintain the monarchical status quo in Piedmont and to carry out France's treaty agreements to the letter of the law. He himself believed that the eventual conversion of Charles Emmanuel's country into a republic was inevitable; and Revelliere-lépeaux could not help thinking wishfully that another friendly republic would in time be formed out of this monarchy. Yet Ginguené was theoretically expected to respect and honor the king.

Ginguené began his diplomatic service by obliging Charles Emmanuel to receive the Citoyenne Ginguené at court without her conforming to the usual etiquette of dress specified for the occasion. Talleyrand at Paris was annoyed and said so, but Ginguené was not abashed. In addition to sending official reports, Ginguené wrote frequently to Revelliere-lépeaux. The

success. Guyot (*Le Directoire et la paix de l'Europe*, pp. 591-592) names Reubell as the only member of the Directory who seriously opposed the Egyptian expedition.

first of these personal letters was dated May 18 (29 Floréal Year VI), two months after his arrival. This initial message was full of stories of factions and strife in Piedmont and of reproaches to his friend in the Directory for not having already sent aid to the obviously righteous group willing to entrust the fate of their country to the French government. He was already warning Revelliere-lépeaux not to believe in false witnesses who were trying to defame him, Ginguené, and his good works at Turin. He protested his own sincerity and in proof of it put forward his willingness to go back to studious retirement, if his work did not in every way please his government. He reported the growth of pro-French sentiment among right-thinking Piedmontese and acknowledged having received contributions toward the campaign against Great Britain from some of these French sympathizers. " It is for you, absolutely for you, Citizen Director, that I write this, for you whom neither intrigue, nor corruption of any kind, nor unfounded opinion, nor injustice can affect. Although far away, I count on your good will. I merit it, and whatever may happen to me, I shall not cease to justify it nor to believe in it." [1]

That same day, May 18, the government at Paris was taking steps to ask Piedmont for the freedom of the insurgents with republican sentiments who had recently risen against the king. In return, France would undertake to disperse hostile movements forming against Piedmont in the neighboring Cisalpine and Ligurian republics. Upon receiving these instructions, Ginguené acted with so much energy that Charles Emmanuel's ministers decided to avoid the issue at Turin and treat directly through their ambassador Balbi at Paris. With his sense of his own importance deeply wounded, Ginguené did not hesitate to explain his side of the story directly to Revelliere-lépeaux as well as to Talleyrand. On May 27 (8 Prairial Year VI), he expressed full confidence that the French government would acknowledge the steps he had taken and would ask for the

---

[1] Ginguené to Revelliere-lépeaux, Collection Pasquier.

insolent Balbi's recall. He even demanded direct interference on the part of France and assistance for the party of true patriots forming in Piedmont to achieve the liberation of their country. He pointed out the needs of every part of Italy and insisted that the Egyptian campaign would be much better postponed a year until the tangle in Italy was straightened out. It would be wiser to set the front yard in order before going off on distant expeditions for which there would always be time. First of all, Venice should be rescued from the clutches of the Emperor and all of Italy saved for freedom.[1]

General Brune over in the Cisalpine republic held the same ideas of applying force as did Ginguené. Revelliere-lépeaux distrusted Brune almost as much as he believed in Ginguené and was inclined to think Brune the champion of ruffians and treasure hunters,[2] while Ginguené befriended men with the qualities of true patriots. Ginguené co-operated with Brune, none the less, through the summer of 1798, openly at times and again by silence and absence from his post at critical moments. Meantime, Balbi in Paris used money and every other influence he could wield to persuade Talleyrand, and others in authority, to maintain the status quo in Piedmont. Revelliere-lépeaux, in part won by his confidence in Ginguené to hopes of forming another Italian republic, on the other hand revolted by the flagrant bribery which Piedmont was undoubtedly attempting in high quarters, balanced the pros and cons and then set himself strongly against the move for reconciliation with the king of Piedmont which Talleyrand and Barras sponsored. Yet the Directory had to take thought of the new coalition then forming. Whether the other Directors thought Piedmont a better ally as a monarchy than as a new struggling republic, or whether the money from Charles Emmanuel's jewels spoke louder than their abstract devotion to liberty, Revelliere-lépeaux was outnumbered in the Directory. It was decided to

---

[1] Ginguené to Revelliere-lépeaux, Collection Pasquier.

[2] MLL, vol. ii, pp. 235, 237, 290 *et seq.*

abandon the revolutionists in Piedmont to their fate, to rebuke Brune, and to sacrifice Ginguené in order that good feeling between France and the kingdom of Sardinia might be revived. Ginguené was therefore removed from his diplomatic post in September, 1798, to be named shortly afterward as a publicist in Italy. Revelliere-lépeaux, always disclaiming any intent to harm the monarchy of Piedmont as long as it represented the wish of the people, was left with regrets that the French republic had been too far corrupted to recognize the will of the true patriots in Turin who were asking only to be brothers of the French in liberty.[1]

The Cisalpine republic, where General Brune was stationed in the spring of 1798, weighed upon Revelliere-lépeaux's mind throughout that year. Conceived by Napoleon Bonaparte as a part of his Italian plan, this republic had been enlarged, consolidated, and officially named by the treaty of Campo Formio. Its government, modeled more or less upon the French Directory, had been dictated by Bonaparte and supplied with administrators of his choice. The unmistakably military character of its origin had not faded from the picture as much as Cisalpine leaders had hoped, and there was a sentiment among certain of their own number as well as in Paris that a carefully planned rearrangement of the Cisalpine republic would be beneficial, and that, if the changes were discreetly carried out, they might result in pacifying the Cisalpine pride as well as in modifications pleasing to the French Directory.

Charles-Joseph Trouvé, Revelliere-lépeaux's protégé, was chosen in February to carry out the Directory's plans for the Cisalpine republic. Of all the diplomats whom Revelliere-lépeaux helped to name, Trouvé was the most completely under his control. Trouvé, not quite thirty years old, was fifteen years younger than his mentor, but his entire and willing submission would not have been warranted by the difference in years alone. Trouvé was almost childlike in his acceptance of the beliefs

[1] MLL, vol. ii, pp. 316-317.

and opinions of his " good and respectable father," as he addressed Revelliere-lépeaux in every one of his frequent letters.[1]
Because of his marriage into the Thouin family, Trouvé had
been all the more adopted into his protector's social circle, and
his relations with Leclerc, of Maine-et-Loire, were likewise
knit closer by the fact that their wives were cousins. Trouvé's
first child, Emma, was nearly the same age as Revelliere-
lépeaux's son Ossian, and no letter, however full of political
import, was concluded without sending a kiss from small
Emma to young Ossian, or making inquiries as to Clémentine
Revelliere-lépeaux's state of health.

At the time of his appointment to the post at Milan Trouvé
was at Naples, where he had served first as secretary of
embassy and then as chargé d'affaires of the French republic.
He was pleased and relieved to be named ambassador to
France's sister republic, for Neapolitan court circles had been
little to his taste. Owing to his obligation to remain at Naples
until his successor arrived, Trouvé reached Milan only on May
15 (26 Floréal Year VI).[2] He found Brune in control, and
gossiping tongues ready to say that the military and civil
authorities could not get along well together. He took pains
to be courteous in his relations with Brune and made it a point
to be seen with him often in public in order to dissipate any
rumors of misunderstanding. The Directory sent Trouvé full
directions as to the changes he was to bring about, and Revelliere-lépeaux added paternal counsels.[3] By the end of June the
plans were made, waiting for the Directory's word as to certain
details. A coup d'état was to be staged, but with infinite care,
so that the initiative would seem to come from the Cisalpine

---

[1] The originals of these letters are at the Bibliothèque Nationale (MSS fr.,
Nouvelles Acquisitions, 21566, 23-175). The correspondence is published
with comparatively few changes—these mostly in respect to affectionate
greetings—in MLL, vol. iii, pp. 200-349. A few letters from the collection,
and the first draft of one letter from Revelliere-lépeaux to Trouvé, have
been omitted from the Pièces Justificatives of the memoirs.

[2] MLL, vol. iii, p. 254.

[3] MLL, vol. iii, p. 256.

republic rather than from France. The plan was to convince some of the respected citizens of the need for changes in their government, to lead them to ask advice of the French ambassador as to how such changes might be accomplished, and then, through the French ambassador, Trouvé, advise the adoption of the changes in constitution and personnel that the Executive Directory at Paris thought most beneficial. Brune promised to co-operate in these measures, but it was intended that the rôle of the army should be as little obvious as possible. Upon this policy Trouvé insisted, at the same time taking care to consult Brune and to keep his good will.

For assistants, Trouvé had Citizen David, secretary of the embassy, and Faipoult, who had been taken from a special mission at Rome and transferred to Milan in order to rearrange the republic's finances to fit the redrafted constitution.[1] Although he had not been able to work miracles, while he held the office of minister of finance under the French Directory, he was generally recognized to be honest. Revelliere-lépeaux had confidence in him and supported him against the criticism of Barras;[2] and without entering into so close a relationship as he maintained with Trouvé, Revelliere-lépeaux gladly received the letters written by Faipoult after his arrival. While Trouvé referred often to the possible danger of a split between French civil and military authorities in Milan, Faipoult came out emphatically on June 30 (12 Messidor Year VI) with the pronouncement that " the military force which has founded everything is bleeding everything white." [3] He supported Trouvé in asking the Executive Directory to provide that final authority should be with the ambassador rather than with the general, in case complications should develop in carrying out the coup d'état. Revelliere-lépeaux, with all his respect for the

---

[1] The correspondence of Faipoult with Revelliere-lépeaux (BN, MSS fr., Nouvelles Acquisitions, 21566, 277-320) is published in MLL, vol. iii, pp. 440-481.

[2] MLL, vol. ii, pp. 297-298.

[3] MLL, vol. iii, p. 453.

army, was entirely of Trouvé's opinion about the necessity of subordinating military to civil authorities in time of peace. Trouvé had learned his motto *Arma cedant togae* from his "good and respectable father."

The struggle was something more, however, than a contest between civil and military authorities. In the case of the French influences at work in the Cisalpine republic, the civil represented the bourgeois interpretation of republican principles, while the military, personified in Brune, fell in with more radical ideas and more radical people. Revelliere-lépeaux pointed out that such demagoguery had only the purpose of soothing the people, until they could be conveniently robbed. The quarrel over methods and expedients involved the Directors themselves and served to separate more widely Revelliere-lépeaux from Barras, who was able to swing the rest of the Directory to his way of thinking.

The essential preliminaries for the coup d'état having been achieved at Milan toward the end of July, Trouvé received assurances from Brune of his readiness, or at least both he and Faipoult reported Brune's acquiescence, and the leading citizens were called into conference as had been agreed. When all was prepared, Brune let news of the expected changes slip out, declared that the affair did not deserve his support, since he had not been heeded in the choice of the government's new personnel, and then left precipitately for Paris to lay his case before the Directory. The Cisalpine leaders were in a difficult position. Trouvé and Faipoult, faced with angry accusations, wrote despairing letters to the Directory, claiming that their careful preparations had been turned against them and that Brune had destroyed all possibility of a salutary coup d'état. Revelliere-lépeaux, unable to convince his colleagues that Brune had erred, was obliged to admit his inability to help his protégé, and Barras won the day. The coup d'état was postponed.

It was September, finally, before the Cisalpine republic was organized. By that time the majority of the Directory in Paris decided that Trouvé had worn out his welcome. In spite of his protests that everybody who amounted to anything held him in the highest respect, it was decided to change him to another post. He stayed on for a short time because of his wife's illness, so that he was at Milan when Fouché, the candidate of Barras, arrived to take charge of the embassy. Profiting by the ignorance or the willing blindness of Fouché, Brune staged a second house-cleaning to remedy the effects of Trouvé's coup d'état. Trouvé objected vociferously in his reports to Revelliere-lépeaux. Resentment, partly at Brune's course of action, partly at the never-ending misunderstandings, led the Directory at length to wipe the slate clean and send an entirely new set of diplomats to Milan. Reubell prevailed this time, and his candidate Rivaud took over the embassy shortly before Trouvé left Milan for his new post at Stuttgart. Rivaud, with General Joubert, was forced to straighten out affairs once more; together they brought about comparative quiet, but by that time everyone knew that the independence of the Cisalpine republic was a travesty and that the French government would not allow a movement against its wishes. Revelliere-lépeaux's hope of managing Cisalpine politics without appearing to do so had proved only a dream. Trouvé found the calmer atmosphere at Stuttgart more to his liking, and before long his pride at being the representative of France in the eastern outpost, while the storms of the second coalition were gathering, helped to soothe his feelings of chagrin.

Between Piedmont and the Cisalpine lay Genoa, capital of the republic reorganized and named Ligurian by Bonaparte in the summer of 1797. Bonaparte, Revelliere-lépeaux believed, was bent upon incorporating Genoa into France at the same time that he transferred Venice to Austria.[1] Revelliere-lépeaux opposed this extension of the territory of the French republic. He preferred to keep France within her natural boundaries, the Rhine, the Alps, and the Pyrenees, and to surround her by a bevy of sister republics. Consequently, he did everything in

[1] MLL, vol. ii, pp. 35-36, 269-270.

his power to keep Genoa independent, and he was convinced that his efforts had something to do with preventing such an annexation. Faipoult, recently resigned from the ministry of finance, was made first French ambassador to Genoa. He was instructed to maintain strict neutrality toward parties in Genoa and not to interfere with Ligurian internal affairs. Bonaparte thought him weak and inconsequential when he followed his instructions as nearly as possible, but Revelliere-lépeaux greatly respected his self-control toward the allied republic. In Revelliere-lépeaux's eyes, Faipoult was already winning back some of the prestige which his inability to cope with the financial situation at home had undermined; Revelliere-lépeaux's confidence in Faipoult's integrity had not failed, for he believed in him and liked him as a person; Faipoult's discretion at Genoa at the end of 1797 won the spontaneous approval which Revelliere-lépeaux was glad to bestow. All the Directors were not of the same opinion, however, and Faipoult was changed for Sotin early in 1798. Revelliere-lépeaux had been one of Sotin's ardent protectors, his enthusiasm having first been aroused by Sotin's praiseworthy conduct in the troubles in the west of France on the eve of the Revolution; [1] Sotin's later success as a member of the central bureau of Paris justified his being named minister of police, as far as Revelliere-lépeaux was concerned; and his willingness to co-operate in his ministry in distributing the Directory's subventions to Theophilanthropy did much to enhance Revelliere-lépeaux's confidence in him. Gradually, however, Revelliere-lépeaux realized that Sotin turned more often to Barras than to him, and by the time Sotin went to Genoa he felt somewhat estranged. Nevertheless, Sotin wrote to Revelliere-lépeaux, consulting him about ways and means of defeating clerical influences in the Ligurian government, [2] even when Revelliere-lépeaux could not help suspecting that Barras had become his guide in more purely political matters.

[1] MLL, vol. ii, pp. 117-119.

[2] Sotin to Revelliere-lépeaux, Collection Pasquier.

Faipoult, on leaving Genoa, was appointed special adviser to the Directory's three commissioners at Rome, Daunou, Monge, and Florent. Their appointment dated from the last day of January, 1798, but by the time they reached Rome at the end of February the Roman republic had been declared. The change in the Holy City's form of government was in no way distasteful to Revelliere-lépeaux, and he approved the removal to France of the many precious objects which he thought had been too long the property of the world's religious capital. He was none the less deeply distressed by the reports of the Directory's commissioners, and especially of his close friend Daunou,[1] exposing the shameless theft going on throughout the city, and the equally shameless graft of commercial companies. The commissioners wrote Revelliere-lépeaux that they were doing their best but were powerless to prevent operations which were proceeding within and without the protection of the French army. The Directory had ordered them to act in concert with the general in charge in whatever matter came up, but especially to set up a workable financial system. The difficulty was that nobody knew where his prerogative began and his colleague's ended; and, since the military was in the habit of commanding, the civil commissioners found their words carrying little weight in spite of their authority from the Directory in Paris. Revelliere-lépeaux at first was able to keep in touch with the developing situation, but soon it went far beyond him. Berthier, a general whom he liked, was replaced by Masséna and Brune. His most reliable informant, Daunou, returned to Paris to resume his legislative career. His next best informant, Faipoult, was transferred to Milan where Trouvé needed the benefit of his added years and experience. The situation at Rome slipped entirely beyond Revelliere-lépeaux's control. He could only protest and claim that he was not at all responsible for the ways in which the latest republic was being despoiled.

[1] Daunou to Revelliere-lépeaux (BN, MSS fr., Nouvelles Acquisitions, 21566, 186-213), MLL, vol. iii, pp. 358-397; AN, AF III, 508, 3215.

Revelliere-lépeaux's attitude toward the kingdom of Naples was less complicated than toward the northern and central regions of Italy. At Naples was a court almost certainly at the beck and call of Great Britain and Austria. Trouvé's stay in southern Italy had only deepened Revelliere-lépeaux's mistrust of Neapolitans, for every letter came back to his protector filled with disgust at court procedures and suspicion of Neapolitan motives.[1] Revelliere-lépeaux was not surprised, therefore, when Naples became one of the focal points of the new coalition against France.

Revelliere-lépeaux was no less positive about French relations with the United States of America than about those with Naples. In principle, he had a great deal of sympathy with the sister republic across the Atlantic; but he believed it had fallen temporarily under evil leadership, and he had no patience with President Adams who seemed to epitomize hateful aristocratic prejudices and pro-English sentiments. Monroe, on the other hand, he found honorable and charming; and Jefferson won his deepest esteem. He even went so far as to assure Logan, who came to Paris shortly before the end of the Adams régime, that the French government would exert every influence which a foreign power could legitimately employ to assure the elevation of Jefferson to the presidency.[2]

IV

The war went badly the first months of 1799, and Revelliere-lépeaux was depressed. He had not approved the appointment of generals to the various armies, but he had been unable to make his voice heard among his colleagues of the Directory; nearly every appointment was carried against him, four to one.[3] The results of the campaign argued against the correctness of the majority's judgment, but Revelliere-lépeaux was not the

[1] MLL, vol. i, pp. 324-339; vol. iii, pp. 210-252.
[2] MLL, vol. ii, pp. 257-262; vol. iii, pp. 179-189.
[3] MLL, vol. ii, pp. 373-382.

more respected because the outcome was what he had pre-
dicted. There was unrest throughout France because the Directory seemed unable to cope with the situation, and the hero of
Italy was too far away to come to the rescue. The protests of
Napoleon Bonaparte's brothers over the sorry state of the
armies was particularly annoying to Revelliere-lépeaux. He had
to admit that military prospects were not bright; but he stoutly
protested that the dark outlook would have been insufficient
to explain the growing anti-Directory sentiment, if this lack
of confidence had not been fostered by evil parties hoping to
promote their own ends by discrediting the government. Foreign difficulties were disheartening for the moment but not half
so serious, to his way of thinking, as the intriguing majority
in the councils, nor half so indicative of ruin as the plottings
within France; failure in the armies abroad only reflected the
corruption at home.[1]

Revelliere-lépeaux was again entrusted with writing the Directory's electoral proclamation in March, 1799, as he had been
the year before; in this proclamation he once more pointed
out the dangers of real and disguised opposition from royalists
and anarchists, and then defined the course which true patriots
should follow. All his alarm at the possible outcome of the
elections and all his faith in the right way of action came out
in this appeal to voters:[2]

The Executive Directory to the French.
Citizens,

You are about to hold your primary assemblies. You should
exercise your prerogatives in them with as much energy as
wisdom in order to safeguard your liberty and guarantee your
tranquillity.

Begin by attending the assemblies punctiliously. Do not abandon
the fate of the republic to a handful of party politicians who would
give it over to the massacres and conflagrations of the Chouans or

[1] MLL, vol. ii, pp. 337-338, 359-367.
[2] AN, AF III, 583, 3994.

to the vengeance of revolutionary despots and the executioners of new decemvirs. Your attendance at the assemblies will be to no avail, however, if you permit yourselves to be reduced to the humiliating and dire rôle of indifferent or timid spectators of the two equally execrable parties. Do not permit insolent, domineering men to overcome you in the name of liberty, to take over the direction of affairs and dictate your choices. These choices should be the result of the votes of a free and enlightened majority. Repress audacity with vigor, oppose firmness to hot-headed persuasion, and pay no attention to evil accusations. If it is honorable for a true republican to be treated as an anarchist and a drinker of blood by royalists, it is no less honorable for him to be accused of royalist sentiments by anarchy, which does not see that these two parties work, one as well as the other, for the reestablishment of despotism, though under different guises.

The ignorant and credulous mass is divided by hatreds, but their leaders are none the less at one; the same hand pays and directs them. Thus it is that in any case the citizens who merit the fullest confidence are precisely those who have drawn upon themselves the hatred of parties, and who are today marked for proscription and the sword by the partisans of the frightful régime of 1793. After having been the target for the friends of royalists before the Eighteenth Fructidor, these pure and courageous men have proved by their conduct that neither self-interest nor fear will cause them to swerve from the true path and that they will always remain aloof from factions. They have given friends of liberty certain assurance of their ardent love for freedom, and those who sigh for repose have a sure guarantee of their conservative spirit, as well as of the efforts they will make to maintain public order.

On the contrary, keep away from the post of elector and from every other public office all those who have figured in the royalist reaction and in the atrocious revolutionary régime. Experience has proved that, in general, nothing can bring these treacherous and insane men to reason. They will betray the most sacred promises. Ambitious, they will risk anything to gain their bloody control. Tormented by remorse, they expect punishment at every turn where they are not in power. Suspicious and vindictive, they cannot credit true patriots with a largeness of spirit which they themselves cannot conceive, nor can they believe any man is ready to forget all else save his dream of strengthening the republic and promoting its happiness.

Be on your guard too against those men who are always in evidence, who hunt ways to keep their names on every tongue. Avoid above all those who make much of you, flatter you, offer you magnificent promises; they are the imposters who will betray you; speaking endlessly of the republic's interest and of the people's happiness, they really dream only of their own affairs. They will betray France into the hands of parties, from whom they hope advancement and fortune.

In a word, choose honest and thinking republicans. Only experience and intelligence assure happy results in all branches of public administration, and the only trustworthy patriotism is that based upon unquestionable honesty.

Rush to your primary assemblies, the Directory urges you again. If traitors should try to usurp your authority there, face bravely their insane furies, and do not fear their threats. Only your weakness would make them strong. Terror should reign in the hearts of factionists, not among true citizens. If they should dare to use violence, have you not the majority, reason, and the law to protect you? Thus you have means directly at hand to command respect for your persons and your wishes. Besides, who of you does not realize that the energetic opposition of one good man suffices to strike fear into a horde of factionists and to ruin their projects. Do not, therefore, surrender in a cowardly fashion to intrigue. A long tranquillity made beautiful by the charms of liberty is well worth a few days of sustained faithfulness and of wise and courageous strength of character.

Finally, citizens, if you wish it, the good will triumph. You have on your side the inflexible justice of your legislators, the unshakable firmness of the Executive Directory, and above all your own force and your own will, if you know how to use them and if you remain united.

On March 9, the day after this proclamation was issued by authority of the Directory, there appeared in the *Moniteur* an unsigned *Lettre sur la signification du mot Représentant du*

Peuple, written by Revelliere-lépeaux.[1] The article was a protest against the encroachment of legislative upon executive
authority. Revelliere-lépeaux released it intentionally at a moment when elections were in the air, for the purpose of instruct-
ing the populace, or at least that part of the populace which
read the *Moniteur,* as to the character of the office for which
they were about to vote. The electoral proclamation proposed
to guide the choice of suitable legislators; this public letter attempted to explain the duties and limitations of the legislators
once they were elected.

In these two short writings Revelliere-lépeaux summed up
one part of his political philosophy to fulfill his self-imposed
obligation of enlightening his constituents. It was a misuse of
the term " Representative of the People," he declared, to limit
its application to members of the Council of Ancients and the
Council of Five Hundred, and this mistake in usage covered
a misconception of fundamental relations of the agents of government. At one moment, namely, during the Convention, the
term was properly used to designate deputies, because the Convention was the sole governing agent of the whole people, combining the duties of administration with the creation of the
nation's constitution and organic laws. After the Constitution
of 1795 was once accepted by the nation and the Directorial
government had been installed, the term " Representative of
the People " could apply rightfully only to the ensemble of
governing agents; since the councils no longer had the exclusive right to be called representatives, they should give up all
idea of being the dominant element in the new government.
They should accept their place as one of several powers, on an
equality with and not superior to the governing agents. The
totality of governmental machinery represented the people, but
the legislator had no more inherent right to call himself representative than did the humblest local administrator, and certainly no more right than a member of the Executive Directory.

[1] MLL, vol. ii, pp. 366-367; vol. iii, pp. 57-63.

Revelliere-lépeaux denounced as fallacious the argument that the Executive Directory was responsible to the councils for its administrative policies because the councils chose the Directors. One might as well refer all the laws back to the electoral assemblies who originally chose the electors. Choosing Directors happened to be one of the duties of the councils, and the performance of that duty did not extend their rôle beyond the constitutional prescriptions; for the most part, the councils should spend their time passing necessary and well-framed laws and not interfering with the execution of the laws.

Revelliere-lépeaux had put in his word to no purpose. The elections of 1799 returned a majority overwhelmingly hostile to the Directory. The bloc which had supported the Directory since the purging of the lists of deputies on the twenty-second Floréal of the year before was finally broken. Many republicans believed that the Directory had forced the constitution out of its essential spirit and intention by the coups d'état of Fructidor and Floréal and that the elections of 1799 should be respected even if the new deputies completely revised the government's policies. The defection of these constitutional republicans from the Directorial bloc made it possible for the new hostile legislative majority to lodge its formal complaint of mismanagement against the Directory and to make of its demand for explanations an occasion for testing the Directory's strength.

The resolution requesting the Directory's justification of its conduct of internal and external affairs within a delay of ten days passed the Council of Five Hundred on June 5. In the meantime, Reubell had drawn the annual fatal lot, he had resigned, and the councils had chosen to replace him Sieyès, then ambassador to Prussia. This election made Revelliere-lèpeaux's heart sink. He had felt no bond of sympathy with Sieyès since the days when they had served together on the Committee of Eleven which formulated the Constitution of 1795. When Sieyès entered upon his duties as Director on June 8, he adopted a very reserved attitude except for making occasional adverse criticisms. To Revelliere-lépeaux's dismay, Sieyès seemed to fall in immediately with Barras, who grew correspondingly colder toward his other colleagues.

Although he was discouraged, Revelliere-lépeaux felt that the situation was not yet irremediable. For days the Directors could reach no decision upon answering the legislative demand for explanations. Barras and Sieyès continued to draw off to themselves. Still, there remained a majority of three Directors who, to Revelliere-lépeaux's way of thinking, were incapable of being deceived or moved by Barras and Sieyès or by the majority in the councils. Revelliere-lépeaux considered himself the spokesman for his colleagues Treilhard and Merlin de Douai, and with the majority of the Directory on his side he hoped that some adjustment yet might be made.

On June 16 the Council of Five Hundred, having received no answer to its demands upon the Directory, resolved to sit in permanent session until the situation could be resolved. That night, June 16-17, the Council of Five Hundred voted to remove the Director Treilhard from his place on a legal disqualification relative to his age. The Council of Ancients concurred in the action, and on Sunday, June 17, the same day that the Directory's message, entirely unsatisfactory to the councils, was at last received, Gohier was elected to take the place of Treilhard. Instead of contesting the issue, Treilhard, when informed of the councils' action, picked up his umbrella, said good-bye to his colleagues, and left the Luxembourg. Revellierelépeaux and Merlin remained to face Sieyès and Barras, and it was obvious that Gohier, newly elected by the councils, would be of the opinion of Sieyès and Barras.

On the same day, June 17, at a special session of the Directory held in the apartments of Merlin, Sieyès advised Revelliere-lépeaux to resign. Revelliere-lépeaux stiffened. He did not have a guilty conscience. He would not resign. If his opponents chose to assassinate him at his post, they would see that he had no fear, but he had accepted the sacred trust of his position as Director, he had sworn to protect the Constitution of 1795 with his life's blood, and he would not yield an inch.

All that day and the next, groups of deputies whom he had always considered his friends came to talk with him, urging him to resign. He refused steadfastly. He could understand his opponents' demand for his resignation, but to have friends urge the same step puzzled him and tried his patience. Time after time he insisted that his friends stand with him and at least try the strength of their cause against their opponents. The answer came repeatedly that by suggesting such a course he was endangering not only his life but theirs as well. Barras took occasion to add the weight of his counsel on June 18, assuring Revelliere-lépeaux that he respected him highly, but that the only possible way out of the impasse was for both Revelliere-lépeaux and Merlin to resign.

Finally, overcome by entreaties and threats, Revelliere-lépeaux yielded and wrote his resignation on June 18, 1799 (30 Prairial Year VI):

When the fatherland is threatened with frightful disruption, those whose presence in public office is an obstacle to public harmony, or serves as a pretext to discord, ought to withdraw from office. That is the only reason which moves me to resign from the Executive Directory. Neither fear for my person nor any hope unworthy of a generous spirit has dictated the decision. I shall remain in the bosom of my family, always ready to render account of a conduct free from every reproach, because it was always directed by the most disinterested of motives and by the most ardent love for the Republic.

Thereupon Merlin asked the privilege of copying his letter and sent in the same resignation, word for word.

Revelliere-lépeaux withdrew to his apartments and before night left for his country house at Andilly. To his mind the Thirtieth Prairial was incomprehensible. He considered it the *journée des dupes*, and for him the First French Republic had met its death.[1]

[1] AN, AF III, 609, 4261; MLL, vol. ii, pp. 362, 389-410.

CHAPTER VII
RETIREMENT

*Dans aucune circonstance de ma vie je ne plierai mon langage
et mes actions au gré des partis, ni pour obtenir leurs faveurs,
ni pour sauver ma tête.*

Revelliere-lépeaux [1]

Ce pauvre imbécile à principes.

Taine [2]

REVELLIERE-LÉPEAUX was forty-five years of age when he resigned from the Directory. He lived to be seventy. Throughout the twenty-five years left to him, he remained a staunch republican, but, since he chose not to join any party of opposition, he was spared political persecution. After a flurry of accusations in the two councils, following his expulsion from the Directory, he was allowed to live in peace.

Renouncing political ambitions and publicity, uninterested in any professional career, he went quietly about his own affairs, husbanding his small fortune as best he could, devoting himself to the education of his children, picking up his pre-Revolutionary occupations and pastimes, and seeing only a few close friends. During the Consulate, the Empire, the Restoration of 1814, the Hundred Days, and the final re-establishment of the Bourbons, while many of his former colleagues shifted their allegiance from one régime to the next, paying for each misjudged move with voluntary or enforced exile or even with imprisonment, Revelliere-lépeaux kept his seclusion. From

[1] *Réponse aux dénonciations portées au corps législatif contre lui et ses anciens collègues*, MLL, vol. iii, p. 157.

[2] A. H. Taine, *Les Origines de la France contemporaine* (Paris, 6 vols., 1876-1894), vol. iv, p. 598 n.

Illustration on opposite page

Bronze medallion, undated, of Revelliere-lépeaux as an old man, by David d'Angers. This reproduction is from a photograph (J. Evers, Angers) of the original in the Musée d'Angers.

1799 to 1824 he left France only twice, once in 1802 on a short trip to Belgium for his health, and again in 1810, when he took his family to Switzerland in the hope that the change of air would cure a nervous disorder of his daughter Clémentine. On leaving the Palace of the Luxembourg, the thirtieth Prairial Year VII, Revelliere-lépeaux went directly to his country house at Andilly. He said that he had never slept so well in his life as that first night after his fall from power and escape from responsibility.[1] He was sensitive, dependent upon the kindliness of friends and family for his own confidence and sense of well-being. He took differences of opinion to heart and was wounded by them, even when he believed he was right and stuck stubbornly to his position. To be shut off suddenly from the countless avenues of disagreement, to be shielded from the contrarinesses of governing, to meet only the appreciation and approval of his wife and children, was a balm and a solace.

He had been assured that his resignation would ease the political situation and prevent attacks against him and his friends in the two councils,[2] but he was not to escape immediate anxiety. Attacks against the expelled Directors began in the Council of Five Hundred in the first days of Messidor (June, 1799) and continued throughout the summer. Some deputies wished only to pass resolutions censuring the conduct of Revelliere-lépeaux and his colleagues. Others were determined to vote a measure declaring the former Directors *hors la loi,* leaving them subject to execution or deportation as the councils might decide.[3] Although Revelliere-lépeaux's life was never actually in danger, he was kept uneasy all the summer of 1799. At first he ignored the attacks, preferring silence to a new controversy. The accumulation of reproaches at length stirred him beyond endurance. All his life he was dominated by the necessity of feeling himself in the right, and to have his

[1] MLL, vol. ii, pp. 409, 413-414.

[2] MLL, vol. ii, p. 407.

[3] *Moniteur,* Messidor-Thermidor An VII ; *Procès-Verbaux du Conseil des Cinq Cents,* Messidor-Thermidor An VII.

motives questioned struck at the very roots of his being. Toward the end of the summer he composed his *Réponse* to the principal charges and had it printed. His former secretary Vallée was allowed to distribute it among the members of the councils.[1] These sixty pages of justification, appearing in August, 1799, were Revelliere-lépeaux's only public reply to his attackers. This *Réponse*, together with his obvious intention to refrain from all further political controversy, may have contributed to stopping threats in and out of the councils. In any case, on Sunday, August 18, 1799, the Council of Five Hundred dismissed the charges against the ex-Directors by the slight majority of two hundred and seventeen against two hundred and fourteen votes.[2] Lafayette, in a letter of October 17, expressed his belief that Revelliere-lépeaux had much less with which to reproach himself than Barras, who was yet in power.[3] In November, the coup d'état of Brumaire and the subsequent stir over organizing the Consulate closed the question of accusing the former Directors more effectively than Revelliere-lépeaux's indignant defense. What had happened before the Consulate lost its interest for the public, while the new government preferred focusing attention upon itself to keeping up old quarrels. A close censorship of the press played its part in consigning the former Directors to oblivion.

Revelliere-lépeaux, detesting Bonaparte in his new rôle, chose to believe that the First Consul was obsessed with the idea of re-enlisting his former chief's sympathy and good will, but that, failing in his object, Bonaparte subjected his former superior to every sort of annoyance. Bonaparte certainly had less time

[1] MLL, vol. ii, pp. 426-427, vol. iii, pp. 113-176; *The Times* (London, September 5, 1799), no. 4580, 3a.

[2] *Cf.* A. Meynier, *Les Coups d'état du Directoire*, vol. iii, *Le Dix-huit Brumaire An VIII et la fin de la République* (Paris, 1928), Chapter III, especially pp. 38-51.

[3] The author owes the copy of this autograph signed letter of Lafayette, addressed in all probability to Latour-Maubourg, to Professor Louis Gottschalk of the University of Chicago. The original letter is in the Archives of the Château of Chavaniac.

to think about Revelliere-lépeaux than the ex-Director had to magnify the new executive's every act. For his part, Bonaparte regarded Revelliere-lépeaux as an honest man, but a little queer and not at all capable of statesmanship. When Bonaparte, through an intermediary, invited Revelliere-lépeaux to call on him at the Tuileries, Revelliere-lépeaux stayed at home, saying that Bonaparte knew where he lived, and that if the First Consul really wished to see him he might make the effort to come to Andilly.[1]

Aside from the business of answering critics, Revelliere-lépeaux's most absorbing preoccupation during the first months of his return to private life was the question of feeding himself and his family. He had entered the Directory a poor man, and he left power without having enriched himself. Forced out of the Directory, he received only what was due him for his current month's salary, and he had difficulty in collecting even that.[2] He had the properties in Maine-et-Loire and in the Vendée, which had come from his own father and his wife's family; but in 1799 these lands were producing no revenue, and the houses on them had been damaged or destroyed by the civil wars. Since 1792 Revelliere-lépeaux had not gone in person to arrange his affairs in the west, and he was not to go until 1801.[3] From 1801 to 1823 he made trips nearly every autumn to oversee his small vineyards and sell his wine and grain; but, with every care, he spent all of ten years in rising out of financial embarrassment into the security of a small dependable income.

Although he remained in modest circumstances the rest of his life, he seems never seriously to have considered exercising

[1] MLL, vol. ii, pp. 440-441, 457-458; *Memoirs of the History of France during the reign of Napoleon, dictated by the Emperor at St. Helena to the generals who shared his captivity* (London, 7 vols., 1823), vol. iii, p. 86.

[2] MLL, vol. ii, pp. 433, 442.

[3] Revelliere-lépeaux twice mentions 1801 as the date of his first return to the west of France (MLL, vol. ii, pp. 452, 454), but two autograph letters (BA, MSS SM 13), addressed by him to his wife seem to be dated in Vendémiaire Year IX, hence in 1800, and sent from the west of France.

a profession in order to gain a more comfortable livelihood. As a young man, he had shrunk from being a lawyer. Now that he was forty-five, the vocation did not appear any more attractive to him. The only political office for which he showed the slightest inclination was a post in the administration of public instruction, and his determination never to co-operate with what he considered a tyrannical régime closed to him even that door.[1]

I

L'aspect séduisant de la ville
Vous cache un destin rigoureux
Ah fuiez ce perfide azile
Volez aux champs pour être heureux.[2]

For five years after his expulsion from the Directory, Revelliere-lépeaux found refuge in the Institut. He built his whole life around this society of learned men, which he had been instrumental in founding and had bent every effort to develop and protect, while he was a member of the Executive Directory. At the Institut he found a circle of friends who, for the most part, continued to receive him without overemphasizing his recent political misfortune. As long as he could go each week to the meetings of his class of political and moral sciences, his isolation was not complete. He found companionship in working on various committees, and he had an audience ready to hear the results of his own intellectual labors. In addition to pleasure and encouragement at the Institut there was also the financial comfort of the stipend that members of the Institut received.[3] Since this payment was contingent in part upon attendance at the sessions, Revelliere-lépeaux had one reason the more for being faithful, though this faithfulness was not

[1] MLL, vol. ii, pp. 444-448.

[2] *Stances adressées à un couple de tourterelles perchées sur les arbres du jardin des tuileries,* autograph poem by Revelliere-lépeaux (BA, MSS SM13, *Poésies fugitives*).

[3] MLL, vol. ii, p. 476.

always easy. Andilly was nearly ten miles from Paris; Revelliere-lépeaux no longer had a carriage and horses, and his only means of going to Paris was on foot. In rain or shine, hot weather or cold, feeling sick or well, he made the journey for the satisfaction of keeping up his part of the Institut and for the sake of adding seventeen or eighteen hundred francs a year to the meagre budget of his family. Sometimes small urchins in the villages he passed on the way hooted at him and teased him and called him names; to them he was only a queer-looking dust-covered or rain-soaked hunchback. To compensate for ridicule and fatigue, he found a hearty welcome each week at the Jardin des Plantes with the Thouin family, where he habitually spent the night on his trips to Paris, in order to avoid the excessive weariness of coming and going in one day. In spite of the precarious state of his health and all the inclement weather, he managed to be present at forty-three of the sixty meetings of his class during the first year he spent at Andilly after his resignation from the Directory.[1]

At the end of that first year friends in Paris came to the rescue. Davalet, receiver-general for the department of the Seine, owed his position to Revelliere-lépeaux's influence and, in spite of various threats, had not been deprived of his office under the Consulate. Connected with his own apartment, at 905 rue de l'Université, Davalet had several rooms which he explained to Revelliere-lépeaux were not rentable but which Revelliere-lépeaux and his family might occupy, if they found it more convenient to be in Paris than out in Andilly. The offer was especially tempting, because Davalet was the son-in-law of Revelliere-lépeaux's very dear friend Pincepré de Buire. The former Director and his wife and children accordingly installed themselves in the rue de l'Université in the autumn of 1800, using the house at Andilly only as a good-weather resort. Their circumstances remained straitened to such a degree that,

---

[1] MLL, vol. ii, pp. 449-451; Lyon-Caen, *Revelliere-lépeaux Membre de la Classe des Sciences morales et politiques, notes cit.*, pp. 2-3.

as soon as it was possible, they sold this country house,[1] hoping to invest the money in some piece of land which would provide a return in rental or produce.

In spite of the hardships he suffered, Revelliere-lépeaux looked back with a certain satisfaction upon his first year of return to private life. He had given way to Bonaparte in no detail, however minute. He had neither signed the register to indicate his approval of the Consulate in the plebiscite nor had he gone to see Bonaparte at the Tuileries.[2] Even when it was rumored that Bonaparte was considering him for a place in the new Senate and was only awaiting an application, Revelliere-lépeaux made no sign; he believed it was a trap to make him bow before Bonaparte only to receive a refusal and a snub.[3] In his own family he could not have hoped that his wife and daughter would adapt themselves more gracefully than they did to the reverses of fortune, and his young son was strong and well. He had received visits from Pléville-le-Pelley and from Talleyrand with equanimity; and, although he had every reason to suspect that Talleyrand came with the purpose of sounding his intentions as to his former colleagues, notably Barras, he could not help being impressed by the consideration Talleyrand showed him as well as by Pléville-le-Pelley's obviously sincere admiration. Revelliere-lépeaux let it be known, however, among his friends that he preferred not to receive visits of political import, from either individuals or delegations, and his wish was respected, whether in submission to his desire or through the natural forgetfulness of those who continued to be occupied with politics.[4]

Another year passed tranquilly; without undue exertion, Revelliere-lépeaux was able to attend sixty-one of the seventy-two meetings held by his class at the Institut. He served on

1 MLL, vol. ii, pp. 451-452, 460.
2 MLL, vol. ii, p. 481.
3 MLL, vol. ii, pp. 443-445.
4 MLL, vol. ii, pp. 414-420.

the committee to award a prize given by the class of moral and political sciences for essays on the subject " Is rivalry a good educational method?"[1] He worked over a series of essays he was preparing on the Vendée. He enjoyed being near Davalet; he went often to the Jardin des Plantes; he had time to see old friends, among them one of his former neighbors of the Vendée, Citizen Loyau from Bazoges-en-Pareds, who was a member of the Corps Législatif. He had no kind feeling towards Bonaparte, but he abstained from public criticism of the Consulate. His frame of mind was calm and fairly hopeful even with the embarrassing state of his finances. He was determined to live within his income, but it became apparent that something would have to be done to ensure even the barest necessities.

In the autumn of 1801, believing the moment had come to attempt repairing his fortunes in the west of France, he undertook the journey. He was nearly beside himself with joy at seeing his mother and sister at Angers after the long separation, but the joy was mixed with bitterness at the thought of his brother's execution during the Terror. From Angers he went to Faye, where he found the house he had rebuilt in the early years of his marriage entirely in ruins. He visited his brother-in-law Boileau at Chandoiseau, and his sister-in-law Madame Moulin in the same neighborhood. Boileau had done what he could to keep up his sister's vineyards and other property, and he was keeping a small amount of money ready to turn over to Revelliere-lépeaux; but the region had suffered deeply during the civil war, and neither the fields and houses nor the temper of the people had yet recovered from the material destruction. Revelliere-lépeaux visited the farmers on his land, gave directions about cultivation and repairs, and wrote to his wife that he saw no reason why in time their

[1] Lyon-Caen, *notes cit.*, p. 3.

revenue should not be brought back approximately to what it had been in 1789.[1]

In the spring of 1802, when it seemed that his family might again look forward to a degree of modest comfort, Revelliere-lépeaux was taken very seriously ill. He suffered from the life-long weakness of his lungs and continued in some danger for months. The acquaintances of his circle at Paris showed him every sympathy, and the class of moral and political sciences sent a representative member, Mentelle, to call on him. When his long and difficult convalescence began, he took a feeble pleasure in books. It was seen, presently, that a change of air might be essential to his recovery, and Pincepré de Buire invited him to bring his family to Buire's house in the country near Péronne until he should be entirely himself again. Revelliere-lépeaux never forgot that summer, when he and his wife and children were able to enjoy country life at its best. At the end of this visit they went with Buire for a short trip through Belgium, to which Buire insisted upon contributing half the expenses, although he was only one and they were four.[2]

In the autumn Revelliere-lépeaux was able again to attend meetings of the Institut. On October 21 he began reading his series of essays on the department of the Vendée; he continued to present sections of his study at meetings through November and December into January, but at that time he fell ill again so that the concluding parts had to be read for him by Daunou on January 27, 1803.[3]

[1] BA, MSS SM 13, Revelliere-lépeaux to Citoyenne Revelliere-lépeaux, 23 Vendémiaire An IX [sic]. The capital source for Revelliere-lépeaux's successive trips to the west of France is this liasse (MSS SM 13) of letters to his wife, given to the Bibliothèque de la Ville d'Angers by his great-granddaughter, Madame Paul Leferme, in October 1901.

[2] MLL, vol. ii, p. 459; Lyon-Caen, notes cit., p. 4; Revelliere-lépeaux to Citoyen Loyau, membre du Corps Législatif, 21 Floréal An X (the author owes to Madame J. Loyau copies of this and other letters from the Collection Loyau at Pulteau par Bazoges-en-Pareds, Vendée).

[3] MLL, vol. ii, p. 460; Lyon-Caen, notes cit., p. 4; BMN, Autographes 238/85, Revelliere-lépeaux to Citoyen Bouron, juge à Fontenay-le-peuple,

At about that time Revelliere-lépeaux began to find less satisfaction at the Institut. He thought Bonaparte was interfering entirely too much with an organization that ought to be intellectual rather than political. Perhaps he was forgetting how completely he had hoped to utilize the Institut as a power to advance republican sentiment; more probably he continued to think it justifiable to have pressed learning into the service of the Constitution of 1795, although it would be sacrilege to demand the Institut's allegiance to the Constitution of 1799, particularly with its modification of 1802. Then Bonaparte found it wise to reorganize the Institut; certain modifications would be more easily accomplished by sweeping changes than by open dictation in details. In the rearrangement, the class of political and moral sciences disappeared, and Revelliere-lépeaux, among others, was transferred to a newly created class of history and ancient literature (today inscriptions and belles-lettres). Although he made it a point to attend the initial meeting of his new class on February 4, 1803, Revelliere-lépeaux because of illness was absent from the two subsequent meetings as well as from two others toward the end of March.[1]

This second long illness left him extremely weak and burdened him with additional financial worries. In order to meet the expenses of medical care, he decided to sell his library, keeping only a few of his most cherished books. To ensure as rapid and sound a convalescence as possible, he rented a small house with a garden in the Valley of Bougival, near the Château of Louveciennes, where he might spend the summer

25 Vendémiaire An XI (October 17, 1802). Revelliere-lépeaux speaks of having presented his essays on the Vendée in the class of literature and ancient languages (MLL, vol. ii, p. 464), but the records of that class (properly called class of history and ancient literature) bear no trace of the essays, while the minutes of the class of political and moral sciences specify the date given here.

[1] MLL, vol. ii, pp. 463-480; Institut National des Sciences et des Arts, *Procès-Verbaux, Classe d'Histoire et de Littérature ancienne, An XI,* Pluviôse, Ventôse, Germinal.

with his wife and children. Even then he did not stop going
to the Institut, and from the end of March until October he
was absent only twice from the meetings of his class.[1]

Absenting himself from nine weekly meetings of the class
of history and ancient literature, he made a really thorough
trip west in the autumn of 1803, inspecting not only his wife's
inheritance near Angers but also his own property in the Vendée. There he saw for the first time in years the cousin he
had once hoped to marry and her husband Clemenceau. They
met on the warmest terms, and the three of them made several
trips to Mouchamps and other spots closely associated with
their earlier days. Once back in Maine-et-Loire, he settled
down to supervise grape-gathering and wine-making, and to
sell his grain. In leisure time he arranged for supplies of butter
and gallons of preserves of which he wrote his wife in Paris,
hoping that his choice of provisions would be pleasing to her.
He visited Leclerc and his wife, the former Louise Thouin, at
Chalonnes. Before he left, he agreed with his sister in Angers
upon the final settlement of their claims upon each other,
especially in view of their mother's death the year before.[2]
Each letter he sent to " Chère Jenny " in Paris was filled with
details of business, accounts of meeting acquaintances, and of
constant regrets that she could not be there to see all the family
and friends. Yet his wife remained in Paris, looking after her
children and her household in the way that fitted her husband's
ideal. If she ever rebelled in spirit at the circumstances of her
life, she made no sign that has endured.

Returning to Paris early in December, Revelliere-lépeaux
resumed assiduous attendance at the Institut, missing not one
session from then until June, 1804, when his refusal to pledge

[1] MLL, vol. ii, pp. 460, 482; Institut National, *Procès-Verbaux, Classe
d'Histoire . . . An XI*, Germinal-Fructidor. The two absences occurred on
8 and 29 Fructidor (August 26 and September 16, 1803).

[2] BA, MS 572, Supplément; BA, MSS SM 13, five letters (Vendémiaire-
Brumaire An XII), Revelliere-lépeaux to Citoyenne Revelliere-lépeaux.

allegiance to the newly-declared Empire cost him his chair.[1] He pretended to take the whole affair calmly, but it was a shock to him. Financial sacrifice apart, leaving the Institut meant isolation from the rank of learned men which was almost dearer to him than had been his membership in the Executive Directory. He had sensed a change of spirit among his associates, partly due, he believed, to the new and undeserving members introduced by Bonaparte's influence. He knew that respect for deism and liberal thinking had given way to conservative devotion to established church and monarchical principles. He knew that to swim against the tide removed him one step farther from the scene of public action. Having taken the step, he went for a short vacation to see Pincepré de Buire,[2] and then returned to Paris to decide upon ways and means of action. While he had been in the west the autumn before, Davalet had died; and shortly afterward Revelliere-lépeaux had removed from the unpretentious apartment that the receiver-general's kindness had provided to another unpretentious apartment at 785 rue du Cherche-Midi, in the house of Senator Lemercier.[3] It was obviously impossible to keep up any standard of living, however simple, in Paris, now that the income from the Institut was removed. The principal from the sale of the house at Andilly was yet intact, and the best solution seemed to be the purchase of some house in the country with an adjacent farm, where living could be reduced to a minimum and where he might rebuild gradually a tiny fortune with revenues accruing from products of his own and his wife's western properties. Revelliere-lépeaux did not shrink from isolation at that moment. Paris had deceived him. He

[1] MLL, vol. ii, pp. 473-480; Institut National, *Procès-Verbaux, Classe d'Histoire . . . An XII*, Frimaire-Prairial. Revelliere-lépeaux attended the Institut for the last time on 5 Prairial (May 25, 1804).

[2] BA, MSS SM 13, Revelliere-lépeaux to Madame Revelliere-lépeaux, 14 Prairial An XII.

[3] *Ibid.*, p. 4, address: "A Madame Revelliere-lépeaux, Rue du Cherchemidi maison du Sénateur Lemercier, no. 785 à Paris"; MLL, vol. ii, p. 463.

looked forward to a renewed communion with nature which
had never betrayed his efforts or his confidence.

II

Ah! du moins la vertu te reste,
Lépeaux, avec la douce paix;
Et de ton azile modeste
Le nom ne périra jamais.

. . . .

Lépeaux, à tes foyers rustiques
Quand je cause avec tes amis,
Aux plaisirs purs des temps antiques,
Près de toi, je me crois admis.
Dans mon Plutarque d'un grandhomme
Cherchant les moeurs et les exploits,
Je t'ai rencontré quelquefois
Dans les murs d'Athène ou de Rome.[1]

In 1806, when Revelliere-lépeaux had been living for two
years on his property La Rousselière, near Orléans in the
region called Sologne, he turned to his friend Bosc. Bosc had
come back to France several years earlier, had been named in-
spector of nurseries at Versailles, and was soon to be admitted
to the Academy of Sciences at the Institut. Revelliere-lépeaux
wrote: "I do not know, my good friend, whether in the
palace of kings, in the midst of your vast and superb gardens,
you still remember a humble dweller of Sologne. For my part,
in my small cottage, lost in the deserts, I forget neither you
nor yours, and every day I make wishes for your well-being." [2]
The rôles had changed. Bosc was no longer fleeing the scene
of misfortunes and heartbreak, beseeching his friend in the
Directory to find some diplomatic post for him in America.
Revelliere-lépeaux, away from all responsibilities of govern-

[1] Poems "Pour la fête du Citoyen Louis-Marie Révelliere lépeaux, le
Dimanche 24 aoust 1806, veille de la Saint Louis, à la Rousselliere, en
Sologne, Commune et Paroisse d'Ardon, Département du Loiret, . . . Par
Jean-François Ducis," fols. 2 v., 3 r. (Author's collection).

[2] Revelliere-lépeaux to Bosc, letter a. s., undated, but, from the context,
probably written in 1806 (Author's collection).

ment, was asking his friend for advice about plants and fence posts.

Revelliere-lépeaux had considered returning to the west of France where the bulk of his property remained; it seemed more advantageous, however, to buy a piece of land with buildings than to reconstruct the ruined house at Faye. For a time he hunted near Saumur and Tours, but anything he considered suitable was beyond his purse. Moreover, the feelings of the west of France were not yet calm enough to make living there comfortable for so outspoken a republican and deist. Pilastre and Leclerc had returned to their properties near Angers, and a few other friends and relatives could be counted upon, but the pleasant pre-war milieu had been broken up. Added to the natural difficulties of returning to the scenes of her childhood, which otherwise might have been a great consolation, were Madame Revelliere-lépeaux's terror and horrible memories of the days of the Convention, which she spent in Angers while her husband was far away and threatened with death.

It was decided, therefore, late in the summer of 1804, to buy La Rousselière, about ten miles from Orléans. There for the sum at hand, about forty thousand francs, Revellierelépeaux could obtain a house and at the same time could be assured of a small income from the adjoining land, perhaps as much as two thousand francs each year.[1] When he went to inspect La Rousselière in August, 1804, he wrote to his wife at Paris that she need never fear for lack of wood, that she might have the house always as warm as she pleased, and that

[1] MLL, vol. ii, pp. 482-483; BA, MSS SM 13, Revelliere-lépeaux to his wife (address lacking), 3 Brumaire An XII.

Illustration on opposite page

Marble bust of Revelliere-lépeaux as an old man, executed in 1823 by David d'Angers. This reproduction is from a photograph (J. Evers, Angers) of the original in the Musée d'Angers.

there was also a splendid cellar for storing wine and vegetables. The house itself was hardly luxurious but certainly large enough for the family and two or three guests. On this visit Revelliere-lépeaux met the three men who were to become his best friends: his nearest neighbor, Légier, who lived at Orléans but came with his family to spend several months each year at Buglain which adjoined La Rousselière; the printer and editor Jacob, of Orléans, whose cordiality was to include an invitation for young Ossian to experiment with type-setting in his shop; and the priest of Ardon, in whose company differences of religious conviction did not prevent Revelliere-lépeaux from finding a great deal of pleasure.[1] Accordingly, in September, 1804, Revelliere-lépeaux and his family came to live in the house under a mansard roof, with whitewashed rooms looking out upon a garden and an alley of linden trees. Sologne was a desert, not in the sense of being a sandy waste, but in its barrenness of human habitation. To be sure, there were fewer springs and brooks than Revelliere-lépeaux was accustomed to see in the west of France, and in consequence the plant life was less luxuriant. Water was not lacking, however, and vegetables, grains, and trees could be grown. It was a lonely country but not a savage wasteland.[2]

---

[1] BA, MSS SM 13, Revelliere-lépeaux to his wife (address lacking), 24 Messidor An XII. Ossian's first attempt at printing, undated, was in honor of the poet Ducis:

ANACROSTICHE
Du Favori de Melpomène
Un mot suffit pour enflammer.
Comment pouvoir lui résister?
Il est si touchant sur la Scène! . . .
Ses vertus y gagnent les coeurs.

Premier essai typographique d'Ossian Révelliere-Lépeaux, dans l'Imprimerie de son Ami Jacob l'Ainé à Orléans.
(Author's collection)

[2] The two best references for the years at Sologne are: Charles Cuissard, *Le Troubadour de Buglain et ses amis*, in the *Mémoires de la Société d'Agriculture, Sciences, Belles-Lettres et Arts d'Orléans* (tome xxxii, 1894), pp. 170-195; Georges Houel, *La Revellière-Lepeaux en Sologne* (Orléans, 1904), 30 pp.

One of Revelliere-lépeaux's major concerns during his annual trip west in the autumn of 1804 was to find suitable servants for La Rousselière. Both he and his wife had more confidence in peasants whose temperament they understood than in the servants they saw near Orléans. After a great deal of searching, he found a man servant and a maid. In that same autumn of 1804 he sold some property in the commune of St. Georges, near Montaigu in the Vendée, to ease his immediate financial situation.

While he was away from La Rousselière, he wrote frequently to consult his wife on every subject. The same man who had presided over celebrations of victory a few years before, in the name of all France, wrote cheerfully about the number of pounds of butter that should be made, or about the success of the grape conserve that the wife of one of his farmers was cooking into a perfect consistency. He was not cheerful, on the contrary, about the separation from his wife and children. He wrote to " Chère Jenny " of visiting their favorite haunts and of stopping to weep as melancholy swept over him. He fretted if delay in the post deprived him of news from La Rousselière. Each of his letters transmitted cordial and tender greetings which their old friends asked him to convey to his wife, each was full of regret that she could not be with him, and he signed each one " Your best friend and faithful husband." [1]

At La Rousselière the days were pleasantly full. Revelliere-lépeaux and his wife supervised personally the care of gardens and poultry and animals. Of the first importance, however, were Ossian's daily lessons in history, geography, Latin, and, above all, botany. During the five years at La Rousselière, Revelliere-lépeaux was with his son almost constantly. Clémentine, already twenty-two years old when they went to Sologne,

---

[1] BA, MSS SM 13, five letters (Vendémiaire-Brumaire An XIII), Revelliere-lépeaux to Madame Revelliere-lépeaux ; BMN, Collection Dugast-Matifeux, MSS 44-41, two letters (12, 29 Brumaire An XIII), Revelliere-lépeaux to Monsieur Brethé, Notaire Public à Montaigu.

felt the isolation of the place more keenly perhaps than any other member of the family; but she was faithful in seconding her mother with household tasks and had her reward each winter, when she was allowed to spend several months at Paris with Madame Guillebert at the Jardin des Plantes.[1] Although the life in the country was the most quiet imaginable and although the amount of money in hand was usually negligible, there was a certain ease in the matter of plentiful food and enough servants; and this was a real relief after the day-to-day anxiety in Paris, where it took a greater amount of money to satisfy indispensable needs. Then, too, although few friends were near, those who did come could be enjoyed to the fullest, without distraction. Revelliere-lépeaux had the great pleasure of offering the poet Ducis a sheltered, kindly retreat for convalescence in 1805, and, as long as the house in Sologne was kept, Ducis came each summer to spend five or six weeks.[2] Revelliere-lépeaux knew only too well the benefits of country air after illness; he felt happy to be able to repay to someone else what Pincepré de Buire had given him. Pincepré de Buire himself came several times to visit the friend whose life he had saved once and perhaps twice. In May, 1806, Revellierelépeaux returned Buire's visit by a short stay with him near Péronne.[3]

Although his refusal to swear allegiance to the Empire ended his membership in the Institut, Revelliere-lépeaux kept

[1] MLL, vol. ii, pp. 486-487; BA, MSS SM 13, Revelliere-lépeaux to his wife (address lacking), 23-26 Octobre.

[2] MLL, vol. ii, pp. 487-488. After the first visit, Ducis was usually accompanied by his sister, Madame de Lagrange. The letters from Ducis to Revelliere-lépeaux for this period are printed in part in the introduction to Revelliere-lépeaux's memoirs (vol. i, pp. xxvi-xxxix). The letters themselves are at the Bibliothèque Nationale (MSS fr., Nouvelles Acquisitions, 21565). An account of Ducis's visits is also to be found in letters from Revelliere-lépeaux to the painter Gérard in the *Correspondance de François Gérard* (Paris, 1867), pp. 298-300.

[3] MLL, vol. ii, p. 487; BA, MSS SM 13, Revelliere-lépeaux to Madame Revelliere-lépeaux, 6 Mai 1806.

up his connections with the Académie Celtique and the Société d'Agriculture at Paris. Even when he lived in the capital, he had never attended the meetings of the two organizations; leaving Paris made no break, therefore, in his relations with these groups. When he had prepared his essays on the Vendée for the Institut, he had sent a related study to the agricultural society. Now that he had more leisure to write at La Rousselière, he busied himself with a memoir on Celtic monuments to present to the Académie Celtique, and, in order to refresh his memory and make his descriptions as accurate as possible, he made a trip in the autumn of 1806, while he was in the west of France, to visit with Pilastre and Leclerc as many of the old remains as they could find in the region they all knew and loved to re-explore.[1]

The year 1807 brought Madame Revelliere-lépeaux's turn for a vacation. In April she took Ossian to join Clémentine, who had been spending the winter as usual with their friends at the Jardin des Plantes. If Revelliere-lépeaux wrote constantly of homesickness for his family when away on his annual trips to the west of France, he was none the less insistent that his wife and children forget him and his difficulties in managing the house at La Rousselière while they were gone. He assured them that everything ran like clockwork, and that his only anxiety was for their visit not to be cut short.[2] The letters exchanged on the occasion of this Paris visit brought to the foreground the parents' wish to see Clémentine happily married. Clémentine was twenty-five years old. What chance had she, asked their friends, of finding a husband, if she was

---

[1] MLL, vol. ii, p. 491; BA, MSS SM 13: Revelliere-lépeaux to " Mon cher ancien collègue," 8 Février 1806; Revelliere-lépeaux to his wife (address lacking), 31 Octobre 1806. Maison Charavay, *Lettres Autographes et Documents historiques, Bulletin d'Autographes, No. 541,* Février 1922, p. 17, no. 94206 " La Revelliere-Lépeaux (Louis-Marie) député de Maine-et-Loire à la Convention, directeur.—L. a. s. à M. Johanneau, secrétaire perpétuel de l'Académie celtique; La Rousselière, 25 janvier 1809, 2 pp. in -8°."

[2] BA, MSS SM 13, five letters, March-May, 1807.

kept buried in the country? Revelliere-lépeaux admitted the appropriateness of their questions; but he felt that his fortune had not yet recovered sufficiently to permit living in Paris, and in truth he was a little loath to leave the country where he and his wife had always been happiest. Still, there was Ossian's education to be considered as well. After a time he would need more instruction than his father could give him, and it was, moreover, not good to keep him too long away from the companionship and competition of other boys his age.

From 1807, therefore, the question of returning to Paris came more and more frequently to the mind of Revelliere-lépeaux. During his autumn visit to the west of France, alone with his vineyards at Faye he had time for reflection; to separate his family, sending the children away, would be unthinkable, even if it were financially possible. Away from home, he could see in retrospect all the scenes of the past year—the fête for his wife, for example, when the neighbors from Buglain had come for dinner, and each member of the party, down to ten-year-old Ossian, had repeated his stanza of poetry in offering a bouquet to the mistress of the house. Pastoral life pleased Revelliere-lépeaux, and it was a struggle to tear himself away from it. He could not reach the decision; he could only write a poem, that tenth day of September, and send it back to La Rousselière to assure his wife and children that all the beauties of nature at grape-gathering time could not make up for the privation of being separated from them.[1]

The problem of Ossian's education had to be faced, however, as well as the more delicate question of finding a husband for Clémentine. With the property in the west of France repaired and in a condition to assure a steady if small income,

[1] BA, MSS SM 13, *Poésies fugitives: Bouquet à ma femme à la Rousselière 1807, nos voisins de Buglin dinant à la maison; Couplets faits en conduisant mes vandangeurs dans leur travail sur le coteau de la cave aux bords du layon commune de faye en maine et loire le dernier jour de mes vandanges le 10 7ᵇʳᵉ 1807.*

Revelliere-lépeaux took his family back to Paris after nearly five years in retirement.[1]

III

Revelliere-lépeaux left his country home, but not his secluded fashion of living. Clémentine had chosen for the family an apartment in the rue du Puits-de-l'Ermite, Faubourg Saint-Marceau, very near the Jardin des Plantes, and there they quickly settled into a quiet routine centering chiefly about Ossian's education. Revelliere-lépeaux chose tutors for his son but took great pains to supervise personally every step of the work.[2] Study with Ossian left enough time, however, for his own intellectual labors; during the first years after his return to Paris, he completed two essays, one a dissertation on the Vendean patois, with grammar, dictionary, and examples of songs with music, the other a description of the monuments he had visited in 1806. Both these essays he sent to be read at the Académie Celtique. In spite of pressing invitations on the part of friends, he refused to attend the meetings of this academy as well as of the Société d'Agriculture in which he preferred to retain his status as correspondent.[3] The régime of tranquil meals at home, of walks in the Jardin des Plantes, of occasional visits with selected friends drawn from a small circle, was admirable as a background for study and for the detachment of Revelliere-lépeaux, who was no longer young and whose delicate health made too crowded a life increasingly inadvisable. It was not a régime calculated to give much relief or diversion to Clémentine, whose very devotion to her parents

[1] Revelliere-lépeaux returned to Paris sometime during the summer of 1809. *Cf.* letter a. s., Revelliere-lépeaux to " Très chers et bons voisins," 16 Août 1809, BN, MSS fr., Nouvelles Acquisitions, Collection Bixio.

[2] MLL, vol. ii, pp. 490-491 ; Collection Loyau, Revelliere-lépeaux to Monsieur Loyau, ex-législateur, 29 Décembre 1809.

[3] The essay on the Vendean patois, inserted in the *Mémoires de l'Académie celtique*, tome iii, pp. 267 *et seq.*, was re-edited in 1868 at Niort and Fontenay (Vendée).

enslaved her. The overdose of retirement either unsettled her nerves or aggravated some nervous maladjustment. Doctors were unable to help her medically, and a mountain trip was suggested as the only possible way of restoring her to normal health. Revelliere-lépeaux's income, though steadier than it had been in some years, was hardly equal to paying for a long journey. Yet the earnest desire to cure his daughter at all costs led him to decide upon taking his wife and both children for a short stay in Switzerland. He could not, of course, have considered sending Clémentine away by herself.

The four left Paris early in May, 1810. The first stage of the journey brought them to Lyons, where for a week they were guests of Revelliere-lépeaux's first cousin, Joseph-Armand Maillocheau. Maillocheau, who had become a priest shortly before the outbreak of the Revolution, had later renounced his vows and left France for England. Returning to Paris when laws against émigrés were relaxed under the Consulate, he had been received cordially by Revelliere-lépeaux and his family. His ability to speak English and his quick intelligence had won him a place as secretary to Fouché for a time, and later he had been named prefect of police for the city of Lyons. He was to be deprived of his place soon after Revelliere-lépeaux's visit, and thereafter he refrained from political endeavors. Clémentine seemed particularly refreshed by the stay at Lyons, so that Revelliere-lépeaux was definitely encouraged as the four embarked upon the second lap of the journey, from Lyons to Grenoble, where they were received by Réal, Revelliere-lépeaux's former colleague in the Convention. Their ten days in and about Grenoble were divided between a visit with Réal in the city and a short stay at the country house of Monsieur Faure, uncle of Toscan, the librarian at the museum of natural history. The trip was continued by way of Chambéry, Aix, and Geneva to Chamonix. At Chamonix, on June 23, the family celebrated with its usual bouquets of flowers and with toasts the eve of St. John's day, Madame Revelliere-lépeaux's fête.[1] After a short stay at Chamonix, they went around Lake Léman to Lausanne, Vevey, and Bex. At Bex Revelliere-lépeaux thought all his dreams of Swiss liberty were fulfilled, when he saw what handsome fire engines the commune could afford because the central government took so small a portion of the taxes away from the locality. His cherished ideal of small states grouped into a federal union seemed to be justified, and he was happier than he had been in a very long time. The return journey was accomplished by way of Geneva to Dijon, where during the Directory Revelliere-lépeaux had named his friend Goupilleau from the Vendée as receiver-general of the department of the Yonne. Goupilleau was still at the same post, and, although he was absent from Dijon at the moment of Revelliere-lépeaux's visit, the former Director was hospitably received by Madame Goupilleau. Back in Paris in July, the four travelers could write their friends truthfully that the trip had been a great success. The mountain air had proved beneficial to them all, and Clémentine was nearly herself again.[2]

Not long after his return to the rue du Puits-de-l'Ermite, Revelliere-lépeaux received the offer of a pension from the government of the Empire. He was left free to ask for the amount he wished, and the only requirement was that he file an application. The offer came in a round-about way, from Fouché through Daunou, who entrusted the announcement to another intermediary, Guiter, a former colleague of the Convention whom Revelliere-lépeaux held in esteem. The reply was predictable, for Revelliere-lépeaux had determined never to have anything to do with the régime that he believed had usurped the powers of government. He refused the offer point blank and thus ended the last official communication he ever had with the Empire.[3]

---

[1] Madame Revelliere-lépeaux's Christian name was *Jeanne*. Therefore she celebrated the day of St. John.

[2] MLL, vol. ii, pp. 491-498; BN, MSS fr., Nouvelles Acquisitions, 21565, 19-20, Jean-François Ducis to Monsieur Revelliere l'epeaux, 28 Juillet 1810.

[3] MLL, vol. ii, pp. 498-500.

Having turned his back upon any and every relation with officialdom, Revelliere-lépeaux, still refreshed from his journey, took up his correspondence with Ducis, who was living at Versailles, and with Loyau of Bazoges in the Vendée. Loyau, who spent much time in agricultural experimentation at his property Pulteau, wished in 1810 to send one of his young gardeners to Paris to be trained in the latest methods, and he besought Revelliere-lépeaux to guide the young man. Calling upon Bosc at Versailles and Thouin at Paris for advice, Revelliere-lépeaux found a place for Loyau's gardener and followed his progress throughout the period of his training.[1]

In October, while on his annual business trip to Maine-et-Loire, overseeing the *vendanges*, selling grain, buying honey for winter consumption, Revelliere-lépeaux sought Leclerc's advice about Ossian's musical education. Leclerc thought that whatever instrument he might wish to take up later Ossian should first acquire a thorough knowledge of the piano, and he recommended a method he had found particularly helpful for beginners. Revelliere-lépeaux wrote immediately to Clémentine to investigate the method indicated and to find out from Méhul whether he considered it valuable or would recommend another.[2]

The next spring, on April 19, 1811, Clémentine gave up direct supervision of her young brother to marry Joseph-Armand Maillocheau, her father's first cousin, who had left Lyons and politics and had retired to live upon his income. Maillocheau was forty-eight years old and Clémentine twenty-nine. The ceremony was witnessed by Clémentine's family and her father's close friends Gérard, Van Spaendonck, Daunou, Guillebert, and Vallée. The bride and groom went to live at Domont near the forest of Montmorency. On the following March 12, Revelliere-lépeaux's only grandchild was born,

[1] Collection Loyau, Revelliere-lépeaux to Monsieur Loyau, 18 Août 1810.

[2] BA, MSS SM 13, Revelliere-lépeaux to Clémentine (address lacking), 20-23 Octobre 1810.

Emilie Jeanne Clémentine Maillocheau, named for her mother and grandmother but always called Emilie.[1]

While Revelliere-lépeaux wrote and translated,[2] Ossian grew tall, resembling his mother's family in stature, for both the Revellieres and the Maillocheaus were traditionally small men.[3] In 1813, at the age of sixteen, he was permitted to accompany his father for the first time to the west of France, though not until 1817 did Revelliere-lépeaux have the pleasure of presenting his handsome son to his relatives and friends in the Vendée.[4]

After Clémentine's marriage, Revelliere-lépeaux had decided to move his family's residence from the rue du Puits-de-l'Ermite to the rue des Fossés St. Victor, number 35,[5] where they remained until 1814, when it seemed advisable for them to join Clémentine and her husband at Domont. Partly to be near their daughter, and partly because country life would always be more agreeable to them than Paris, Revelliere-lépeaux and his wife retired to Domont with the intention of spending the rest of their days near the forest of Montmorency.[6] Ossian was judged old enough and of sufficient prudence to

[1] Collection Viénot, Act of Marriage of Joseph-Armand Maillocheau and Clémentine de la Revellière, copied from the Préfecture de la Seine, Ville de Paris, Douzième Mairie, Extraits des Actes de Mariage de l'An Mil huit cent onze.

[2] BMHN, MS 292, *Rapport à son Excellence le ministre de l'intérieur du royaume d'Italie sur l'état du jardin d'agriculture de l'université roiale de Bologne, à Milan Chez Jean Silvestoi, 1812, Traduit par M. Revelliere Lepeaux.*

[3] Collection Viénot, H. Leferme (great-granddaughter of Revelliere-lépeaux) to Monsieur John Viénot, 28 Octobre 1912.

[4] MLL, vol. ii, pp. 452, 462.

[5] In a letter of January 26, 1812, Revelliere-lépeaux announced to Loyau the intended change (Collection Loyau). The earliest use of the new address noticed by the author is in a letter from Madame de Lagrange to Revelliere-lépeaux, on March 22, 1812 (BN, MSS fr., Nouvelles Acquisitions, 21565, 3-4).

[6] Revelliere-lépeaux announced his new address at Domont to his friend Loyau in a letter written from Paris on September 3, 1814 (Collection Loyau).

be left in Paris continuing his studies to become a lawyer. In Paris, therefore, rue de la Vieille Estrapade, he occupied a three-room apartment with his cousin Victor Revelliere.[1]

No plan could have been more appropriately laid, but the struggles of the Empire, which up to this time had interfered very little with Revelliere-lépeaux's private life, brought pandemonium into his seclusion. When the Bourbons entered for the second time with the armies of the Allies, at the end of the Hundred Days, the house at Domont was overrun with foreign soldiers. Escaping hastily, Revelliere-lépeaux and his wife took refuge in the student lodgings of their son, rue de la Vieille Estrapade, while he rented a room nearby. At the end of August Revelliere-lépeaux wrote to his " dear compatriot and very good friend " Loyau that for six weeks past six officers, six soldiers, and seventeen horses had been living at their own discretion in and about the house at Domont. In November he wrote again that the soldiers were still quartered at Domont, to the great discomfort and financial ruin of the countryside. For the first time in years, Revelliere-lépeaux was forced by the uncertainty of conditions to forego his annual trip west.[2] The uncertainty was not dispelled in 1816. The law of January, 1816, condemning former regicides to exile did not technically apply to Revelliere-lépeaux, because, with a gesture of forgiveness, it restricted the penalty to those regicides who had signed the *Acte Additionnel* and supported the régime of the Hundred Days.[3] Nevertheless Revelliere-lépeaux did not escape suspicion and close observation from early spring until the question was dropped in the summer. On April 30, having

<hr />

[1] MLL, vol. ii, pp. 504-505; Collection Viénot, H. Leferme to Monsieur John Viénot, July 10; Collection Loyau, Revelliere-lépeaux to Monsieur Loyau, 3 September 1814.

[2] Collection Loyau, Revelliere-lépeaux to Monsieur Loyau, 27 Août 1815 and 14 Novembre 1815. BA, MSS SM 13: Revelliere-lépeaux to Monsieur Boyleau, 25 Août 1815 and 28 Septembre 1815; Revelliere-lépeaux to Monsieur Pincepré Buire, 11 Septembre 1815.

[3] *Bulletin des Lois*, Série 7, vol. 50, no. 58 (no. 349), pp. 17-19.

heard that he was being made the subject of inquiry, Revelliere-lépeaux wrote two letters, one to the minister of police and the other to the prefect of police, announcing frankly his address and claiming his right to freedom from all persecution by reason of his constant refusal to take part in political affairs for the preceding seventeen years.[1]

Although Revelliere-lépeaux's position was more uncomfortable than dangerous, the inquiries to which he was subjected were inconvenient for his son-in-law. Clémentine's health was showing the strain of the difficult year, and her husband hoped to restore her by a sojourn in Switzerland, counterpart of the trip she had taken with her family in 1810. To his great annoyance, his passports were delayed because authorities suspected him of leaving the country to prepare a refuge for his father-in-law in Switzerland, where émigrés were no longer permitted to go.[2] Eventually the passports were granted, and by the middle of June Revelliere-lépeaux could write to Loyau that Clémentine was in Switzerland with her husband and small daughter, waiting for the season to take a cure at Aix.[3]

The spring was saddened, too, by the death of Ducis at the end of March. Although he had been in declining health for some time, his death came as a shock. He and Revelliere-lépeaux had delighted in exchanging memories of the summers at La Rousselière whenever they had met or written to each other in recent years. Ducis had preserved the shepherd's cap

[1] AN, F⁷ 6715, 245-248; Archives de la Préfecture de Police, 49777: 278-282, 284-293, 300. In March, 1816, Revelliere-lépeaux was included in a list of those who would be obliged to leave the realm in accordance with the provisions of the law of January 12, 1816 (AN, F⁷, 6707, plaquette 5). There is no accompanying indication of the date at which his name was removed from the list. In another list, July 28, 1818, classifying the regicides of the Convention in five categories, the name "Laréveillere Lépeaux" appears under the heading "Non atteints par la loi" (AN, F⁷, 6707, plaquette 1).

[2] AN, F⁷, 6715, 247; Archives de la Préfecture de Police, 49777: 280-282, 284-287, 290, 291.

[3] Collection Loyau, Revelliere-lépeaux to Monsieur Loyau, 12 Juin 1816.

made for him by Clémentine with as much care as Revelliere-lépeaux had in March, 1814, set up the bust of Ducis beside that of Pincepré du Buire, in the salon of the apartment, rue Fossés St. Victor.[1] The death of the poet was associated poignantly with the end of the pastoral life with its simple fêtes made gay by impromptu verse; and it was the beginning of last things for Revelliere-lépeaux. The trip with Ossian to the Vendée in the autumn of 1817 was the last visit to his native town Montaigu, the last time he saw his friend Loyau or his cousin Madame Clemenceau. He had only the most discouraging news of his daughter's health to give solicitous friends, but with pride he presented the stalwart son of twenty who was succeeding in his law courses and, according to Revelliere-lépeaux's own word, was showing promise of a " vigorous honesty and a solid character." [2]

Ossian passed his examinations for the *licence* in law in 1819 and was ready to practise. He had only to conclude the formality of being registered for his new estate. His reception, when he himself presented himself for this registration, gave his father food for bitter reflection throughout the remaining years of his life. The secretary to whom the credentials were presented took exception to Ossian's Christian name on the ground that it was not Christian at all. The matter would have to be referred to higher authorities, he decided. Ossian was notified that, if he would change his name or simply add to it one of the names in the Christian calendar,

---

[1] Revelliere-lépeaux to " Monsieur Ducis Membre de l'institut des sciences et arts," 18 Mars 1814. This letter was added to the author's collection through the kindness of Mademoiselle M. De Chaux. Ducis speaks of " le petit chapeau pastorale " in his letter of March 21, 1812, to Revelliere-lépeaux (BN, MSS fr., Nouvelles Acquisitions, 21565, 7-8), offering congratulations upon the birth of his granddaughter.

[2] MLL, vol. ii, p. 462; Collection Loyau: On May 18, 1817, Revelliere-lépeaux wrote to Loyau about his anxiety over Clémentine and his joy at Ossian's progress. When Clémentine returned from Plombières to Paris the following August, Revelliere-lépeaux wrote again of his despair at his daughter's still unimproved health.

he would be admitted to the bar. He stubbornly resisted. The matter trailed from office to office and finally came to nothing. Revelliere-lépeaux was doubly offended by the attack upon liberty of thought and by what he considered a hidden insult to his own political persuasions.[1] Whether this rebuff was final, with no possible redress, or whether like his father Ossian did not really wish to practise law, he never was any more of a lawyer than Revelliere-lépeaux himself. His talent for languages and literature became to him what botany had been to his father.

In the tiny apartment of the rue de la Vieille Estrapade, where their financial straits forced Madame Revelliere-lépeaux to do the household work, the former Director began writing his memoirs.[2] In the hurried escape from Domont, his papers had been left behind, and many of his important letters had been mislaid or stolen by the soldiers who occupied the house. He was obliged to rely very greatly, therefore, upon his memory. He realized the danger of errors in factual matters; but, utilizing what papers he had, he recounted his career as straightforwardly as he could remember it. On March 29, he suffered a new bereavement in the death of his son-in-law;[3] and then, as if to end his days in recapitulation, he gathered his family about him, wife, daughter, and son, in an apartment at number 28, rue de Condé, only a few steps from the Luxembourg. If it had not been for the young Emilie he might have believed they had always been together, only four of them. Clémentine's health was a little less precarious, but she was far from able to care for her young daughter. Also Revelliere-lépeaux lacked the energy to direct the studies of his granddaughter as he had those of his own children. Therefore little Emilie was

[1] MLL, vol. ii, pp. ∪06-511.

[2] MLL, vol. i, p. 1.

[3] Archives du Département de la Seine, Extrait du Registre des Actes de Décès, 11eme arrondissement de Paris, 1821, reconstitué par la Commission (Loi du 12 Février 1872) : Acte de décès, J. A. Maillocheau, copie faite et collationnée sur une minute carbonisée.

placed in a boarding school for children, directed by Madame
Servier, a Protestant from Geneva. Although he would have
liked his only grandchild near him continuously, Revelliere-
lépeaux approved thoroughly his daughter's decision for bringing up Emilie, not that he believed in all the ramifications of
Protestantism but that to his way of thinking it was the nearest practical approach to the natural religion in which he had
brought up his own children. Emilie remained with Madame
Servier until she was seventeen years old, and two years later,
in 1831, she was married to the sculptor David d'Angers.[1]

Revelliere-lépeaux was an old man. He spent the year 1822
completing his memoirs. He finished by telling the story of
Ossian's failure to be admitted to the bar. "Now our son
occupies himself at translations. I hope, however, that in time
he may devote himself to his rightful vocation." He then
affixed the date, January 1, 1823. On the following April 6,
he placed with the memoirs his own directions for editing and
publishing.[2] In the autumn of 1823 he took Ossian as usual
to look after their vineyards in Anjou. He saw Leclerc and
Pilastre, but his sister had died the year before. Ossian described their visit to the ruins of the old house at Faye:

The scantiness of our income had never permitted him to rebuild it; but the memory of the happy days he had passed there
with my mother and my two young sisters before the confusion of
Europe was at the time very near and dear; he always visited with
a melancholy pleasure what was left of his former garden, where
the blackberry briars of today choked back the roses of former days
without entirely hiding them.[3]

[1] MLL, vol. ii, pp. 505-506; Collection Pasquier, letter a. s., Emilie
Maillocheau to her cousin Victor Revelliere, 3 Septembre 1829; Archives
du Département de la Seine, Extrait du Registre des Actes de Mariage de
l'an mil huit cent trente un, Reconstitution des actes de l'état civil entrée
le 24 mai, 1873: Acte de mariage, Pierre Jean David et Emilie Jeanne
Clémentine Maillocheau.

[2] MLL, vol. ii, p. 511; vol. i, p. iv.

[3] MLL, vol. i, pp. xxxix-xl.

Father and son returned to Paris late in November. A few days later, in spite of the damp, cold weather and his family's warnings, Revelliere-lépeaux walked to see Daunou who lived in the rue Ménilmontant. The chill and fatigue were too much for his strength, and he was obliged to go to bed to nurse his weak lungs and sore throat.[1] Every care was unavailing. He was ill all through the winter, and his familiar figure, always dressed in a suit of the same grey color, was missed from the Jardin des Plantes. The illness, which seemed more painful than severe, was made more difficult by the knowledge of Clémentine's failing health. His few friends, though, were faithful. Daunou, in particular, came to call when he could. Toward spring he failed rapidly. On Friday, March 26, 1824, Ossian wrote to his cousin, Victorin Revelliere that his mother, sister, and father were all three very ill, and that in the last four or five days his father had suffered chills, fever, and hemorrhage from the lungs.[1] The nearness of the end was apparent. The next morning calmly and without apparent suffering Revelliere-lépeaux died.[2] On Monday he was buried in

[1] Collection Pasquier, letter a. s., Clémentine Maillocheau to Victor Revelliere, 9 Décembre 1823.

[2] Ossian wrote immediately to Victorin Revelliere, describing the death of Revelliere-lépeaux.

"The most cruel blow has struck me. I expected it. I hope that I may bear up under it. Heaven will sustain me. It must, for my lot is bitter. Two hours ago we lost the one whom we shall always love and whose gentle and noble memory will sustain us through life. My father died with an inconceivable calm. His features are pale but unchanged. There is no trace of suffering to be seen.

"My sister, who is dangerously ill, my mother unwell, are asleep, both of them. They know nothing. They must be told, sustained, consoled! What a predicament! But I trust in myself and in God.

"Adieu. If you would like to return, come; it would help us. Tell our friends. Adieu."

Ossian's two letters to his cousin, dated March 26 and March 27, are now in the Collection Pasquier.

In BN, MSS fr., Nouvelles Acquisitions, 21887, 99, a letter from Ossian to Daunou praying him to say a few words at the funeral on the following Monday with the interment at Père Lachaise. See also *Le Constitutionnel, Journal du commerce, politique et littéraire*, Paris, Lundi 29 Mars 1824, p. 3.

Père Lachaise. The Jardin des Plantes went into mourning, but the court of Louis XVIII and the general public of France took no note of the passing of one Director of the fallen republic.

CHAPTER VIII
COMMENT AND CRITICISM

A man is as many men as there are men to meet him; as
many men as there are days which pass; perhaps one more, the
man he himself thinks he is.

IN 1895, exactly a century after the installation of the Executive Directory in the Luxembourg, appeared the memoirs of two of the five Directors, Barras and Revelliere-lépeaux. The stories of aristocrat and bourgeois alike had been kept from the public, but, while the record of each man waited, the manuscript of Barras suffered many vicissitudes, whereas Revellierelépeaux's memoirs led the peaceful and traceable kind of existence which critics of texts greet with joy and relief. The simultaneous appearance of these two versions of the history of the Directory was not premeditated, but it was appropriate. Revelliere-lépeaux had constantly disapproved of Barras and his train, and Barras had often smiled at Revelliere-lépeaux and finally betrayed him, but there had been at times a bond of sympathy between the two men, and a respect of each one for the other, which none of their misunderstandings could quite efface.

The memoirs of Revelliere-lépeaux, having been completed in 1823, a year before his death, lay for half a century in their author's own carefully penned writing, undisturbed except for occasional consultation by some historian and for his son Ossian's painstaking preparation of the manuscript for the press. Mahul had access to all Revelliere-lépeaux's papers as he was preparing the *Annuaire nécrologique* of 1824. Thiers consulted the papers in 1827, when he had nearly finished writing his account of the period of the Directory in his *Histoire de la Révolution française*, (Paris, 10 vols., 1823-1827); he expressed regret at not having known earlier that the manuscript existed. Lamartine, nearly twenty years later, made use of Revelliere-lépeaux's own account of proscription under the Terror in composing his *Histoire des Girondins* (Paris, 8 vols., 1847).

Ossian made no attempt to edit the memoirs in the years immediately following his father's death, because Revellierelépeaux had wished his work to remain unpublished as long as the men under comment were living. Yet, even when the death of his father's contemporaries seemed to make publication incumbent upon him, Ossian continued to hesitate; he himself explained the failure to present his father's work on the ground that he did not wish to expose the constitutional monarchy to what might have been construed as ill-timed criticism. For this reason, or for others, Ossian did not complete his preparation of the manuscript for publication until about 1847. At that time, on leaving France for an extended trip to South America, he entrusted the corrected papers to his cousin Victorin, son of Revelliere-lépeaux's brother Jean-Baptiste beheaded during the Terror. On returning, he received these papers intact from the hands of Victorin, but at the same period, in the process of moving his own household belongings from Paris to Maine-et-Loire, Ossian lost supplementary papers bequeathed to him by his father. His marriage to Madame Cesbron de Nerbonne in 1856 added a personal deterrent to whatever political scruples the Director's son might yet have entertained with regard to publishing the memoirs. Ossian was devoted to his wife, who was a devout Catholic and mother-in-law of Theobald de Soland, a man with pronounced monarchical convictions, soon to become a deputy. Calling up old ghosts, by bringing Ossian's regicide and deist father into the limelight, seemed to them embarrassing and needless, and their influence was sufficient to prevent Ossian from overcoming his own hesitancy.

In 1873, when the Third Republic seemed to promise a more flattering audience for Revelliere-lépeaux's musings and justifications, Ossian went so far as to have his father's memoirs put into print. Having made that conscientious concession, he still could not bring himself to order the public distribution of the work. With reluctance he deposited the required copy at the Bibliothèque Nationale and at the same time scattered a dozen sets among relatives and close friends. Though sincerely happy in having saved his father's work from the threat of destruction by multiplying the number of copies in existence and pleased by the congratulations of certain distinguished persons, among them the historian Michelet, Ossian never decided to have the bulk of the printed copies transferred from their storeroom to the open shelves of booksellers. When he died, in 1876, he left the injunction that the memoirs were not to be published until after the death of his wife. The manuscript passed into the hands of Revelliere-lépeaux's granddaughter, Emilie David d'Angers who, at her death, in turn laid Ossian's injunction upon her son Robert David d'Angers.

The death of Madame Larevellière-Lépeaux in 1891 released Robert David d'Angers from the last family obligation to keep the memoirs in hiding; but in 1891 the president of the French Republic was Sadi Carnot, grandson of Carnot the Director, and in his memoirs Revelliere-lépeaux had reserved the most severe diatribes, not for Barras who had been instrumental in forcing him from the Directory, but for Carnot whom he and Barras had together put out of power. Perhaps it was easier for Revelliere-lépeaux to forgive the man who had unquestionably wronged him than to refrain from justifying his own course of action toward the man whom he had helped to drive from the Directory. In any case, on confiding his memoirs to the care of his son, Revelliere-lépeaux had recommended that they be edited so as to soften those criticisms of Carnot which might seem unfair or unrestrained. Neither Ossian, however, nor his grandnephew Robert David d'Angers was willing to amend the text with a view to carrying out these instructions. So it happened that after time had invalidated all other possible reasons for delaying the memoirs' publication, Robert David d'Angers decided to postpone the appearance of the volumes until after the term of Carnot's grandson as president of the French Republic should be concluded. The assassination of Sadi Carnot in 1894 removed the grounds for this last reticence. Revelliere-lépeaux's narrative in two volumes was finally published in 1895 with an accompanying third volume of selected writings and correspondence.

Already, in 1888, Robert David d'Angers had given to the Bibliothèque Nationale the manuscript upon which the printed edition was based, but with the restriction that it was to be opened for public consultation only in 1910. His wish was obeyed. Today the original manuscript of the memoirs is subject to no other reserve than the usual regulations governing all manuscripts belonging to the Bibliothèque Nationale. The memoirs and accompanying papers are bound in five volumes; all except letters addressed to Revelliere-lépeaux are clearly written in ink in his own unmistakable hand and corrected for publication by Ossian with an indelible pencil. For the most part these changes would appear to have been made not with a view to modifying the sense but rather in an effort to improve the smoothness of the style. In any event, the papers remain available for comparison with the printed text whenever that expedient may seem advisable, and there can be no difficulty in distinguishing Ossian's words from his father's.

Three events marked the end of Revelliere-lépeaux's political career: he was forced against his wish to leave the Directory in June, 1799; the Constitution of 1795, sacred to him, was discarded a few months later, carrying with it the régime of the Directory; within two years after the Directory's fall, the cult of Theophilanthropy was officially disbanded. Acceptance of these facts has been inescapable, but their explanation and interpretation have given rise to the principal controversies over Revelliere-lépeaux's place in the sun. His reputation has de-

---

Illustration on opposite page

Autograph signed letter from the historian Michelet to Ossian Larevellière-Lépeaux, son of the Director. The envelope (not reproduced here) is postmarked at Paris, with the date of February 1, 1873. Collection Pasquier.

2 - d'Alfar 74

Monsieur,

plusieurs personnes me parlent des
mémoires et s'affligent de ne pas les voir
paraître.

je les annonce ces jours ci dans mon
histoire du Dix-neuvième siècle, où j'admire

la modération de votre père pour tous
ses ennemis, pour Carnot qui l'accable
d'injures — Moi même je suis resté très

modéré sur tout cela

je vous en prie: Veuillez donc mettre
en tête le Superbe portrait gravé de votre
père qui est ici, au cabinet des estampes

je vous remercie de nouveau, et vous salue
affectueusement.   J. Michelet.

— le portrait seul est un abrégé. Il rattache tous les ennemis.

pended very largely upon the views taken of the triple failure, of his personal exclusion from politics, of the end of the régime he worshipped, and of the death of his preferred form of deism. However diverse the conclusions of Revelliere-lépeaux's biographers have been, no estimate has ignored the sharp truth that in the eyes of the world he failed.

He has never enjoyed the honor or notoriety of a violent public controversy over his reputation. He has never arrived at the point of dividing the academic world into armed camps as have Danton and Robespierre. Yet there has never been a time when either public opinion or learned pronouncements have succeeded in reducing him to a formula universally acceptable. With equanimity, and sometimes with smugness, he has been called incompetent or unfortunate, or both. Simple condemnation based upon his failure to survive has been mingled with more astute disapproval of his motives and achievements. Yet he has rarely failed of a defendant to point out that he possessed qualities transcending his fall from the Directory. From 1799, therefore, until today, there has persisted in the judgments passed upon Revelliere-lépeaux a strain of the age-old controversy over the respective merits of virtue and actual outcome. Also certain interpreters of his personality have expressed their views as to the futility of good intentions and middle-class morality, such as his, in a world of action.

While Revelliere-lépeaux's career has been taken as one more case in point in the classic apposition of utility and principle, his reputation has been involved in two more immediate nineteenth century issues: on one hand, the struggle over a form of government for the French state, and, on the other hand, the relation between church and state. Biographers of monarchical leanings have tended, in their lighter moods, to dub him an impractical dreamer, and, when they felt more serious, to accuse him of treason in promoting so absurd a government as the Directory. Since 1870 he has been more often charged with incompetence than with a mistaken political philosophy. Catholic sentiment, in the earlier part of the nineteenth century, was still irate at Revelliere-lépeaux's share in the Directory's persecution of priests, but later this feeling faded more or less into a habit of ridiculing his attempts to institutionalize deism. In this connection, it is interesting to note that two of the most recent attempts to rehabilitate Revelliere-lépeaux's reputation have been made by Protestant clergymen.

At least three distinct schools of thought arose to explain Revelliere-lépeaux during his lifetime. The poet Ducis expressed the belief of many personal friends when he was unable to find any flaw in the virtues and abilities of Revellieve-lépeaux as Director and was forced to fall back upon the explanation that the times were out of joint, that the age was unworthy.[1] At the other extreme stood Carnot-Feulins, brother of Carnot the victim of Fructidor, believing firmly that the times had been manageable if not entirely propitious and that, owing to his peculiar position of holding the balance of power in the Directory, Revelliere-lépeaux with reasonable firmness and clearsightedness could have saved the day for the constitutional republic; Carnot-Feulins thus blamed not the age but Revelliere-lépeaux's inadequacy. Carnot-Feulins is one of the first of a long line of biographers who denounced what they called domestic virtues as not only insufficient baggage for statesmen but a positive menace in that such qualities blind the public to the political shortcomings of the person in question.[2] A third point of view, midway between Ducis and Carnot-Feulins, was held by Paganel, fellow regicide at the Convention with Revelliere-lépeaux but in 1815 pleading for a constitutional monarchy. Paganel was inclined to attribute the Directory's failure to the inherent human inability of five men to form a working executive power. In attempting to fix precise responsibility for failure in the Directory, Paganel cast no aspersions upon Revelliere-lépeaux's intelligence or uprightness but rather upon the special form of jealous desire for serving the fatherland, which

[1] MLL, vol. i, p. xxxvi.

[2] *Histoire du Directoire constitutionnel* (Paris, An VIII), pp. 238-241.

his patriotism took. Paganel [1] credited Revelliere-lépeaux with a sense of devotion which would have led him to dispute with every republican the privilege of sacrificing himself for the good of the country; but, Paganel pointed out, Revelliere-lépeaux's very love for France re-enforced the rigidity of his ways so that he found it difficult to work with other people. Less through personal egotism than through disbelief in the virtue and ability of others, Revelliere-lépeaux wished every plan of action drawn according to his specifications and was therefore incapable of those adjustments without which committee government is out of the question.

Revelliere-lépeaux's death opened to biographers the possibility of consulting his memoirs, and those persons who did see the manuscript during the period of fifty years before its publication seem in each case to have adopted a charitable if not indeed a sympathetic attitude toward the former Director. It may have been, however, that only those biographers already possessed of a kindly feeling toward Revelliere-lépeaux and his family were very likely to have access to the memoirs. A suitable example of this is Thiers, who had once met and been favorably impressed by Revelliere-lépeaux. When the printed memoirs were at length available, they cast no magic spell to win historians from their preconceptions. Taine, in *Les Origines de la France contemporaine* (Paris, 6 vols., 1876-1894), turned Revelliere-lépeaux's own words against him in the eighteen eighties, and none of Revelliere-lépeaux's justifications or explanations could make Sciout (*Le Directoire,* Paris, 4 vols., 1895-1897) vary one particle from his anti-Directorial prejudice.

The *Annuaire nécrologique* of Mahul carried the first important account of Revelliere-lépeaux's career to be published after the former Director's death. Mahul had access to all Revelliere-lépeaux's papers and correspondence, but instead of writing the account himself he accepted for publication the

[1] *Essai sur la Révolution française* (Paris, 3 vols., 1815), vol. ii, pp. 478-480.

story of someone whose name he withheld; it is probable that Ossian either wrote or carefully revised the article for Mahul. The story of the *Annuaire*, at all events, is written entirely in the mood of the memoirs and avowedly refrains from passing judgment upon Revelliere-lépeaux's chief political actions. Mahul himself, on the contrary, was not so detached. In a signed note he criticized severely Revelliere-lépeaux's voting the death of Louis XVI, his part in the Fructidor coup d'état, and his attitude toward the Catholic Church. At the same time Mahul remarked that the seriousness of these mistakes had been unduly exaggerated by the government of the Empire. In closing his note Mahul asserted that few statesmen had deserved so richly as Revelliere-lépeaux to have their errors forgiven.

Because of his position in the Directory, Revelliere-lépeaux could not be omitted from the important biographical dictionaries and encyclopedias that appeared through the nineteenth century. The detailed account in the *Biographie universelle* (Paris, 1842), is typical of the public attitude toward Revelliere-lépeaux outside the small circle of his descendants and his close friends' descendants. The point of view of the *Biographie universelle* was quite in line with the tradition crystallized in the words of Carnot-Feulins, with emphasis on the inadequacy of personal and domestic virtue in meeting crises of state administration. Durozoir, author of the sketch, was patently monarchical and Catholic in sympathy. His estimate was not inordinately severe until it reached the period of the Directory, but from then on the only ungrudging approval he could bestow upon Revelliere-lépeaux was on the score of honesty in refraining from self-enrichment during the course of his years in power. Durozoir took Mahul strongly to task for slurring over Revelliere-lépeaux's relations with Theophilanthropy and laid great stress upon Revelliere-lépeaux's hatred of the Pope as the factor responsible for his attitudes in Italian affairs. Durozoir's criticism was not a tirade, but it was far from satisfactory to Revelliere-lépeaux's sincere admirers. Through a coincidence, the sketch was replaced by a more favorable story in 1859 in a new edition of the *Biographie universelle*. Revelliere-lépeaux's great-granddaughter, Hélène David d'Angers, had married a certain Doctor Gubler who, in the course of his practice, had occasion to treat an editor of the *Biographie*. The two men became friends, and one day Doctor Gubler was asked to re-write the account of his wife's great-grandfather for the *Biographie*. This work he did gladly, and in some haste, owing to the shortness of time before the new edition's appearance. He was able to use not only family tradition but also papers and résumés put at his disposal by Ossian Larevellière-Lépeaux.

The *Annuaire nécrologique,* the *Biographie universelle* and other dictionaries and encyclopedias were enterprises of Paris, the capital; but away in the west of France divergent traditions about Revelliere-lépeaux were being handed down. In April, 1840, François Grille, local historian, read at the Société industrielle at Angers an essay on the life and works of Revelliere-lépeaux, listing his interests and deeds in panegyric style, suggesting the publication of an edition of his works, and urging the erection of a bust in marble of the former Director and of his friend Leclerc. Three years later, on the occasion of Ossian Larevellière-Lépeaux's gift of the Gérard portrait of his father to the museum of Angers, the *Journal de Maine-et-Loire et de la Mayenne* carried a short life story of Revelliere-lépeaux, friendly in tone and written probably by the Director's nephew Victorin. These two accounts, however, represented only one side of Angevin feeling. To begin with, among Revelliere-lépeaux's own relatives and those of his wife there were many who had never forgiven him for leaving the religious traditions of his family nor for voting the death of his king. Then, too, the civil strife which had broken families and friendships all over the west of France had been too bitter an experience to be forgotten even after fifty years and more; Revelliere-lépeaux was to many Angevins the representative of that hateful government which had persecuted their fathers and grandfathers. Belonging to the hostile tradition, M. Bougler, in his *Biographie des députes de l'Anjou depuis l'Assemblée Constituante jusqu'en 1815,* which appeared first serially in the middle eighteen fifties in the *Revue de l'Anjou et de Maine-et-Loire,* wrote a severe but, granting the author's point of view, honest criticism, treating specifically the stages of Revelliere-lépeaux's political career.

Still farther to the west, at Montaigu in the Vendée, Revelliere-lépeaux's birthplace, another local historian, Dugast-Matifeux, was developing an interest in the Vendean who had not only become a Director of the First Republic but after the close of the Directory had continued to demonstrate his attachment to his native province by studies of its Celtic remains and its linguistic peculiarities. Although he communicated with Ossian Larvellière-Lépeaux by letter, Dugast-Matifeux did not meet the Director's son. Ossian could scarcely frown upon Dugast-Matifeux's zealous work in editing Revelliere-lépeaux's study on the Vendean patois and publishing it in 1867 with a short biographical sketch copying the story as told by Mahul's *Annuaire nécrologique.* Nevertheless, he was made uncomfortable by the forthright republicanism of the Montaigu patriot. At the same time he felt that Dugast-Matifeux's eager proposal, in the style of Grille, to set up a public monument to the Citizen Director, was precipitate and unwise. France was yet under the Second Empire. In 1870 the Third Republic was established; and in 1876 Ossian Larevellière-Lépeaux died. Dugast-Matifeux worked on, and in 1886 his efforts were successful. René Goblet, minister of public instruction and of cults, came on June 14 to preside over the unveiling of the bust of Revelliere-lépeaux, set in front of the town hall of Montaigu, where it stands today. The town was in a bustle; the unveiling was followed by a banquet. Nantes newspapers told of the occasion. The *Journal officiel* carried all over France its preliminary announcement of the event by Léon Bienvenu, former deputy from the Vendée, and a few days later the complete text of Minister Goblet's address. Dugast-Matifeux published a revised version of his 1867 biography of

Revelliere-lépeaux, illustrated with a photograph of the newly displayed bust.

The occasion was a fête for Montaigu, but it brought bitterness in its train. Ossian Larevellière-Lépeaux had died ten years before. Robert David d'Angers, Revelliere-lépeaux's great-grandson and only surviving male descendant, expressly or by accident had been omitted from the list of invited guests. He learned what was about to happen only through the letters of friends from Paris who planned to pass through Angers on the way to Montaigu. The publicity given the event raised questions about what had really happened to Revelliere-lépeaux's memoirs, because many people did not know that the volumes had been printed in 1873 or that one copy had been given to the Bibliothèque Nationale. Robert David d'Angers felt called upon to explain in the columns of the *Phare de la Loire* of Nantes what had happened to his great-grandfather's writings.

A description of the printed memoirs available at the Bibliothèque Nationale, published by Jean Destrem in the *Revue historique* in 1879, was unknown to the inquirers who caused Robert David d'Angers trouble, in spite of the fact that this review, composed very largely of quotations from the memoirs, had closed with exhortations to students not to neglect the volumes in making any serious study of the Revolution. Destrem's conclusions recalled, unwittingly it would seem, the estimate of Paganel, describing Revelliere-lépeaux as " an honest man, sincerely impassioned for liberty, very devoted to the Revolution provided that it be conceived exclusively in a certain fashion, little inclined to indulgence for the other man, a cultivated mind, a limited brain, . . ."

The public appearance of the memoirs in 1895 was the signal for a flood of disapproving reviews. It is impossible to find in the avalanche any example of unqualified praise for Revelliere-lépeaux. Aulard (*Revue d'Histoire moderne*), one of the more restrained critics, attempted to suggest ways in which the volumes presented new material for historians, but he con-

cluded that the memoirs were mediocre and almost insignificant
for the Convention and merely curious for the Directory and
that any testimony found therein would have to be carefully
checked. Charavay (*Revue bleue*) took the trouble to begin
the process of checking, pointing out several of Revelliere-
lépeaux's obvious though, he was willing to admit, possibly
honest misrepresentations, notably in the case of a description
of the last days of the Committee of Public Safety. Perhaps
the most thorough-going condemnation came from Eugène
Melchior de Vogüé, who frankly aligned himself with Bougler
and Taine and found Michelet's indulgence explainable only
by the fact that the historian had been an aging man when he
passed comment upon Revelliere-lépeaux and his memoirs. De
Vogüé (*Revue des Deux Mondes*) described Revelliere-lépeaux
as combining the naïveté of a child with an old employee's capacity for grudges. To him, Revelliere-lépeaux's sole historical
interest was as a specimen for students of moral zoölogy.
Carrying the figure of Revelliere-lépeaux's devotion to botany
into a final estimate, de Vogüé concluded: " Our living and
mysterious flower, the genius of France, is not to be gathered
by naturalists who catalogue dead objects in their herbarium."

Robert David d'Angers was wounded by the severity and
ridicule of the reviews. He saw his great-grandfather's reputation bedraggled once more, not only by the adversaries from
whom he might have expected unfriendliness but also by literary men of note. In indignation he wrote to Henri Camerlynck, who was about to present a more friendly picture of
Revelliere-lépeaux to the academy of sciences, letters, and arts
of Amiens: " Do what they may, the great and austere figure
of Larevellière will remain none the less the model of uprightness, of honesty, and of devotion to the fatherland and to the
Republic! "

After fifteen more years, the manuscript of the memoirs was
at last open to the public at the Bibliothèque Nationale.   Albert
Mathiez, having paid especial attention to Revelliere-lépeaux in
his dissertation *La Théophilanthropie et le Culte Décadaire*

(Paris, 1903) seized the moment to point out important letters from Volney to Revelliere-lépeaux to be found among the newly opened papers. In this article of 1910 (*Annales révolutionnaires*), Mathiez, unwilling to accept as final any previous judgment upon Revelliere-lépeaux, spoke of his personality as not yet fully divined and then went on to say that Revelliere-lépeaux, like Volney, loved the people, but at some distance. "They feared the unleashed crowd. They were first of all men of order, property owners. *Sans-culotterie* disgusted them and enraged them. They were Girondins." Mathiez never conceived Revelliere-lépeaux as anything but a negligible quantity in political affairs, and the estimate in his posthumously published volume *Le Directoire* (Paris, 1934) varies little from the opinion expressed by critics in 1895. " Unfortunately, that man of the balanced middle course, well-intentioned, had neither a grasp of politics nor the quality of firmness. He allowed himself to be guided alternately by hatreds and by fears. Thus, vain and grudge-holding, stubborn and mediocre, he will be for the Directory only a very feeble force, or rather a dead weight."

It is to be remarked that not one of the eleven decades since Revelliere-lépeaux's death has passed without the appearance of some biographical sketch, but in all these years he attracted general public attention only twice, in 1886, when his bust was unveiled before the town hall of Montaigu, and in 1895, the year his memoirs finally appeared. These two occasions brought out a large number of periodical articles and controversial statements to add to the accumulating encyclopedic summaries and the infrequent biographical paper read before some learned society. In 1905, ten years after the memoirs were published, the very first historical essay of book size appeared in the form of the doctoral dissertation of Albert Meynier who, during residence of several years at Angers, had re-created and put into words an image of Revelliere-lépeaux, deputy to the Constituent Assembly and to the Convention, as he appeared against his Angevin background. Meynier's study, sympathetic but not uncritical, is carried only to the beginning of the Directory. In

1916, John Viénot began publishing in *La Revue Chrétienne* in serial form his unreservedly favorable version of Revelliere-lépeaux's life story, but the greater part of his chapters have never been printed. Jean Meinadier's doctoral dissertation in theology, also a friendly account, completed in 1928, has likewise remained in manuscript.

Many of Revelliere-lépeaux's critics have ridiculed him for attempting to change the world overnight by childish devices, but scarcely a nation today fails to utilize one or another of the methods he pressed forward tirelessly while he was Director. Shrugs and epithets bestowed upon Revelliere-lépeaux by his contemporaries would be easily understood by today's world. The self-conscious twentieth century would join the equally self-conscious eighteenth century in judging the well-meaning but unsuccessful Director as naïve and incompetent, in smiling at the way he sometimes missed the facile play of influence behind the scenes. Yet now, nearly a century and a half after Revelliere-lépeaux laid down his program of reorganizing society, rulers and would-be rulers are adopting methods he urged upon the Directory. In the future, he may be remembered less for his political successes and failures than for his preoccupation with the problem of developing and adapting techniques of social control.

APPENDIX A

REVELLIERE-LEPEAUX'S NAME

Revelliere-lépeaux was christened Louis-Marie de la Revelliere, but his father had been the first of his family to use the particle and the definite article and even signed this second son's baptismal registration with the one word *Revelliere*. The second part of the compound name was added, in accordance with the custom of the time, to distinguish Louis-Marie from his elder brother Jean-Baptiste. L'Epeaux was the name of a small farm owned by the family near Montaigu in the Vendée.

Revelliere-lépeaux's name has been spelled in many fashions, and he himself set the example of orthographic inconsistency. By 1795, however, when he entered the Executive Directory, he seems to have adopted a form he used, with rare exceptions, throughout the rest of his life. The author has chosen the spelling *Revelliere-lépeaux*, therefore, not only because the subject of the study so signed political documents of the Directory but also because his signature at various subsequent dates indicates that he maintained his preference for this spelling as long as he lived.

The varying traditional spellings of the name differ chiefly with respect to one or more of five points: the use or rejection of the definite article, the use of a capital or a small letter to begin the first part of the name, the placing or omission of an accent over the third *e* in the first part of the name, the placing or omission of the hyphen, and the use of a capital or a small letter to begin the second part of the name.

Revelliere-lépeaux's son, Ossian, chose for himself and for the published memoirs of his father the spelling *Larevellière-Lépeaux*, and a number of historians have followed him. Beginning with the period of the Directory, however, Revelliere-lépeaux certainly did not incorporate the definite article in his name, and it was unquestionably his habit to begin the name with a capital *R*. The omission of an accent over the third *e* in Revelliere is perhaps more questionable than are the first two points. It is difficult to tell, in scrutinizing various examples of Revelliere-lépeaux's signature, whether or not the dot over the *i* may have been intended to continue with one stroke of the pen to form an accent over the *e* immediately following. Etienne Charavay, however, in *La Revelliere-Lépeaux et ses mémoires*, says that in all his experience he never saw a signature with an accent over the *e* in question, and as a merchant of autographs he handled an unusually large number of important documents. The present author has observed a great many autograph, signed letters of Revelliere-lépeaux and in only one case has seen a separate mark that might be an accent. In this case, however, the letter (dated August 16, 1809), belonging to the Bixio Collection at the Bibliothèque Nationale, has for some years been under so strict a reserve that the director of the library has been able to communicate only a photostatic copy of the document. From this copy it is impossible to tell whether the mark is really an accent; whether it is a scratch on the paper; or whether it may have been added by some hand other than Revelliere-lépeaux's. Considering the evidence of many signatures, the author has decided to omit the accent. The question of the hyphen might have been settled one way or the other. About half the time Revelliere-lépeaux used the hyphen and the other half ran the two parts of his name into one without raising his pen. Since there is as much ground for using the hyphen as for omitting it, and since the use of the hyphen makes the name easy to grasp at a glance, the author has chosen to retain it. As for the letter *l*, the majority of historians have made it a capital, but Revelliere-lépeaux himself without exception did use a small letter.

APPENDIX B

REVELLIERE-LEPEAUX AND DEPART-
MENTAL APPOINTMENTS

ARCHIVES NATIONALES, SÉRIE AF III, CARTONS 314-637

Charente. 324, 1327; 345, 1556; 347, 1585; 356, 1673; 358, 1695; 378, 1912; 379, 1921; 398, 2123; 416, 2316.

Charente-Inférieure. 320, 1286; 327, 1352; 347, 1583; 349, 1595; 350, 1611; 351, 1620; 368, 1795; 376, 1888; 376, 1891; 383, 1966; 387, 2001; 389, 2029; 392, 2064; 393, 2069; 395, 2094; 397, 2115; 400, 2151; 405, 2211; 415, 2312; 471, 2884.

Corrèze. 342, 1523; 371, 1826; 400, 2155; 412, 2275; 414, 2300; 470, 2881.

Creuse. 326, 1348; 349, 1595; 379, 1918; 381, 1936; 381, 1944; 389, 2022; 390, 2042; 398, 2133; 400, 2151; 403, 2192; 459, 2758.

Deux-Sèvres. 347, 1585; 358, 1691; 367, 1788; 379, 1921; 383, 1967; 394, 2082; 394, 2085; 396, 2103; 410, 2260; 450, 2659.

Dordogne. 320, 1290; 324, 1330; 339, 1491; 345, 1564; 352, 1630; 355, 1659; 357, 1675; 364, 1762; 376, 1891; 377, 1905; 378, 1912; 379, 1918; 380, 1930; 383, 1966; 384, 1974; 403, 2195; 404, 2202; 412, 2276; 416, 2321.

Gers. 316, 1255; 344, 1546; 344, 1550; 345, 1561; 352, 1634; 355, 1662; 380, 1933; 381, 1940; 395, 2094; 413, 2285; 441, 2565.

Gironde. 322, 1306; 346, 1573; 356, 1668; 366, 1776; 366, 1785; 383, 1959; 383, 1963; 384, 1971; 384, 1974; 387, 2001; 387, 2004; 388, 2011; 395, 2094; 398, 2123; 399, 2141; 402, 2174; 402, 2180; 405, 2217; 406, 2226; 414, 2300; 443, 2590; 614, 4312.

Haute-Garonne. 329, 1379; 341, 1521; 346, 1570; 347, 1581; 360, 1718; 361, 1730; 387, 2008; 388, 2011; 389, 2025; 390, 2035; 402, 2180; 412, 2276.

Haute-Vienne. 358, 1689; 382, 1951; 383, 1967; 387, 2006; 388, 2015; 395, 2094; 403, 2186; 520, 3349.

Indre. 316, 1256; 323, 1314; 330, 1391; 341, 1521; 346, 1567; 347, 1583; 354, 1652; 363, 1741; 377, 1905; 378, 1912; 386, 1991; 387, 2004; 394, 2082; 404, 2022; 415, 2312; 520, 3350.

Indre-et-Loire. 329, 1381; 360, 1718; 360, 1719; 368, 1795; 374, 1858; 377, 1905; 386, 1991; 398, 2123; 399, 2147; 402, 2180; 415, 2312; 418, 2236; 454, 2699; 455, 2721; 456, 2727; 520, 3350; 599, 4145.

Landes. 328, 1368; 344, 1546; 347, 1578; 347, 1585; 357, 1678; 380, 1927; 383, 1963; 386, 1997; 392, 2064; 398, 2123; 399, 2144; 400, 2151; 403, 2186; 406, 2226; 428, 2433; 438, 2541; 527, 3427.

Lot. 345, 1556; 349, 1606; 358, 1689; 374, 1867; 381, 1936; 381, 1940; 392, 2064; 393, 2075; 405, 2214; 412, 2276; 415, 2312.

Lot-et-Garonne. 316, 1260; 344, 1551; 355, 1662; 359, 1706; 363, 1739; 365, 1771; 373, 1844; 376, 1892; 383, 1963; 385, 1981; 390, 2042; 391, 2045; 392, 2064; 395, 2094; 403, 2188; 404, 2202.

Maine-et-Loire. 320, 1291; 331, 1407; 354, 1652; 357, 1674; 360, 1718; 374,
    1854; 382, 1954; 391, 2046-2047; 391, 2051; 397, 2115; 400, 2151; 410,
    2260; 420, 2349; 426, 2409; 433, 2489; 434, 2496; 435, 2499; 439, 2545;
    443, 2587; 445, 2606; 454, 2699; 466, 2835; 466, 2840; 471, 2886; 478,
    2950; 479, 2959; 482, 2991; 483, 3004; 490, 3068; 495, 3114; 501, 3170;
    502, 3175; 505, 3195; 507, 3205; 513, 3259; 518, 3321; 526, 3413; 527,
    3427; 542, 3596; 554, 3730; 575, 3913.
Vendée. 330, 1396; 347, 1581; 354, 1653; 355, 1665; 360, 1712; 361, 1730;
    366, 1782; 375, 1875; 381, 1946; 382, 1952; 385, 1982; 386, 1995; 387,
    2006; 387, 2007; 389, 2022; 392, 2060; 393, 2071; 394, 2092; 395, 2097;
    396, 2109; 403, 2187; 407, 2233; 412, 2277; 508, 3212; 512, 3250; 520, 3349.
Vienne. 317, 1269; 342, 1526; 346, 1571; 351, 1624; 352, 1634; 358, 1691;
    368, 1796; 373, 1844; 385, 1982; 387, 2001; 395, 2094; 399, 2137; 458,
    2749; 481, 2981; 491, 3076; 503, 3182; 520, 3349.

Paris. 328, 1360; 343, 1535; 344, 1546; 345, 1560; 361, 1726; 363, 1739; 381,
    1937; 384, 1968; 430, 2447; 457, 2738; 460, 2770; 617, 4353.
Seine. 324, 1323; 338, 1474; 355, 1662; 355, 1663; 368, 1796.
Jura. 342, 1525; 455, 2711; 459, 2758.
Loire-Inférieure. 388, 2011; 395, 2097; 396, 2103; 399, 2141; 407, 2233;
    431, 2467.
Loiret. 342, 1525; 348, 1588.
Marne. 428, 2433; 429, 2443; 440, 2558; 526, 3418.
Morbihan. 321, 1299; 428, 2434; 446, 2623.
Pas-de-Calais. 325, 1336; 342, 1531; 520, 3353; 537, 3549.
Sarthe. 358, 1693; 419, 2343; 454, 2709; 511, 3247; 516, 3297; 516, 3300;
    517, 3310; 520, 3348.
Seine-et-Oise. 315, 1250; 341, 1519; 383, 1959; 447, 2634; 447, 2635; 481,
    2982.

Aisne. 315, 1247; 458, 2749.
Calvados. 516, 3300; 530, 3469.
Côte-d'Or. 514, 3271; 518, 3319.
Ille-et-Vilaine. 322, 1303; 520, 3350.
Loir-et-Cher. 344, 1550; 346, 1567.
Seine-Inférieure. 445, 2608; 460, 2770.
Yonne. 327, 1358.

Ain. 426, 2413.
Aude. 412, 2274.
Eure. 338, 1484.
Haute-Loire. 333, 1421.
Isère. 333, 1419.
Manche. 333, 1425.
Mayenne. 518, 3321.
Meurthe. 482, 2999.

Meuse. 337, 1462.
Moselle. 325, 1334.
Nièvre. 321, 1300.
Nord. 355, 1663.
Oise. 349, 1603.
Seine-et-Marne. 358, 1696; 361, 1724; 363, 1744.
Somme. 437, 2530.
Vaucluse. 337, 1466.

Hautes-Alpes. 524, 3390.
Haut-Rhin. 542, 3596.
Orne. 520, 3352.
Sambre-et-Meuse. 533, 3510.

BIBLIOGRAPHY

I. MANUSCRIPT SOURCES

A. PUBLIC COLLECTIONS

1. Paris

Archives Nationales:
   Cartons: AA 44; AA 64. AE II, 1475. AF III: 1-17, 20A, 21D, 71,
      75, 112, 296, 314-637. Bᵃ 13. C 347; C 353. F⁷: 3832, 4774, 6707,
      6715. F¹⁷: 1021ᴬ, 1055, 1275, 1279.
   Registres AF III* 116, 118.
Archives de l'Institut de France:
   *Procès-Verbaux de la Classe d'Histoire et de Littérature Ancienne An
      XI, An XII.*
Archives de l'Opéra:
   Cartons: A 44, A 49, A 50.
   Registres: 116, 117, 121.
Archives de la Préfecture de Police à Paris:
   Liasse 49777.
Archives du Bureau des Longitudes:
   Procès-Verbaux des Séances 1795-1804.
Archives du Département de la Seine:
   Registres des Actes de Décès, 1821, 1824.
   Registres des Actes de Mariage, 1831.
   Registres des Actes de Naissance, 1797.
Archives du Ministère des Affaires Etrangères:
   Correspondance politique, Gênes, 170, 33.
   Correspondance politique, Hollande, 590: 155, 240, 294.
   Mémoires et Documents, 1414 (Affaires intérieures, 674).
Archives historiques du Ministère de la Guerre:
   Registres: B* 3: 119, 124, 125, 186. G 2.
Archives du Musée du Louvre:
   *Correspondance de l'Administration du Musée Central des Arts An V-
      An VIII.*

*Procès-Verbaux de l'Administration du Musée Central des Arts An V–
An VIII* (2 vols.).
Bibliothèque Nationale:
    MSS français, Nouvelles Acquisitions: 9533, 123, 124, 125; 21562-21566;
        21887; Collection Alexandre Bixio.
Bibliothèque de l'Institut de France:
    MSS 1275: 85-90.
Bibliothèque du Muséum d'Histoire Naturelle:
    Procès-Verbaux des séances, vols. ii, iii.
    MSS 292; 309; 1975, tome v, 747; 1998, tome ii, 202-203.
Bibliothèque du Protestantisme française:
    Collection Viénot.

2. French Provinces

Archives du Département de la Loire Inférieure, at Nantes:
    Série E, Etat Civil, Nantes, Parish Register Saint-Saturnin.
Archives du Département de Maine-et-Loire, at Angers:
    Séries C 192; D 23; E 3773; L 152-153; L 918.
    Parish Registers: Faveraye, Le May-sur-Evre, Montigné-sur-Moine,
        Notre-Dame de Cholet, Notre-Dame de Montfaucon-sur-Moine,
        Trinité d'Angers.
Archives du Département de la Vendée, at La Roche-sur-Yon:
    Parish Registers: Saint-Jean-Baptiste de Montaigu, Mouchamps.
Bibliothèque municipale de la Ville d'Angers:
    Archives Anciennes de la Mairie d'Angers, Registres de la Capitation,
        CC 169, 170, 171.
    MSS SM 13; SM 78; 572; 1031; 1035.
Bibliothèque municipale de la Ville de Nantes:
    Autographes 238/85.
    MSS Dugast-Matifeux 44=41.
Bibliothèque municipale de la Ville de Reims:
    Collection P. Tarbé, Carton XXIII, 156.
Bibliothèque municipale de la Ville de Saint-Dié:
    MSS 75.
Bibliothèque nationale et universitaire de Strasbourg:
    MSS 1539.
Mairie de Faveraye, at Faveraye, Maine-et-Loire:
    Parish Registers.
Mairie de Faye, at Faye, Maine-et-Loire:
    Parish Registers.
Mairie de La Bruffière, at La Bruffière, Vendée:
    Parish Registers.
Mairie de Montaigu, at Montaigu, Vendée:
    Parish Registers, Saint-Jean-Baptiste de Montaigu.

3. London

British Museum:
  Additional Manuscripts 21513: 48, 49, 82, 83, 84, 85, 86, 87.
Public Record Office:
  F. O. 27/48, 27/49, 27/50.

B. PRIVATE COLLECTIONS

Collection Loyau, at Pulteau, Bazoges-en-Pareds, Vendée.
Collection Pasquier, at Externat Saint-Maurille, Angers, Maine-et-Loire.
Collection Pilastre, at Salidieu, Mareuil-sur-Lay, Vendée.

II. WRITINGS OF REVELLIERE-LÉPEAUX

A. PUBLISHED WORKS

Lettre à un seigneur d'Anjou, accusé de tromper le peuple (Angers, 1789). Pamphlet.

Adresse à la noblesse et au clergé de la Province d'Anjou (Angers, 1789). Pamphlet, included in *Correspondance de MM. les députés des communes de la Province d'Anjou, avec leurs commettans* (Angers, 10 vols., 1789-1791), vol. i.

Plaintes et désirs des communes tant de ville que de campagne (S. l. n. d. [Angers, 1789]). Pamphlet, included in *Correspondance de MM. les députés. . .*, vol. i.

Doléances, voeux et pétitions, pour les représentants des paroisses de*** aux assemblées de la nation pour les Etats-Généraux, rédigés par un laboureur, un syndic et un bailli de campagne (Angers, 1789). Pamphlet, written in collaboration with Pilastre and Leclerc, included in *Correspondance de MM. les députés. . .*, vol. i.

Opinion sur la sanction royale prononcée à l'Assemblée nationale, dans la séance du 2 septembre 1789 (S. l. n. d. [Paris, 1789]). Pamphlet.

Adresse aux citoyens du département de Maine-et-Loire (Angers, 1791). Pamphlet; authorship not indicated.

Les Citoyens de la ville d'Angers à leurs frères, les citoyens de la ville de Paris (Angers, 1791). Pamphlet.

Département de Mayenne et Loire — Roi des François (Angers, 1791). Pamphlet, with twenty signatures.

Rapport du voyage des commissaires de la Société des Amis de la Constitution d'Angers au club ambulant établi dans les Mauges, fait à la séance du Ier avril, l'an IV de la liberté [1792] *(S. l. n. d.).* Pamphlet.

Procès-Verbal de la cérémonie funèbre qui a été célébrée à Angers en l'honneur de Jacques-Guillaume Simoneau, maire d'Etampes, mort pour le maintien des lois, le 10 avril 1792 (S. l. n. d.). Pamphlet.

A mes frères d'armes, les citoyens composant la légion du district de Vihiers, département de Maine et Loire (Orléans, 1792). Pamphlet.

La Société des Amis de la Liberté et de l'Egalité d'Angers à celle de Paris (Angers, 1791). Pamphlet, signed *La Révellière, Cordier, Papin.*

Convention Nationale. *Opinion sur la question de savoir si Louis XVI peut être mis en jugement* (Paris, 1792). Pamphlet.

Convention Nationale. *Opinion sur la question de l'appel au peuple du jugement de Louis* (Paris, 1793). Pamphlet.

"Le Cromwellisme," in *Chronique de Paris*, 11 février 1793, no. 42, p. 166, and in MLL, vol. iii, pp. 3-6.

Louis-Marie Revellière-Lépeaux . . . à ses commetans (Paris, 1793). Pamphlet.

Déclaration des citoyens La Revellière-Lépeaux, Pilastre, Leclerc et Le Maignan, relativement aux évènemens du 31 mai dernier (Laval, An II [1793]). Pamphlet.

Convention Nationale. *Discours sur les relations extérieures, prononcé dans la séance du 26 Ventôse* (Paris, An III). Pamphlet.

Convention Nationale. *Opinion sur le jury constitutionnaire, prononcée dans la séance du 24 Thermidor* (Paris, An III). Pamphlet.

Convention Nationale. *Rapport et projet de décret concernant l'ordre des délibérations et la police du Corps législatif, présentés à la Convention nationale, au nom de la commission des onze* (Paris, An III). Pamphlet.

Le Directoire exécutif aux habitants des départements de l'Ouest [February, 1796], in Debidour, *Recueil des Actes du Directoire exécutif* (Paris, 4 vols., 1910-1917), vol. i, pp. 659-661.

Proclamation du Directoire exécutif aux Lyonnais [April, 1796], in Debidour, *Recueil des Actes . . .*, vol. ii (1911), pp. 166-168.

La Vérité (Paris, s.d. [1796]). Pamphlet.

Réflexions sur le culte, les cérémonies civiles et les fêtes nationales, lues à l'Institut le 12 Floréal An V (1er mai 1797), dans la séance de la classe des sciences morales et politiques (Paris, An V). Pamphlet, included in MLL, vol. iii, pp. 7-27; in *Révolution française, Revue*, vol. ii, pp. 1076-1100; in Dubroca, Jean-François, *Discours sur divers sujets de morale et sur les fêtes nationales, précédés des Réflexions sur le culte, les cérémonies, etc. lues à l'Institut national, le 12 Floréal An V, par L.-M. Reveillère-Lépeaux* (Paris, An VII), pp. 1-45; and in *Opuscules moraux de L.-M. Revellière-Lépeaux et de J.-B. Leclerc* (Paris, An VI).

Betrachtungen über den Gottesdienst, bürgerliche Gebräuche und National=Feste, aus dem Französischen übersetzt von C. Fabricius (Hamburg, 1797). Translation of *Réflexions sur le culte*. . . .

"Réponses de La Revellière-Lépeaux, président du Directoire exécutif, dans la séance publique du 10 Fructidor An V, au discours de Visconti, ministre plénipotentiaire de la république cisalpine, et à celui du général Bernadotte, présentant les drapeaux conquis par l'armée d'Italie," in *Le Moniteur*, 13 Fructidor An V, and in MLL, vol. iii, pp. 49-56.

Discours prononcé par . . ., président du Directoire exécutif, à la fête de la République, le 1er Vendémiaire An VI. Discours prononcé à la cérémonie funèbre exécutée en mémoire du général Hoche, au Champs de

Mars, le 10 Vendémiaire An VI (Paris, An VI).   Pamphlet, included in MLL, vol. iii, pp. 40-44, 45-48, and in *Opuscules moraux de L.-M. Revellière-Lépeaux et de J.-B. Leclerc.*

Essai sur les moyens de faire participer l'universalité des spectateurs à tout ce qui se pratique dans les fêtes nationales, lu à la Classe des Sciences Morales et Politiques de l'Institut de France, dans la séance du 22 Vendémiaire An VIe de la République (Paris, An VI).   Pamphlet, included in MLL, vol. iii, pp. 28-39, and in *Opuscules moraux . . . .*

Du Panthéon et d'un théâtre national (Paris, An VI).   Pamphlet, included in *Opuscules moraux . . . .*

Opuscules moraux de L.-M. Revellière-Lépeaux et de J.-B. Leclerc (Paris, Pluviôse An VI).

Adresse du Directoire exécutif aux électeurs sur le choix qu'ils auront à faire dans leurs nominations des législateurs de l'An VI, 2 Germinal [March 22, 1798].   Printed in *Messages, arrêtés et proclamations du Directoire exécutif* (Paris, s.d., 7 vols.), vol. v, pp. 1-4.

Des Dangers de la résolution proposée sur l'enceinte des deux Conseils (Paris, An VI).   Pamphlet.

Le Costume des Représentans conforme à la religion de nos pères [signed] *Sandalo-Philos* (Paris, s. d.).   Pamphlet.

Au Citoyen Texier-Olivier, membre du Conseil des Cinq-Cents. Mémoire réfutant une lettre adressée par Texier, député d'Indre-et-Loire, au Directoire exécutif, à l'occasion de destitutions de fonctionnaires publics faites dans ce département...Signé N.-E. Lacour (S. l. n. d.).   Pamphlet, included in MLL, vol. iii, pp. 64-92.

"Lettre adressée au rédacteur du Moniteur sur la signification du mot représentant du peuple," in *Le Moniteur*, 10 Ventôse An VII, and in MLL, vol. iii, pp. 57-63.

Proclamations du Directoire exécutif aux français relatives aux assemblées primaires de l'An VII, 17 Ventôse An VII [March 7, 1799].   Reprinted in *Messages, arrêtés et proclamations du Directoire exécutif*, vol. vi, pp. 305-308.

Réponses de L.-M. Revellière-Lépeaux aux dénonciations portées au Corps législatif contre lui et ses anciens collègues, 15 Thermidor An VII (Paris, 1799).   Reprinted in MLL, vol. iii, pp. 113-176.

Rapport fait par les citoyens Hallé, Desessarts, Toulongeon, Revellière-Lépeaux, Lesblond et Camus, commissaires chargés par l'Institut national des sciences et arts de l'examen des mémoires envoyés au concours proposé par le gouvernement sur les questions relatives aux cérémonies funéraires et aux lieux des sépultures. Jugement porté par l'Institut et proclamation des prix (Paris, s. d.).   Pamphlet.

L.-M. Revelliere-lépeaux to François Gérard, two autograph, signed letters, written from La Rousselière, 12 Messidor An XIII [July 2, 1805] and 21 Janvier 1807, in *Correspondance de François Gérard* (Paris, 1867), pp. 298-300.

"Notice sur divers objets trouvés dans une tourbière de la commune de Buire," in *Annales du Muséum d'Histoire Naturelle* (Paris, 1807), vol. ix.

"Notice des monuments celtiques visités dans le département de Maine-et-Loire, par Louis-Marie Revellière-Lépeaux, J.-B. Leclerc et Urbain Pilastre, en Octobre 1806," in *Mémoires de l'Académie Celtique* (Paris, 6 vols. in 5, 1807-1810), vol. ii (1808), pp. 169-203.

"Extrait d'une lettre de M. Revellière-Lépeaux, sur une hache de pierre et autres monuments druidiques," in *Mémoires de l'Académie Celtique,* vol. ii (1808), pp. 458-462.

"Notice du patois vendéen, adressée à l'Académie Celtique, et extraite d'un Essai sur le département de la Vendée; lue à la Classe des Sciences Morales et Politiques de l'Institut National, en l'an onze," in *Mémoires de l'Académie Celtique,* vol. iii (1809), pp. 267-290, 370-398.

Notice du patois vendéen, précédée d'une biographie de l'auteur par Ch. Dugast-Matifeux (Paris, Niort, Fontenay, 1867, 1869).

Mémoires de Larevellière-Lépeaux, membre du Directoire exécutif de la République française et de l'Institut national, publiés par son fils sur le manuscrit autographe de l'auteur et suivis de pièces justificatives et de correspondances inédites (Paris, 1873), 3 vols. in-8°.

"La Théophilanthropie par Larevellière-Lépeaux," reprinted from MLL, vol. ii, pp. 157-184, and vol. iii, pp. 7-27, in *La Révolution française, Revue,* 14 Juin 1882, pp. 1076-1100.

"La Première Rencontre de l'Ancien Régime et de la Révolution, La Revellière-Lépeaux et le Marquis de Dreux-Brézé," reprinted from MLL, vol. i, pp. 66-69, in *La Révolution française, Revue,* 14 Novembre 1883, pp. 408-411.

"Extraits des Mémoires de la Revellière-Lépeaux," reprinted from MLL, vol. i, pp. 21, 40-44, and vol. ii, p. 462, in *Echos du Bocage Vendéen,* 1886, No. I, pp. 193-197.

Mémoires de Larevellière-Lépeaux, membre du Directoire exécutif de la République française et de l'Institut national, publiés par son fils sur le manuscrit autographe de l'auteur et suivis des pièces justificatives et de correspondances inédites (Paris, 1895), 3 vols. in-8°.

B. UNPUBLISHED WORKS (NOT INCLUDING CORRESPONDENCE)

Observations envoyées par la municipalité de Faye au district de Brissac, touchant les chemins pour être jointes aux instructions demandées à la ditte municipalité, 7 Mars 1788.   Archives de Maine-et-Loire, Série C 192, fols. 17 r., v., 18 r.

Plan de monuments pour perpetuer le ressouvenir des evenements d'italie, 7 brumaire an 6 [October 28, 1797], 1 p. in-4°. Bibliothèque de la Ville d'Angers, MS 572.

Quelques idées sur la Morale, 3 pp. Collection Pasquier.

Poésies fugitifs, Bibliothèque de la Ville d'Angers, MSS SM 13:
"A Mlle Ernestine Darlot."

" A Clémentine."

" Bouquet a ma femme a la Rousseliere 1807, nos voisins de Buglin dinant a la maison."

" Couplets faits en conduisant mes vandangeurs dans leur travail sur le coteau de la cave aux bords du layon commune de faye en maine et loire le dernier jour de mes vandanges le 10 7bre 1807."

" Morceaux écrits pendant mon refuge a Buyre pendant la terreur."

" Romance, sujet tiré du roman anglais le vicaire de wakefield."

" Stances adressées a un couple de tourterelles perchées sur les arbres du jardin des tuileries."

Rapport à son Excellence le ministre de l'intérieur du royaume d'Italie sur l'état du jardin d'agriculture de l'université royale de Bologne, par J. Bertolini, à Milan chez Jean Silvestoi, 1812, traduit par M. Revelliere Lépeaux. 24 *feuillets.* Bibliothèque du Muséum d'Histoire Naturelle, MS 292.

Notice sur ma vie jusqu'en 1817. BN, MSS fr., Nouvelles Acquisitions 21565, fols. 78-85.

III. WRITINGS ABOUT REVELLIERE-LÉPEAUX

Audra, M. E. " La Réveillière-Lépeaux," in *Revue de l'Anjou* (Angers), Nouvelle Série, vol. xxxi (1895), pp. 123-129.

Aulard, Alphonse. " Mémoires de La Revellière-Lépeaux," in *Revue d'Histoire moderne et contemporaine,* vol. xxviii (1895), pp. 278-283.

Bémont, Ch. " Mémoires de La Revellière-Lépeaux," in *Revue historique,* vol. lvii (1895), pp. 354-355.

Berthe, J. A. " Louis Marie Revelliere-lépeaux," in *Extraits historiques sur l'Anjou et le Département de Maine-et-Loire* (2 vols., Bibliothèque de la Ville d'Angers, MS 1031), vol. ii (1846), fol. 81 r.

Bienvenu, Léon. " La Révellière-Lépeaux," in *Le Temps,* 14 Juin 1886.

Biographie moderne, Lives of remarkable characters who have distinguished themselves from the commencement of the French Revolution to the present time (London, 3 vols., 1811), vol. ii, pp. 243-246.

Biographie nouvelle des contemporains (Paris, 20 vols., 1820-1825), vol. xi (1823), pp. 28-34.

Biré, Edmond. " Larevellière-Lépeaux," in *Mémoires et souvenirs (1789-1830) La Révolution, l'Empire et la Restauration* (Paris, 3 vols., 1896), vol. ii, pp. 45-82.

Blordier-Langlois. " La Revellière-Lépeaux," in *Angers et le département de Maine et Loire, de 1787 à 1830* (Angers, 2 vols., 1837), vol. ii, pp. 229-236.

Bougler, M. " Larevellière-Lépeaux," in *Biographie des députés de l'Anjou depuis l'Assemblée Constituante jusqu'en 1815* (Paris, 2 vols., 1865), vol. i, pp. 170-222, reprinted from " Larevellière-Lépeaux," in *Revue de l'Anjou et de Maine-et-Loire,* 4e Année, vol. ii, pp. 336-374.

Bougler, M. Answer to a letter of O. Larevellière-Lépeaux, in *Revue de l'Anjou et de Maine-et-Loire,* 5e Année, vol. i, pp. 242-245.

Boursin, E. et Challamel, A. "La Réveillère-Lépeaux," *Dictionnaire de la Révolution française* (Paris, 1893), p. 400.

Camerlynck, Henri. "La Théophilanthropie et les Théophilanthropes," in *Mémoires de l'Académie des Sciences, des Lettres et des Arts d'Amiens 1897* (Amiens, 1898), pp. 145-176.

Camerlynck, Henri. "Les Mémoires de Larevellière-Lépeaux," in *Mémoires de l'Académie des Sciences, des Lettres et des Arts d'Amiens* (Amiens), vol. xlv (1898, published 1899), pp. 185-218.

Chanonie, C. de la. *Larevellière-Lépeaux d'après ses Mémoires* (Vannes, 1895), reprinted from the *Revue du Bas-Poitou* (Vannes), vol. viii (1895), pp. 197-212.

Charavay, Etienne. *La Revelliere-Lépeaux et ses mémoires* (Paris, 1895), reprinted from *Revue bleue*, 4e Série, vol. iii (1895), pp. 104-111, 146-152.

Cosnier, L. Answer to a letter of O. Larevellière-Lépeaux, in the *Revue de l'Anjou et de Maine-et-Loire*, 5e Année (1856), vol. i, pp. 125-128.

Cuissard, Ch. *Le Troubadour de Buglain et ses Amis* (Orléans, 1894), reprinted from *Bulletin de la Société d'Agriculture, Sciences, Belles-Lettres et Arts d'Orléans*, vol. xxxii (1894), pp. 170-195.

Daudet, Ernest. "Larevellière-Lépeaux," in *Poussière du Passé* (Paris, 1896), pp. 62-68.

Debidour, A. "La Révellière-Lépeaux," in *La Grande Encyclopédie* (Paris, 31 vols., *s. d.* [1886-1902]), vol. xxi, p. 961.

Despaze, Joseph. "Revelliere Lepaux," in *The Five Men; or, a review of the proceedings and principles of the Executive Directory of France: together with the lives of its present members, S. F. L. H. Letourneur, J. Rewbell, L. M. Revelliere Lepaux, P. F. I. N. Barras, and L. N. M. Carnot, translated from the French of Joseph Despaze by John Stoddart* (London, 1797), pp. 55-78.

Destrem, Jean. "Les Mémoires de Larevellière-Lépeaux," in *Revue historique*, 4e Année, vol. x (1879), pp. 68-91.

Dugast-Matifeux, Ch. (editor). "Demande de renseignements historiques, archéologiques et statistiques sur la Vendée, par La Revellière-Lépeaux," in *Echos du Bocage Vendéen*, (Montaigu, Nantes), 2e Année (1885), No. VI, pp. 164-168.

——. "Fête de Montaigu, en l'honneur de La Revellière-Lépeaux," in *Echos du Bocage Vendéen*, 3e Année (1886), No. II, pp. 225-240.

——. *Notice du patois vendéen, précédée d'une biographie de l'auteur par Ch. Dugast-Matifeux* (Paris, Niort, Fontenay, 1867, 1869).

——. *Notice sur Revellière-Lépeaux, Député aux Etats-Généraux, Membre de la Convention nationale, Directeur de la République française. Nouvelle édition, revue et augmentée, publiée pour l'inauguration de son buste, sous la présidence de M. René Goblet Ministre de l'Instruction publique et des Cultes à Montaigu-Vendée, le 14 Juin 1886* (Paris et Nantes, Niort et Fontenay, 1886).

Durozoir, "Larévellière-L'Epaux," in Michaud (editor), *Biographie universelle, ancienne et moderne. Supplément, ou suite de l'histoire, par ordre alphabétique, de la vie publique et privée de tous les hommes qui se sont fait remarquer par leurs écrits, leurs actions, leurs talents, leurs vertus ou leurs crimes. Ouvrage entièrement neuf, rédigé par une société de gens de lettres et de savants* (Paris, 85 vols., 1811-62), vol. lxx (1842), pp. 267-284.

The Encyclopedia Britannica, a dictionary of arts, sciences, literature and general information (Cambridge, New York, Eleventh Edition, 1911), vol. xvi, p. 216, " La Révellière-Lépeaux."

Fête patriotique de Montaigu (Vendée) en l'honneur de La Revellière-Lépeaux (14 Juin 1886) ornée d'un portrait de M. René Goblet, ministre de l'Instruction publique, des Beaux-Arts et des Cultes et du buste de l'Ancien Directeur de la République française (Nantes, 1886), reprinted from *Phare de la Loire* (Nantes), 16-17 Juin 1886.

Fleischmann, H. " La Révellière Lépeaux et Volney, lettres inédites," in *Annales révolutionnaires*, 3ᵉ Année (1910), pp. 581-584.

Goblet, René. "Discours prononcé par M. René Goblet, ministre de l'Instruction publique, des beaux-arts et des cultes, à Montaigu (Vendée), le 14 Juin, pour l'inauguration du buste de La Révellière-Lépeaux," in the *Journal officiel de la République française, Jeudi, 17 Juin 1886,* and in *Echos du Bocage Vendéen,* 1886, No. II.

Goldsmith, Lewis. *The revolutionary Plutarch, exhibiting the most distinguished characters, literary, military and political in the recent annals of the French Republic, the greater part from the original information of a gentleman resident at Paris* (London, Fourth Edition, 3 vols., 1806), vol. ii, p. 129.

Grabit (Joseph Despaze). *Vie privée des cinq membres du Directoire; ou les puissans tels qu'ils sont* (Paris, s. d. [1796]), pp. 4-5.

Grille, François. *Revellière-Lépeaux, essai sur sa vie et ses oeuvres* (Angers, 1840), read at Angers on April 22, 1840, at the Société Industrielle.

Grün, Albert. " La Revellière-Lépeaux et Napoléon," in *Feuilles d'Histoire du XVIIᵉ au XXᵉ siècle,* 3ᵉ Année, vol. vi (1911), No. VIII, pp. 155-163.

Gubler, F. *Larevellière-Lépeaux* (Paris, 1859), reprinted from *Biographie universelle* (Michaud, editor), *ancienne et moderne, ou histoire, par ordre alphabétique, de la vie publique et privée de tous les hommes qui se sont fait remarquer par leurs écrits, leurs actions, leurs talents, leurs vertus ou leurs crimes. Nouvelle édition, revue, corrigée et considérablement augmentée d'articles omis ou nouveaux, ouvrage rédigé par une société de gens de lettres et de savants* (Paris, 45 vols., 1854-1865), vol. xxiii, pp. 248-260.

Houel, Georges. *La Revellière-Lepeaux en Sologne* (Orléans, 1904).

L'Intermédiaire des Chercheurs et Curieux, 20 Novembre 1893; 10 Janvier 1894; 20 Mai 1906; 30 Mars, 30 Avril, 20 Mai, 10 Juin, 20 Juillet 1914; 10, 20, 30 Août, 10, 20, 30 September 1926.

Kuscinski, Auguste. "La Revellière-Lépeaux," in *Dictionnaire des Conventionnels* (Paris, 1916), pp. 373-376.

Laborie, L. de Lanzac de. "Le Journal d'un Constituant et les Mémoires d'un Directeur, d'après deux récentes publications," in *Le Correspondant* (Paris), vol. clxxviii, Nouvelle Série vol. cxlii (1895), pp. 334-339.

Larévellière, Victorin. "Larévellière-Lépeaux (1753-1824)," in *Andegaviana* (Angers), 10e Série (1911), pp. 13-20, in *L'Anjou historique*, vol. x (1909), pp. 254-261, and in the *Journal de Maine-et-Loire et de la Mayenne*, 7 Février 1843.

Larousse, Pierre (editor). "Larevellière-Lépeaux," in *Grand Dictionnaire universel du XIXe siècle* (Paris, 17 vols., 1866-1890), vol. x, p. 197.

Lenotre, G. "La Révellière-Lépeaux," in *Le Temps*, 6 Mars 1906, and in *Vieilles Maisons, vieux papiers*, 5e Série (Paris, 1924), pp. 85-117.

Louvet. "Une lettre de Louvet (1796) au Citoyen La Revellière, Membre du Directoire exécutif, au Luxembourg," in *La Nouvelle Revue rétrospective*, XVIIe Année, No. 90 (10 Décembre 1901), pp. 429-430.

Mahul, A. (editor). "Revellière-Lépeaux," in *Annuaire nécrologique, ou complément annuel et continuation de toutes les biographies, ou dictionnaires historiques; contenant la vie de tous les hommes remarquables par leurs actes ou leurs productions, morts dans le cours de chaque année, à commencer de 1820* (Paris, 7 vols., 1821-1826), 5e Année (1824, published in December, 1825), pp. 252-266.

Mathiez, Albert. *Lettres de Volney à La Révellière-Lépeaux (1795-1798)* (Le Puy, 1910), reprinted from *Annales révolutionnaires*, 1910, pp. 161-194.

Meinadier, Jean. *La Revellière-Lépeaux*, doctoral dissertation presented before the Faculté de Théologie Protestante de Paris, 1928. Unpublished.

Merland, C. *Illustrations Vendéennes—Larevellière-Lépeaux* (Niort, Paris, 1869), reprinted from *Mémoires de la Société de Statistique, Sciences et Arts de Deux-Sèvres*.

Meynier, Albert. *Un Représentant de la bourgeoisie angevine à l'Assemblée Nationale Constituante et à la Convention Nationale—L.M. La Revellière-Lépeaux (1753-1795)* (Angers, Paris, 1905).

Phare de la Loire, Journal quotidien, politique, littéraire et commercial (Nantes), "M. Goblet à Montaigu," Mercredi, 16 Juin 1886; "Les Mémoires de la Revellière-Lépeaux," Jeudi-Vendredi, 17-18 Juin 1886.

Port, M. Célestin. "Révellière-Lépeaux," in *Dictionnaire historique, géographique et biographique de Maine-et-Loire* (Paris, 3 vols., 1874-1878), vol. iii, pp. 247-249.

Regnard, E. "Larevellière de Lépeaux," in *Nouvelle Biographie générale depuis les temps les plus reculés jusqu'à nos jours, avec les renseignements bibliographiques et l'indication des sources à consulter* (Paris, 46 vols., 1862-1866), vol. xxix, columns 589-597.

Robert, A. (editor). "La Révellière-Lépeaux," in *Dictionnaire des parlementaires français, comprenant tous les membres des assemblées françaises, et tous les ministres français depuis le 1er Mai 1789 jusqu'au 1er Mai 1889* (Paris, 5 vols., 1889-1891), vol. iii (1890), pp. 594-596.

Robinet, Robert et Chaplain (editors). "La Révellière-Lépeaux," in *Dictionnaire historique et biographique de la Révolution et de l'Empire (1789-1815)* (Parıs, 2 vols., s.d. [1899]), vol. ii, pp. 324-325.

Rocheterie, M. de la. "Mémoires de La Revellière-Lépeaux," in *Revue des questions historiques,* vol. lviii (1895), pp. 283-284.

Roussel, Auguste. "La Réveillère-Lépeaux," in *L'Univers* (Paris), Jeudi, 17 Juin 1886.

Stephens, H. Morse. "Recent Memoirs of the French Directory," in *The American Historical Review,* vol. i (1896), No. III, pp. 473-489.

Uzureau (editor). "Larévellière-Lépeaux dans la Vendée Angevine (1792)," in *L'Anjou historique,* 14e Année (1914), pp. 365-378.

——. "La Révellière-Lépeaux et le 'cahier' de Faye (1789)," in *L'Anjou historique,* 29e Année (1929), pp. 221-224.

——. "La Soeur de Larévellière-Lépeaux (1749-1822)," in *L'Anjou historique,* 35e Année (1935), pp. 199-206.

——. "Une Lettre de Bourmont à Larévellière-Lépeaux (1796)," in *L'Anjou historique,* 22e Année (1922), pp. 168-170.

Viénot, John. "Un honnête homme sous le Directoire, La Revellière-Lépeaux," in *La Revue Chrétienne,* 63e Année, IVe Série, vol. i (1916), pp. 367-379, 447-453, 551-561. The concluding chapters of this book remain in manuscript.

Vivier, Alphonse. "Inauguration du buste de La Revellière-Lépeaux à Montaigu (Vendée)," in *La Révolution française, Revue,* 6e Année, vol. xi, No. I (14 Juillet 1886), pp. 32-40.

Vogüé, Eugène-Melchior de. "Un Plaidoyer pour le Directoire, Les Mémoires de Lareveillère-Lépeaux," in *Revue des Deux Mondes,* vol. cxxvii (1895), pp. 662-678.

Welvert, Eugène. "La Scellé La Révellière-Lépeaux," in *Feuilles d'Histoire du XVIIe au XXe siècle,* 3e Année, vol. vi (1911), pp. 72-82.

——. "Une Lettre de Bourmont," in *Feuilles d'Histoire du XVIIe au XXe siècle,* 6e Année, vol. xi (1914), p. 182.

ICONOGRAPHY

This list of busts, medallions, paintings, prints, and engravings of Revelliere-lépeaux has been compiled from the following public and private collections:

Bibliothèque Nationale, Bureau d'Estampes, Paris
British Museum, London
Collection Comte Jean de Villoutreys, Angers, Maine-et-Loire
Collection Paul Clemenceau, L'Aubraie, Réorthe, Vendée
Musée Carnavalet, Paris
Musée d'Angers, Angers
Musée du Jeu de Paume, Versailles.

I. Busts

A. David d'Angers. 1823.
   1. Marble. Musée d'Angers. See *supra*, p. 240.
   2. Bronze. Musée d'Angers.

B. Eude, Louis-Adolphe. 1883.
   1. Marble. Musée du Jeu de Paume.
   2. Bronze. Montaigu, Vendée. See *supra*, frontispiece.
   3. Terra cotta. Musée d'Angers.

II. Medallions

A. David d'Angers. Undated.
   Bronze, 9 cm., signed. Cadre no. 13, Musée d'Angers.

B. David d'Angers. Undated.
   Bronze, 9 cm., unsigned. Cadre no. 38, Musée d'Angers. See *supra*, p. 227.

III. Portraits in Oil

A. Gérard, François. 1795-6. Flowers by Van Spaendonck. Oil on canvas, 1m.52 x 1m.09, Musée d'Angers. See *supra*, p. 197. The Gérard portrait, used as the frontispiece of Revelliere-lépeaux's memoirs (Paris, 1895), was also reproduced in the catalogue *Le Musée d'Angers* (Paris, 1928), p. 48. The painting, shown in London in 1932, was described in the *Royal Academy of Arts, Exhibition of French Art 1200-1900, January-March 1932* (London, 1932), p. 253. A detail of the portrait appeared in *L'Illustration* of November 4, 1933, p. 308.

B. Pilastre, Madame Urbain, née Adelaide Lejay. Flowers by Van Spaendonck. Oil on canvas, copy of the Gérard portrait. Musée Carnavalet.

IV. Portraits—Prints and Engravings

A. In Folio.

1. Lithograph by Delpech of drawing by Maurin, published in *Iconographie des contemporains,* vol. ii (Paris, 1832), Plate LII. This portrait is traditionally considered a good likeness of Revelliere-lépeaux. Bibliothèque Nationale; Collection Villoutreys; Collection Clemenceau.

2. Colored engraving by Chereau, full-length portrait of Revelliere-lépeaux in Director's costume. Legend: " Reveilliere-Lépeaux. Membre du Directoire Executif avec le costume de Président. Né à Montaigu Dept. de la Vendée le vingt cinq aout 1753." Bibliothèque Nationale; Collection Villoutreys.

3. German engraving, sepia, full-length portrait of Revelliere-lépeaux in Director's costume, standing on a terrace decorated in classical fashion. Author's collection. See *supra,* p. 131.

4. Lithograph by Gibert of the Gérard portrait, published by the Imprimerie de Vᵉ Pigne, Château Angers. Legend: " La Revelliere-Lepeaux (Louis-Marie) né le 25 août 1753 à Montaigu (Vendée). L'un des trois députés du Tiers-état de la sénéchaussée d'Anjou aux Etats-généraux; président de la convention nationale; l'un des cinq membres du Directoire exécutif; Protecteur du Musée d'Angers, et l'un des Fondateurs du Jardin Botanique de cette ville." Collection Villoutreys.

5. Sketch by Eric Pape from the Gérard portrait, made to illustrate W. M. Sloane's *Life of Napoleon,* appearing first in the serial form of that work *(The Century Magazine,* 1895, p. 808) and again when the biography was published in four volumes (New York, 1896, vol. i, p. 165).

B. In Smaller Formats.

1. Lithograph by Delpech, in quarto, apparently identical with IV. A. 1 (See *supra,* p. 31), except that the artist's signature is here omitted and the lithographed signature *Revellierelépeaux* appears as a legend. This lithograph was chosen by Meynier for the frontispiece of his *Un Représentant de la bourgeoisie angevine* (Angers, Paris, 1905). Bibliothèque Nationale; Collection Villoutreys.

2. Engraving by J. B. Compagnie of drawing by F. Bonneville, published in quarto and in octavo, Paris, rue St. Jacques, no. 195. Revelliere-lépeaux in Director's costume, bust, three-quarters toward right. Legend: " Revelliere-lépeaux. Membre du Directoire. Né à Montaigu, dept. de la Vendée, le 25 août 1753." Bibliothèque Nationale; Collection Villoutreys.

3. Engraving in 1846 by Jules Perreau of drawing from life by Gabriel, published in quarto by Vignères, Paris, rue du Carrousel, no. 4. Bust, profile, of Revelliere-lépeaux as an old

man with hat and coat. Legend: "L. M. Reveilliere-Lepaux Botaniste. Dép. et Présid. à la Conv. Natle. Membre du Directoire Executif. Chef des Théophilantropes. Né en 1753. + en 1824." Bibliothèque Nationale, Collection Alexandre Bixio; Collection Villoutreys.

4. Engraving by P. Adam from the Gérard portrait, published in octavo by F. Chardon ainé, Paris, rue Hautefeuille, no. 30. Legend: "La Reveillère Lepaux." Collection Villoutreys.

5. Engraving by Couché fils, published in duodecimo by Baudouin Frères, Paris, rue de Vaugirard, no. 36. Bust of Revellière-lépeaux in Director's costume. Bibliothèque Nationale; Collection Villoutreys.

6. Engraving of Revelliere-lépeaux in Director's costume, bust, slightly toward left, oval frame, published in duodecimo. No indication of artist or editor. Legend: "Revellière-Lépeaux." Bibliothèque Nationale. This portrait is reproduced in sextodecimo in Johann Christian Dieterich's *Revolutions=Almanach von 1798* (Göttingen, 1798), p. 186.

V. CARICATURES

A. Fragonard, Th., and Massard, L. Colored engraving, 110 mm. x 160 mm., reproduced in black and white in *Réimpression de l'Ancien Moniteur* (June 8, 1797), vol. xxviii, facing p. 722. Legend: "Un Théophilantrope." Author's collection. See *supra*, p. 161.

B. Gillray, J. Colored engraving, 245 mm. x 355 mm., published by Humphrey, St. James Street, London, on June 20, 1799. Legend: "French Generals retiring on account of their health;—with Lepaux presiding in the Directorial Dispensary." Collection Villoutreys.

C. Gillray, J. Colored engraving, also printed in black and white, 170 mm. x 620 mm., published by J. Wright, no. 169 Piccadilly, London, on August 1, 1798. Legend: "New Morality, or The Promis'd Installment of the High-Priest of the Theophilanthropes, with the Homage of Leviathan and his Suite." *Anti-Jacobin Review and Magazine* (London, July, 1798), p. 114. British Museum, Caricatures, 1868-8-6761. See *supra*, p. 180.

D. Prudhon (drawing attributed to). Engraving, in quarto, of Revelliere-lépeaux, dressed in classical costume and without a hat, standing by a stone wall and looking sternly to the left. The head is in profile. Legend: "Le Directeur Reveillere Pape des Theophilantropes. Ce Burlesque Pontificat étoit placé dans le Directoire. Français de Nantes. Rapport des Onze." Author's collection.

E. Colored English engraving (artist not indicated), 240 mm. x 252 mm., published in London on April 16, 1798. Legend: "The French Mahomet (1797)." Reproduced as frontispiece of *Etrennes aux amis du Dix-huit* (Paris, An VII, 108 pp.). Exhibited at the Bibliothèque

Nationale in January-March, 1928, and reproduced in the catalogue of the exhibition, *La Révolution française* (Paris, 1928), Plate XXIII, opposite p. 209, with a description on p. 191. Bibliothèque Nationale, Etampes, Qb. 109. See *supra*, p. 156.

Brief iconographies relating to Revelliere-lépeaux are to be found in the following volumes:

American Library Association Index to Portraits contained in Printed Books and Periodicals (Washington, 1906), p. 833.

Dugast-Matifeux. *Notice sur Revellière-Lépeaux* (Paris, Nantes, Niort, Fontenay, 1886), pp. 21-22.

Duplessis, George, et Lemoisne, P.-A. *Catalogue de la collection des portraits français et étrangers conservée au Département des Estampes de la Bibliothèque Nationale* (Paris, 6 vols., 1896-1907), vol. vi, p. 53.

Lieutaud, Soliman. *Liste de portraits dessinés des députés à l'Assemblée nationale de 1789, avec l'indication de leur format et le nom des artistes auxquels ils sont dûs, précédés d'une courte notice biographique sur chaque personnage* (Paris, 1854), pp. 184-185.

INDEX

293